GREAT BRITAIN

&

PRUSSIA

in the Eighteenth Century

GREAT BRITAIN

PRUSSIA

in the Eighteenth Century

Being the FORD LECTURES

delivered in the University of Oxford

Lent Term 1922

BY

SIR RICHARD LODGE

M.A., LL.D., LITT.D.

HONORARY FELLOW OF BRASENOSE COLLEGE AND
PROFESSOR OF HISTORY IN THE UNIVERSITY OF EDINBURGH

OCTAGON BOOKS

A DIVISION OF FARRAR, STRAUS AND GIROUX

New York   1972

50925

Originally published by Oxford University Press in 1923

Reprinted 1972
by special arrangement with Oxford University Press

OCTAGON BOOKS
A DIVISION OF FARRAR, STRAUS & GIROUX, INC.
19 Union Square West
New York, N. Y. 10003

Library of Congress Cataloging in Publication Data

Lodge, Sir Richard, 1855-1936.
    Great Britain & Prussia in the eighteenth century.
    (The Ford lectures, 1922)
    Reprint of the 1923 ed.

        1. Gt. Brit.—Foreign Relations—Prussia.
        2. Prussia—Foreign relations—Gt. Brit.   I. Title.
        II. Series: Oxford University. Ford lectures, 1922.
DA47.2.L55   1972   327.42′043   76-159208
ISBN 0-374-95077-6

Manufactured by Braun-Brumfield, Inc.
Ann Arbor, Michigan

Printed in the United States of America

PREFACE

In the choice of a subject for the Ford Lectures I was guided
partly by the advice of Professor Firth and partly by the memory
of the war. Professor Firth urged that I should deal with foreign
relations, to which I was sufficiently inclined by my own studies
and predilections. And the particular foreign relations were
suggested by two considerations connected with the war.
Germany has been so dominated and inspired by Prussia during
the last half-century that in common usage the two terms have
come to be regarded as almost synonymous. The recent
struggle against Germany seemed to give a peculiar interest to
our earlier relations with the predominant province of our late
enemy. Also I was impressed by the danger that the retrospect
of the past might be coloured by the hostility aroused during
the conflict. Against this danger—already conspicuous in the
course of the war—and against the degradation of history
to be the handmaid of political passion I could, at any rate,
offer a passive protest. And there was a further consideration
which had some weight. It was in our relations with Germany
in the eighteenth century that the often divergent interests of
Britain and Hanover were most conspicuous. The difficulty
of regulating the foreign policy of a ruler who has to safeguard
the welfare of two imperfectly united states is one which
confronts the British Empire, now that it has become more
and more a mere ' personal union ' in which great self-governing
units claim a share in the direction of what should be a common
policy.

In grappling with my subject I have been impressed by the
difficulty of interesting either hearers or readers in the details
of obsolete diplomacy. I have sought, and have found for

myself, some relief from this difficulty by forming an intimate acquaintance with the humbler agents of diplomacy, and especially with the successive British envoys at Berlin. This intimacy has been rendered more attractive by the fact that the most notable of these envoys—Lord Hyndford, Andrew Mitchell, Hugh Elliot, and Joseph Ewart—were all Lowland Scots; and it is not a little noteworthy that, at a time when the Union was still unfamiliar and unpopular, Scotsmen should have played so prominent a part in the diplomatic service of Great Britain. It is impossible in a necessarily curtailed sketch of a long period to convey to others that sense of personal familiarity which the perusal of their handwriting has brought to myself. But I have hopes that I may add touches to their portraits in subsequent studies; and also that I may complete my subject by tracing the relations of Britain and Prussia during the great French wars, and so bringing the story down to 1815, which is its most natural termination.

In conclusion, I should like to express my gratitude to the faithful members of my audience, and especially to those old colleagues and old pupils who were induced by past associations to come to my lectures.

RICHARD LODGE.

EDINBURGH, 1 *January* 1923.

CONTENTS

LECTURE I

INTRODUCTORY, 1688-1740

LECTURE II

THE WAR OF THE AUSTRIAN SUCCESSION, 1740-8

Frederick reverts to policy of Klein Schnellendorf—Battle of Chotusitz (17th May)—Treaties of Breslau (11th June) and Berlin (28th July)—British guarantee of treaty—Treaty of Westminster (29th November)—Apparent triumph of British policy.

Altered character of war in 1743—Maria Theresa's policy of revenge—Carteret supports it—Frederick's efforts to secure terms for Charles VII—Conference at Hanau—Treaty of Worms (13th September)—Frederick's alarm.

Invasion of Alsace in 1744—Renewed intervention of Prussia—League of Frankfort—Frederick conquers and loses Bohemia—Importance of Saxony and Russia—Attack on Silesia repulsed—Fall of Carteret.

Quadruple Alliance of Warsaw (8th January 1745)—Death of Charles VII (20th January)—Frederick opens negotiations with Britain—Vacillation of British Ministers—Renewed invasion of Silesia—Hohenfriedberg (4th June) —British Ministers return to policy of 1742—Convention of Hanover (26th August 1745)—Obstinacy of Austria and Saxony—Battle of Soor (30th September)—Election of Francis I—Prussian invasion of Saxony—Villiers negotiates Treaties of Dresden (25th December 1745).

Mission of Villiers to Berlin in 1746—Failure to effect an alliance between Britain and Prussia—Quarrels about Prussian ships and Silesian Loan—Alarm excited by French successes and invasion of Holland—Renewed effort to gain Prussian alliance—Mission of Henry Legge, 1748—Its failure—Treaty of Aix-la-Chapelle (18th October 1748).

Additional Notes : A. Lord Hyndford at Berlin. B. The Vacancy in the Empire, 1745. C. The House of Brunswick Wolfenbüttel. D. The Holstein Marriages. E. The Foreign Secretaries of Frederick.

LECTURE III

THE DIPLOMATIC REVOLUTION—THE ORIGIN OF THE SEVEN YEARS' WAR IN EUROPE—THE ANGLO-PRUSSIAN ALLIANCE

The ' old system' apparently intact after Aix-la-Chapelle—The first assault by Prussia fails—Strained relations between Britain and Prussia, 1748–55—The second attack on the system by Austria fails—Colonial quarrels in North America—Imminent war between Britain and France—Danger to Hanover and the Netherlands—Breakdown of Anglo-Austrian Alliance—Possibility of aid from Prussia—The Convention of Westminster (16th January 1756)—Anglo-French War—The first Treaty of Versailles (1st May 1756) completes the diplomatic revolution.

Exultation in London and Berlin over Convention of Westminster—Gradual disillusion—Prospects of continental peace—Frederick's invasion of Saxony—Formation of anti-Prussian Coalition—The outbreak of war in Europe.

LECTURE IV

THE QUARREL

LECTURE V

THE PERIOD OF ALIENATION, 1763–86

LECTURE VI

THE RECONCILIATION IN 1787 AND THE TRIPLE ALLIANCE OF 1788-91

I

INTRODUCTORY, 1688–1740

AMONG the first things which strike the student of diplomatic history is the love of all Foreign Office bureaucrats—as of other bureaucrats—for a system, for a regular groove along which their activities can proceed with the minimum both of worry and of risk. Any complete or sudden departure from tradition is regarded with the gravest misgivings, and nothing pleases the worshippers of routine better than the failure of the experiment and the contented slipping back into the well-worn ruts. During the sixteenth and seventeenth centuries the main grouping of European states had been determined by their respective relations to the two great rival powers of the Continent, France and the house of Habsburg. More and more Europe had tended to split into two considerable groups ; the powers which supported Spain on the one side, and those which inclined to back the Valois or the Bourbon on the other. It must not, however, be hastily concluded that the various states included at any time in one or other of the two groups were therefore of necessity friendly to each other. If that had been the case, both the practice and the study of diplomacy would be fatally dull and depressing. Among the members of each group there was every variety of friendship, every variety of envy, malice, and all uncharitableness. The most exhilarating exercise of the diplomatic art was to drive a team of plunging mules, each eager to bite and kick its neighbour. The familiar illustration is that of France—the past master of cunning and acute diplomacy— maintaining its grip for a century and a half over three client states, Sweden, Poland, and Turkey, in spite of the fact that Poland during most of the time was at daggers drawn with both its northern and its southern neighbour. And the groups were no more constant than they were united. Incessant and frequently successful efforts were made by the great powers to detach states from the hostile group or even to bring them over altogether to their own side. And from time to time lesser states under a daring or a reckless ruler, especially those states whose geography assured their importance and their impunity, ventured to play their own game with the hostile leviathans, and to extort gains for themselves by selling their services to the highest bidder. The supreme instances of this are to be found in the history of the house of Savoy.

The Revolution of 1688 is in many ways a greater revolution in the foreign policy of England than in its domestic affairs. Hitherto, except for a short time under Wolsey and Elizabeth, and for a still shorter time under Charles I and Cromwell, England had held herself somewhat aloof from the main current of continental contentions. This had been facilitated by its insularity and encouraged by its absorption in its own religious and constitutional problems and in the expansion of its industries, trade, and plantations. After 1688 this absorption notably diminished. Religious disputes were lulled, though not stilled, by the Toleration Act, and the Revolution itself settled the main principles of constitutional development, leaving to later generations the task of determining its details. And commercial and colonial expansion, which had made such notable progress in the seventeenth century, proved to be a fertile cause of quarrel with jealous and encroaching rivals. But it was the circumstances in which the Revolution took place, the resolute policy of its protagonist, William III, and the close association with the United Provinces (creating almost a new unit in Europe, 'the Maritime Powers'), which bridged the Channel and threw England into the vortex of European politics.

One result of the Revolution, therefore, was to make England a member of the European states-system in a sense in which it had never been before. Another result was to transfer it from one of the great groups of powers to the other. In the sixteenth century circumstances had driven England into hostility to Spain, and Spanish bigotry and persecution forced most Protestant states, and England with them, into an alliance or *entente* with France. As late as the middle of the seventeenth century

Cromwell—a representative of English and Protestant prejudice —could say, 'The Spaniard, there is the natural enemy.' Only four notable attempts were made to draw England out of the anti-Spanish groove in which it was fixed by Elizabethan traditions. James I set himself to terminate the quarrel with Spain and to pose as a mediator between the contending forces on the Continent, but the attempt was a ludicrous failure. At the Restoration it seemed likely that the Stewarts would endeavour to punish their French relatives for their recognition of the Protectorate by transferring English support to the side of Spain, which had never deserted them. And later in 1668, when he joined the Triple Alliance, and in 1677, when he married his niece to William III, Charles II seemed about to translate the threat of 1660 into action. But on none of these occasions, although public opinion clamoured for such a change of policy, was England detached for more than a moment from association with France, either avowed or concealed.

All this was changed by the Revolution. Louis XIV had prepared the way for the change by abandoning the traditional alliance with foreign Protestantism, and by endeavouring, not only to suppress the Huguenots in France, but to take the place of Spain as the champion of the Roman Catholic interest in Europe. It is a time-honoured contention—consecrated in our Universities by a long succession of examination questions—that wars of religion ceased with the treaty of Westphalia, and that wars of commerce took their place. The contention is not in itself quite accurate, and if it implies that religion ceased in 1648 to be a substantial force in inter-state relations, it is demonstrably untrue. Possibly by the middle of the eighteenth century 'the Protestant cause' had become a stereotyped formula in the diplomatic language of certain states, but it was a formula whose value lay in its appeal to public opinion, and this rendered it worth while to pay more than mere lip-homage to the phrase. And in the later years of the seventeenth century the religious impulse was still powerful, and Louis himself recognized this by endeavouring to divide his opponents upon religious grounds. Thanks to his own blunders, to the adroit policy of William III, and to the alienation of Pope Innocent XI, he failed in his immediate object, and only succeeded in alienating from France most of the Protestant states whom it had hitherto patronized. When England decided that it must get rid of a Roman Catholic king, it also decided that it must seek support from the enemies of France.

In the first Grand Alliance of 1689, provoked by Louis XIV's invasion of Germany, and in the second Grand Alliance, formed to restrict Bourbon gains in the Spanish succession, England was committed to that hostility to France which, with the exception of some fourteen years, dominated its foreign policy during the whole period with which these lectures deal. In the first of the two coalitions William III was the predominant leader, because Austria, in spite of the imperial obligation to defend Germany, could not be induced to terminate its war with the Turks, and was thus unable to employ its full forces in the west. In the second Austria was more prominent, partly because the treaty of Carlowitz freed Eugene and his army to fight against France, and partly because the claim of the Archduke Charles provided the chief pretext for the war. But in both the backbone of the league was the combination against France of Austria with the two maritime powers, and this became the basis of the 'system' to which England was committed in 1689 —the 'old system', as it was affectionately called by disgruntled diplomatists after 1756, when it seemed almost hopeless to restore it. With the decline of Spain, and still more definitely after the transfer of Spain to a Bourbon prince, it seemed to be the obvious and the necessary balancing force against the might of France. This was the conviction of the Whigs, who in the main dictated English foreign policy for more than half a century.

In the two Grand Alliances England was for the first time associated with two German states, Brandenburg and Hanover, whose relations with England and with each other form the main subject-matter of these lectures. With both of them William III was very closely connected. The young Elector of Brandenburg, Frederick III, who succeeded in 1688, was his first cousin, and, under the will of Frederick Henry, the heir presumptive to the Principality of Orange. No foreign state did more than Brandenburg to facilitate William's expedition to England. At the same time Sophia, the wife of Ernest Augustus of Hanover, was the nearest Protestant descendant of the Stewart line after

Mary, Anne, and William himself. Her insertion in the legal order of succession was suggested when the Bill of Rights was adopted, and was ultimately effected in the Act of Settlement. The two houses of Welf and Hohenzollern were also closely associated with each other by geographical propinquity, by common Protestant interests in Germany, and by frequent inter-marriage. Unfortunately the association was not always friendly. Both families were dominated by the characteristic German passion for territorial expansion, and their ambitions and claims were not infrequently conflicting.[1] Neighbourhood and relation-ship gave to their differences, when they did arise, a personal bitterness which might not have been felt if the connexion had been less close. Of the two, Brandenburg was at the outset the more powerful and the more dignified. One of the original electorates, it had added to its territorial strength in the early part of the seventeenth century the duchy of East Prussia and a share of the Rhenish provinces of the former dukes of Cleve. Later in the century the Great Elector, by acquiring in the settlement of 1648 a large share of Pomerania with the secular-ized bishoprics of Magdeburg, Halberstadt, and Minden ; by freeing East Prussia from its vassalage to Poland; by his famous victory over the hitherto invincible Swedes at Fehrbellin ; and by the foundation of an administrative unity which counteracted the evils of geographical separation, had raised the Hohenzollerns to be incontestably, both in territory and prestige, the second dynasty in Germany. The Brunswick dukes had no such brilliant suc-cesses to chronicle, but they too had made substantial progress, to which Ernest Augustus, the husband of Sophia, had been the chief contributor. By discarding the old custom of partition, which had been so damaging to the Welfs, in favour of indivisi-bility and primogeniture, by securing the duchy of Lauenburg, and by preparing the way for the union of Celle with Hanover, which took place in 1705, Ernest Augustus elevated his house to

[1] A notable illustration of this was the prolonged dispute as to East Friesland, with its attractive harbour of Emden, which caused endless heart-burnings for half a century. Hanover claimed it by virtue of a treaty of mutual inheritance made by Ernest Augustus with the reigning duke in 1692, whereas the Hohenzollerns pleaded an imperial expectative granted by Leopold to Frederick III in 1695.

something like equality with the Wittelsbachs and the Wettins, and justified the grant of a ninth electorate, with which the Emperor Leopold in 1692 rewarded the loyal services of the house in the Turkish wars and purchased its continued support in the wars against France. His son-in-law in Brandenburg was not slow to follow his example and to claim, with equal success, a proportionate elevation in rank to the kingship of Prussia. Both powers supported each other's pretensions to these higher ranks, and both were backed by the potent influence of William III. Thus, in spite of undercurrents of personal and family jealousy, it seemed that to previous links between Hanover and Brandenburg-Prussia there were added their common alliance with England, their common obligations and gratitude to the Habsburg emperor, and in addition a certain elementary German patriotism, which it is as easy to exaggerate as to depreciate, and which showed itself mainly in a dogged resentment of French patronage and French aggression.

A word in passing should be given to the choice of the title which transformed the elector Frederick III into Frederick I, king of Prussia. The Prussia from which the title was taken was a mere fragment of the older Prussia of the Teutonic Knights. Within the last half-century it had been a fief of Poland. It lay far away from the main bulk of the Hohenzollern dominions; and it could hardly be defended in case of war with either Poland or Russia. Yet this outlying fragment of his dominions, the least valuable as it appeared, which had come to his family by a title still contested, was chosen for association with the royal rank because it lay outside Germany, owed no obligations to the Empire or to any other external authority, and thus gave to the new monarchy an independence which it could hardly have claimed if the title had been affixed to his older and far more important dominions. And through the influence of the title the name of Prussia and of Prussians has come to be applied to and adopted by the other territories and subjects of the Hohenzollern dynasty, who have no other connexion with the historic Prussia strictly so called. There are very few instances of so complete, and perhaps none of so rapid, a transfer of an alien name to a large area and a numerous people. The nearest parallel I can suggest is the expansion of the names Scotia and Scoti, belonging originally

to the small body of settlers from Ireland on a fragment of
Caledonia, first to the land and people north of the Forth and
Clyde, and later to the provinces and inhabitants of the Lowlands,
who had no association whatever, except the recognition of a
common king, with the original Scots. Technically, at the
outset, the union of Prussia with Brandenburg was a mere
personal union, like that of Great Britain and Hanover after
1714. This was acted upon by Frederick William I, the second
king. In the year of his accession he signed the treaty of
Utrecht as king of Prussia, while as Elector and as a German
prince he remained at war with France for another year. His
successors were careful to avoid the blunder, and, by insisting
upon treating their dominions as one indivisible unit, they
facilitated the acceptance by all their subjects of the name of
Prussians, which might otherwise have been resented as bitterly
as Scotsmen would resent being called Englishmen, or as they
do resent the use of the term England to include Scotland.

The accession of the house of Hanover to the British throne
in 1714 is almost as great a landmark in the history of our
foreign policy as the Revolution had been a quarter of a century
earlier. It restored power to the Whigs with their craving for
the 'old system' which the recent Tory ministry had so completely abandoned. But in no respect was it more important
than in our relations with Prussia. From 1688 to 1714 those
relations had been friendly but not intimate. They were distinctly
less intimate in the reign of Anne than in that of William III;
and they were somewhat strained when Oxford and Bolingbroke
set themselves to bring the war to a speedy close. There was,
however, no actual rupture, and British diplomatists at Utrecht
helped to secure for Frederick William a substantial portion
of Spanish Gelderland, which was the only reward for the
valuable services of Prussian troops during the war. These
friendly but distant relations might have continued indefinitely
so far as Great Britain was concerned, but their whole character
was changed by the accession of George I. Prussia was as
resolute a champion of the Protestant succession in 1714 as it had
been in supporting William III in 1688, and Frederick William
was the first European sovereign to intimate his recognition
of the new dynasty. George I was both his uncle and his

father-in-law, and at the moment both princes had almost identical interests in the northern war which had broken out before the war of the Spanish Succession and continued after its close.

It is impossible to evade the vexed question of the influence of Hanover upon British policy, because the relations of George I with Prussia were far more dictated by Hanoverian than by British interests. In theory the two states were as distinct and autonomous in foreign affairs as in domestic administration. George I and George II both held that their actions as electors were quite apart from their actions as kings, and bitterly resented anything that looked like interference by British ministers with the external relations of Hanover or indeed with German affairs of any kind. But in practice this complete severance proved to be impossible. It was inevitable that a Hanoverian king should succumb to the temptation to use the resources and prestige of his kingdom to strengthen his position as elector; it was equally inevitable that British ministers should endeavour within limits to gratify the sovereign who could deprive them of office; and it is certain that Hanoverian ministers, especially in the early years of George I, hardly concealed their attempt to guide both the foreign and in some measure the domestic policy of the British crown. But, even if there had been a more honest and resolute effort, the separation between the two states could only be complete if it was accepted by foreign powers, and such acceptance might be demanded but could not be enforced. If they chose to punish the king for his conduct as elector, or the elector for his conduct as king, no one could prevent them. It was this dependence upon the action of foreign states which made it impossible to enforce the famous clause of the Act of Settlement which forbade that England should be involved in war on behalf of the foreign dominions of its future rulers. Considerations of honour compelled a reluctant public opinion to admit that the electorate could not be allowed to suffer for its association with the kingdom, and it was always possible with a little ingenuity to contend that the interests of the two states were identical. The confusion between what professed to be two policies was the more obvious because Hanover had a very incomplete diplomatic organization. At several courts, and notably at that of Berlin, the electorate was for considerable periods unrepresented, and in such circumstances the British minister perforce acted also as the agent of Hanover, and sent his reports to the Hanoverian Regency as well as to the Secretary of State at Whitehall.

The northern war,[1] in which Sweden was confronted by a hostile confederation of Russia, Saxony-Poland, and Denmark, was the first episode in which Britain, Hanover, and Prussia were closely associated. In 1713, when George I ascended the British throne, Charles XII, now a virtual prisoner in the hands of the Turks, had lost all his trans-Baltic possessions except Pomerania, and there his troops were engaged in an apparently hopeless struggle when the sudden reappearance of the king in November 1714 revived their spirits and their hopes. Hanover and Prussia, freed by the conclusion of the Spanish Succession war to turn their attention to northern affairs, acted at the outset in complete concord. Although they had no immediate quarrel with Sweden, they could not allow their neighbours to aggrandize themselves without asserting their own claim to a share in the spoil. With the reluctant assent of the Danes, Hanoverian troops occupied the duchies of Bremen and Verden, while the Russians and Saxons allowed Frederick William to take over Stettin and the adjacent part of Pomerania. In both cases the occupation professed to be only provisional for the duration of the war, and was represented as not unfriendly to Sweden. But Charles XII bitterly resented the intrusion into his territories of states which he had in no way injured, and his hostility forced Hanover and Prussia into an alliance with each other and with the enemies of Sweden.

[1] The northern war has been fully treated by Mr. J. F. Chance in *George I and the Northern War*, London, 1909 ; by Professor Wolfgang Michael in *Englische Geschichte im achtzehnten Jahrhundert*, of which two volumes have appeared (Hamburg and Leipzig, 1896, and Berlin and Leipzig, 1920 ; a new edition of the first volume has recently appeared) ; and in the fourth volume of J. G. Droyson's great work *Geschichte der preussischen Politik* (Leipzig, 1869 and 1872). A very useful summary of its main features is to be found in Sir A. W. Ward's *Great Britain and Hanover* (Oxford, 1899), which embodies the Ford Lectures for that year. I did not realize, until my subject had been chosen and announced, that one of my most distinguished predecessors had covered so much of our common ground.

These events placed the British ministers in an awkward dilemma. Great Britain had no substantial reason for hostility to Sweden, and in fact Charles XII was entitled under a treaty of 1700 to claim English aid against his enemies. But it was clear that George I as king of Great Britain could not be expected to compel George as elector to restore Bremen and Verden or to break his treaty with Prussia by demanding the evacuation of Stettin. Britain must therefore remain neutral, but Hanoverian pressure demanded some course by which this neutrality should be associated with indirect service to the interests of Hanover. An excuse was found in the Swedish encouragement of privateering and in the severe measures adopted by Charles XII to prohibit trade with the ports in the eastern Baltic which were now in the hands of Russia. This made it easy to justify the sending of a British fleet to the Baltic to protect British shipping, to convoy traders to their respective ports, and to take reprisals for outrages committed by Swedish men-of-war. If, in carrying out these defensible instructions, the fleet also aided the besiegers of Stralsund by keeping Swedish transports in harbour and cutting off reinforcements from Pomerania, or if, by extreme mischance, it came into collision with the Swedish navy and sent it to the bottom, no blame could be attached to British ministers who had given no instructions to this effect.

That the protection of British trade was largely *camouflage* to conceal the defence of Hanoverian interests is demonstrated by what passed between Hanover and Prussia. When Frederick William made his treaty with Hanover for the mutual guarantee of their respective gains, he assumed, and was encouraged by the Hanoverian representative to assume, that he would thereby secure British support against Sweden. When the fleet entered the Baltic, the Prussian king both expected and demanded that it should take an active part in the reduction of Rügen and Stralsund. He refused to separate the king from the elector, and paid little attention to the (to him) unintelligible contention that British ministers might be impeached if they used British forces in a Hanoverian quarrel. And when he complained that Hanover was doing too little in the joint war, Bernstorff did not hesitate to point to the indirect services of the British fleet as if they were a Hanoverian contribution. It is no wonder that Charles XII found it equally difficult to distinguish between the action of the elector and that of the king. When the elector was at war, the alleged neutrality of England was a mere farce. Hence it was held that Sweden was justified in sheltering and encouraging the Jacobites, and they were led to expect that the Swedish king would punish the unprovoked seizure of Bremen and Verden by leading an expedition to England for the expulsion of its Hanoverian ruler. When Gyllenborg was seized in his London embassy, and Charles retaliated by the imprisonment of the British envoy, it seemed that the Hanoverian union must inevitably involve Britain in war with Sweden.

Thus the first result of the accession of George I was a close alliance between Hanover and Prussia, the entry of both powers into a war with Sweden, and the ill-disguised complicity of Great Britain in the prosecution of their designs. But in 1716 the northern war entered into a wholly new phase. The Swedish war continued, a British fleet was again in the Baltic, Wismar shared the fate of Stralsund, but the coalition against Sweden was practically dissolved by internal dissension. Again the first impulse came from Hanover. George I resented the intrusion of Russian troops into Mecklenburg, where they were employed to assist the duke (who married Peter the Great's niece) in a quarrel with his subjects. It was feared that Peter might follow the example of Gustavus Adolphus, and found a Russian principality within Germany. Hanover demanded the complete evacuation of Mecklenburg, and refused to continue the war against Sweden until the demand was complied with. Britain had no direct concern in this purely German dispute, but it was interested in opposing the establishment of what might be a dangerous supremacy of Russia in the Baltic, whence came so many commodities essential for shipbuilding. Hence in this Russian dispute the co-operation between Britain and Hanover became closer and more avowed than it had been in the Swedish war, and Hanoverian influence in London made a notable gain when the schism in the Whig party led to the retirement of Townshend and Walpole from office in 1717.

Hostility to Russia brought about a crisis in the relations with Prussia. Frederick William was the ally both of Peter and of

George I, and to both of them his adhesion was of vital importance. The Prussian king was no great master of European
affairs, and he had little conception of the might of Russia and
of the dangers that might be caused by Russian expansion. His
son was probably the first European statesman who adequately
comprehended these matters. But Frederick William knew that
East Prussia was now only severed from Russia by the little
duchy of Courland, and that a rupture with Peter might cost him
the province from which he took his title. And he was readily
influenced by personal motives. He had no great love for his
uncle and father-in-law. He had welcomed his accession to the
British throne because he thought it would benefit Prussia.
But his uneasy jealousy, always a prominent Hohenzollern
characteristic, was excited when he found that the parvenu
elector had become a more powerful monarch than himself.
And the more prominent George I became, the more bitter
became Frederick William's resentment. The French alliance,
the dependence of Austria upon British naval power for the
defence of the Italian provinces, the so-called Quadruple
Alliance,[1] the destruction of the Spanish fleet off Cape Passaro,
the triumph of British diplomacy in mediating the peace of
Passarowitz—all these things which combined to give to George
and Stanhope an almost dictatorial position in Europe, were gall
and wormwood to Frederick William. It is not surprising that
when he asked himself whether it was better to increase the
power of Peter the Great or that of George I, he preferred to
adhere to the alliance with Russia.[2]

During 1717 and 1718 the tension between the two groups

---

[1] When the ' Quadruple Alliance' was made between Austria, France, and
Great Britain, it was assumed, as a matter of course, that the Dutch would
join it. Hence the name. But the States General continually postponed
signature, and ultimately evaded it altogether; so that they took no part
in the coercion of Spain, and kept their hold on Spanish trade. The term
' Quadruple' is, therefore, a misnomer.

[2] This was settled at a personal interview between Peter and Frederick
William at Havelberg in September 1716 (*Recueil des Instructions données
aux Ambassadeurs de France, Suède*, p. 280). Droysen (iv. 2, p. 207) quotes
a marginal note by Frederick William (5 February 1717): 'Gut, mit dem
Zaaren zusammen Frieden. England will ich mit dem grössten Plaisir, und
wenn ich auch etwas Schaden dabei haben sollte, im Stich lassen.'

among the northern powers steadily increased, and at the end of the latter year everything seemed to point to an open rupture, in which Russia and Prussia would come into collision with Denmark, Saxony, and Hanover-Britain, while Sweden would hold the balance in its hands. It was this state of things which encouraged Alberoni in Spain to scheme for a reconciliation between Sweden and Russia, and for their joint action in expelling George I from the British throne. But the situation was suddenly and completely changed by the death of Charles XII, and the transfer of a now limited monarchy in Sweden, first to Charles's younger sister Ulrica Eleanor, and in 1720 to her husband, Frederick of Hesse Cassel. It was now imperative that Sweden should purchase peace at almost any price, and the only question was which of the rival groups would give the best terms. Britain, acting in close agreement with France, determined to make sure of a satisfactory settlement by detaching Prussia from its alliance with the Tsar. The great obstacle was the personal antipathy to Prussia on the part of George I and still more on that of his Hanoverian advisers. But Stanhope and Sunderland at last determined to take a strong line in the interests of Great Britain and to thrust Bernstorff and his colleagues into the background.[1] Sooner than submit to their dictation they were prepared to reunite the Whig party by restoring Townshend and Walpole to office. Negotiations were opened both at Stockholm and at Berlin. The Hanoverian agents hitherto employed were superseded by sending Carteret to the Swedish capital and Sir Charles Whitworth to that of Prussia.

Peter the Great attempted to anticipate his opponents by coercing Sweden into a separate peace with himself and his ally. Russian transports were landed on the Swedish coast, and the terrified citizens of Stockholm could see flames devour devastated villages. In despair the Swedish government appealed for British aid, and Norris brought up his ships, prepared to treat the Russian fleet as Byng had treated that of Spain in the previous year. But Peter was too cunning to be entrapped, and the

---

[1] 'Les choses sont venues à ce point-ci que les Ministres anglois ont pris le dessus sur les Hanovriens dans les affaires du Nord, qu'ils ont pris la résolution de ne plus dépendre de ceux-ci sur les affaires.' Report of Bonnet, 28 March 1719, quoted by Droysen, iv. 2, p. 261.

Russian vessels had already retired to the shallow waters of the eastern Baltic, where Norris could not follow them. Naval power, however, had done its work, Sweden accepted British mediation, and Frederick William grudgingly and ungraciously consented to receive the coveted Stettin through the agency of his unloved kinsman.[1] The Russo-Prussian alliance came to an end, and George I seemed to hold a commanding position both in the north and in the south. There had been some divergence of view between France and Britain as to the terms of the northern settlement. Britain at first adhered to the Hanoverian policy of expelling Sweden altogether from Germany, whereas France clung to the Westphalian tradition which made Sweden a sort of French agent within Germany. In the end a compromise was adopted, and was indeed forced upon the disputants by the danger that excessive demands would drive Sweden into the arms of Russia. The outline of the joint scheme was that Hanover and Prussia should retain the territories they had occupied, that the Danes should give up Stralsund and the part of Pomerania which they had occupied since 1715, and be compensated with Sleswick at the expense of the house of Holstein ; and that Poland, which for some years had taken no part in the war, should be pacified by the recognition of Augustus and the abandonment by Sweden of his rival, Stanislas Leczinski. This scheme was embodied in a series of treaties, arranged and guaranteed by the mediating powers, France and Britain, by which first Hanover, then Poland, then Prussia, and finally Denmark were reconciled with Sweden.[2] Russia was as isolated in 1720 as Spain had been in 1719.

[1] The treaty between Britain and Sweden was signed on 22 July 1719 ; that with Prussia on 14 August, but the latter, on Whitworth's proposal, was antedated to 4 August, in order to conceal the fact that it was concluded after the Swedish treaty, which made no reference to the cession of Stettin, had reached Berlin. Droysen (iv. 2, pp. 276-7) quotes a marginal note in which Frederick William expressed his undiminished enmity to Hanover : 'lieber mit Hannover mit grossem Plaisir Krieg anfangen ; würde mich gleich gesund machen, wenn ich im Hannövrischen etliche hundert Dörfer brennen sähe'.

[2] The treaty with Hanover was signed at Stockholm on 20 November 1719; that with Poland at Stockholm on 7 January 1720 ; that with Prussia at Stockholm on 1 February 1720 ; and that with Denmark, the most obstinate enemy of Sweden, on 14 June 1720, also at Stockholm.

But no such triumph was to be gained over Peter the Great as that over Alberoni. Both Great Britain and France were suddenly paralysed by the collapse of inflated credits in the two countries. The ministry of Stanhope and Sunderland, hitherto so triumphant, came to an ignominious close with the deaths of Stanhope and Craggs and the enforced retirement of Sunderland in the midst of financial chaos. Townshend and Walpole, who had previously returned only to minor offices, now regained complete ascendancy in the British ministry, and Hanoverian influence, already shaken, received a set-back from which it never completely recovered. The new ministers were desirous of peace, and had no intention of continuing the aggressive and venturesome policy of Stanhope. In fact they could not have done so if they had wished. The allies of Great Britain could no longer be relied upon for support. France, which had only minute commercial interests in the Baltic, had never been so hostile to Russia as England had been. And relations between the two powers were strained by the recent settlement with Spain. France was annoyed because it had been led to give promises to Spain as to the cession of Gibraltar which George I, in spite of his personal assurances, had been unable to fulfil. A strong party in France, which Orleans could not afford to disregard, had always denounced the war against a grandson of Louis XIV in the interests of England and of the hated house of Habsburg. Austria, the other member of the Quadruple Alliance, had been uneasy in the novel co-operation with France into which it had been dragged by British diplomacy and the pressing dangers in Italy. Now that these were over, Austria not only drew away from France, but also ventured to alienate the maritime powers by encouraging Flemish merchants to start a lucrative trade with India. The Dutch, who had refused to take any part in the Spanish war, were not likely to risk the interruption of their Baltic trade by a quarrel with Russia. Denmark and Prussia, both content with their recent gains, were equally unwilling to endanger their security by venturing into open opposition to the Tsar. Thus Great Britain was left alone to fulfil or abandon the virtual assurances of support against Russia which had induced Sweden to make such sacrifices to its other enemies. Nothing but force could compel the Tsar to restore Livonia and Esthonia, and at the last moment Britain decided to withhold active assistance from Sweden. Thus Peter was enabled with security to play the last trump card in his hand. Ulrica Eleanor and her husband had gained the Swedish crown by the exclusion of Charles Frederick of Holstein, the son of Charles XII's elder sister. But the Holstein claim was not without supporters in Sweden, and their numbers and zeal were increased by the efforts of Frederick to recover some of his lost prerogatives. Peter took up the young duke's cause, and proposed to marry him to his own daughter, Anna Petrovna.[1] This danger, combined with the virtual desertion of Great Britain and Hanover, forced Sweden to accept the hard terms dictated by Russia. By the treaty of Nystad (10 September 1721) Peter surrendered Finland and a fragment of Carelia, but retained all his other conquests, on condition that he would abstain from intervention in the domestic affairs of Sweden. The supremacy in the Baltic had passed from Sweden to Russia, and Russia had entered the lists as one of the great powers of Europe. Peter celebrated his own triumph by assuming the title of Emperor of all the Russias.

In 1721 both the northern and the southern disturbances came to an end, and Europe enjoyed the first interval of real peace since 1700. But the force of the recent disturbances was still felt, and they had produced a general unsettlement of inter-state relations which did not promise a prolonged continuance of peaceful conditions. The 'old system' had for the time completely disappeared; and even the Quadruple Alliance, the nearest approach to it which Stanhope had been able to bring about, had collapsed with the disappearance of the conditions which had created it. Charles VI had begun to repent of his promise to satisfy Elizabeth Farnese with regard to the succession of her son in Parma and Tuscany. The Bourbons already held two great European crowns, and it seemed inconsistent either with Austrian interests or with the balance of power to allow the rival house to found a new principality in Italy. Still more serious were the differences which the transfer of the Netherlands

---

[1] This marriage took place in 1725 after the death of Peter the Great, and resulted in the accession to the Russian throne in 1762 of the ill-fated Peter III, the offspring of the marriage, and of his wife Catharine II.

had generated between Austria and the maritime powers. Under pressure Charles VI had agreed to the Barrier Treaty of 1715, in spite of its serious encroachment upon his sovereignty, but he refused to be bound by the restrictions which his former allies endeavoured to impose upon the trading rights of his new subjects. Flemish merchants had already commenced a flourishing trade with India and had secured a factory for their goods in the neighbourhood of Madras. In defiance of the protests of the maritime powers, based upon the treaty of Westphalia, Charles proceeded to take this commerce under his patronage by granting a charter in 1722 to a privileged company at Ostend.

The three members of the Triple Alliance, each of which had an East India Company of its own, resented the intrusion of the Ostend Company and demanded its suppression. They were also pledged to enforce the terms of the Italian settlement which the emperor had acceded to in 1718. But the Triple Alliance, though it still survived, was no longer closely knit together. The Gibraltar dispute had alienated France from Britain; and French mediation in the treaty of Nystad, together with the discovery that France had thwarted British efforts at Constantinople to induce the Turks to attack Russia, had irritated Britain against France. Orleans and Dubois, the originators of the Triple Alliance, were beginning to draw closer to Spain, and a double marriage scheme, by which Philip V's daughter was betrothed to Louis XV, seemed to foreshadow the family compacts of later decades. Still more alarming was the possibility of a Franco-Russian alliance. The intrusion of Russia brought a new and as yet incalculable disturbing force into European politics. France and Austria were both bidding for the support of Peter the Great. Whichever decision was come to at St. Petersburg must be dangerous to Britain, as it was notorious that Peter had never forgiven George I for the Mecklenburg episode or for his undisguised opposition to Russia in the later stages of the Swedish war. The Dutch, in spite of their close association with Britain, had not proved trustworthy allies in the recent conflict with Spain, and were not likely to give more substantial backing in any new disputes.

The British ministry began to feel uncomfortably isolated.

C

Both Whig and Hanoverian traditions pointed to a vigorous effort to restore harmonious relations with Austria as a balance to the house of Bourbon. But Walpole, who jettisoned so many Whig traditions, was never a keen supporter of the Austrian alliance. He was also resolutely opposed to Hanoverian influence in foreign policy, and Townshend, who was more directly concerned with foreign affairs, could hardly seek reconciliation with Austria so long as the Ostend Company and a possible Austro-Russian alliance stood in the way. In these circumstances the Prussian alliance assumed a value and an importance which it had never previously possessed. And contemporary circumstances rendered its conclusion a comparatively easy matter. Charles VI had bitterly resented the settlement of so many German problems in the Swedish treaties without the participation of imperial authority. He especially resented the aggrandizement of Prussia by the unearned acquisition of Stettin. His indignation showed itself in a policy of pin-pricks, to which Frederick William was inordinately sensitive. In a series of legal questions before the *Reichshofrath*, decisions were given against Prussia, in many cases without a full hearing of the evidence in her favour. When Frederick William protested, the emperor threatened to entrust execution to neighbouring princes. Religious interests were involved in the quarrel. Systematic persecution of Protestants in Poland and in the Palatinate revived the suspicion of a new Roman Catholic league under imperial patronage. Frederick William was the most efficient and outspoken champion of the Protestant cause, and this increased his estrangement from the court of Vienna. Behind these minor disputes was the Prussian claim to Jülich and Berg on the extinction of the Palatine house of Neuburg. It was clearly to the interest of the Roman Catholic church to prevent these principalities from falling to a Protestant prince, and, in view of Austrian relations with the Palatine Wittelsbachs, it was practically certain that the imperial authority would be thrown into the balance against the Prussian claims.[1] In these circum-

---

[1] Another reason for Austrian support of the Palatine house was the desire to induce them to withhold support from the prospective claims of the Bavarian Wittelsbachs to the Austrian succession, if Charles VI should leave no male heir.

stances it was not difficult for the British ministers, during the king's visit to Hanover in 1723, to conclude the treaty of Charlottenburg, the first direct treaty between Britain and Prussia since 1690. It was a purely defensive alliance, but it included the German dominions of George I, and Britain undertook, when the occasion arose, to support the just claims of Prussia to Jülich and Berg. The treaty made no mention of a project which was mooted at the same time and regarded as practically settled. This was a proposal, eagerly advocated by the Prussian queen, that the matrimonial connexion between the Welfs and the Hohenzollerns should be continued for another generation by a marriage of the Crown Prince to one of the daughters of the Prince of Wales, and by the marriage of the Princess Wilhelmina to her cousin Frederick.

The treaty of Charlottenburg had the effect of dragging Prussia into European complications with which it had singularly little concern. The failure of the Congress of Cambray to settle the outstanding quarrels between Austria and Spain alienated Elizabeth Farnese from France and Britain, which were pledged to gain the emperor's recognition of her son's claims to succeed in Parma and Tuscany. At the same time the dispute about the Ostend Company had caused the same two powers to quarrel with Austria, and the division was widened by their obvious reluctance to accept the Pragmatic Sanction, by which Charles VI endeavoured to secure the undivided Austrian succession for his own daughters in preference to those of his elder brother. These circumstances drew Austria and Spain together, and the deadly insult inflicted upon the latter power when the Infanta was repudiated and Louis XV was hastily married to Maria Leczinska gave the final impulse to the strange negotiation. Europe was startled to learn, in April 1725, that an actual alliance had been concluded at Vienna between Charles VI and Philip V, the two claimants who had fought against each other throughout the great war, whose rivalry had generated a subsequent smaller war, and who had hitherto seemed to be irreconcilable. The two powers most directly threatened, Britain and France, deemed it necessary to renew their alliance, and Prussia, which had hitherto had nothing to do with these southern disputes, was drawn into the net during George I's visit to Hanover.

There, on the 3rd September 1725, a new triple alliance—
joined later by Holland, Sweden, and Denmark—was formally
signed. The links between Prussia and Britain seemed
to be strengthened and the double marriage alliance fully
secured.

The story of the wiles by which Seckendorf, the Austrian
envoy, seduced Frederick William from the League of Hanover,
and so from the British alliance, is told with much gusto and at
great length by Carlyle. But, as a matter of fact, no great
cunning was needed. If Frederick William had been a competent statesman, he would never have signed the treaty, and
when he found that the rival League of Vienna had been joined
by Catharine I of Russia—disgusted by the refusal of the proffered
hand of her own daughter and by the French king's marriage
to the daughter of the ex-king whom Peter the Great had
expelled from Poland—he began to see that his action was
dangerous as well as foolish. The treaty of Wusterhausen
(12 October 1726), Seckendorf's first achievement, proved futile,
because Austria never carried out nor attempted to carry out its
provisions. For two years Prussia relapsed into sullen neutrality,
and the rival groups continued to compete for its support. But
the British ministers made a fatal blunder in trying to use the
proposed marriage treaty as a bribe to bring Prussia back to
the Hanoverian fold. Frederick William resented the intrusion
of domestic concerns and influences into foreign politics, and the
accession of George II, whom he regarded with ill-concealed
detestation, did nothing to improve the relations between the
two courts. Thus Seckendorf, who had detached Prussia from
Britain in 1726, was enabled to adjust an Austro-Prussian alliance
by a secret treaty on the 23rd December 1728.

The alliance was to be perpetual, and both states were to
guarantee the territories of each other. In case of war the
Prussian contingent was to be 10,000 men, the Austrian 12,000,
but in extremity each was to employ its full force. On the
extinction of the Neuburg line, Austria was to support Prussia
in gaining Berg and Ravenstein, and was to transfer to Prussia
its own claim to this much-disputed inheritance. On the other
hand, Prussia was to guarantee the Pragmatic Sanction, and the
Prussian vote in the imperial election was to be given to the

German prince who should be chosen as the bridegroom for Maria Theresa.[1]

Before the conclusion of this treaty, which dominated Prussian policy for the rest of Frederick William's reign, the danger of war between the rival leagues had almost disappeared. The Austro-Spanish alliance of 1725 was so hollow and unnatural that it could not be lasting, and would probably have perished earlier but for the rather provocative opposition of the hostile combination formed at Hanover. First Austria and then Spain consented to negotiate, and in the end Spain was induced in the treaty of Seville (9 November 1729) to accept the terms laid down by the Hanover allies. It was anticipated that Charles VI, now finally deserted by his principal ally, would at once give way. But to the astonishment of the allied courts he refused to be intimidated. The unnatural combination of the maritime powers with the two branches of the house of Bourbon was confronted by a new league between Austria, Prussia, and Russia. The clouds of war, which had cleared away since the preliminary treaty of 1727, rolled back again in 1730. Spain welcomed the prospect of war, as opening the way for the recovery of the lost Italian provinces. Even France could hardly resist the temptation to humble the house of Habsburg with the help of the very powers which had fought its battle in two great wars. Townshend was in favour of war as he had been in 1727. But Walpole stood firm, and the long and intimate connexion between the two brothers-in-law was broken by Townshend's retirement in 1730. His place as Secretary of State was taken by William Stanhope, who had been made Lord Harrington as a reward for his success in negotiating the treaty of Seville. But Harrington was no Townshend, and henceforth Walpole took the control of foreign policy into his own hands. His first expedient for the preservation of peace was a supreme effort to detach Prussia from the Austrian alliance. The two queens, Caroline and Sophia Dorothea, were the ardent patronesses of the scheme. The Prussian queen had found supporters in the ministry, Knyphausen and von Borcke, who, she hoped, might prove a match for the formidable combination of Grumbkow with

[1] For a full analysis of the treaty, and of the motives which induced Frederick William to conclude it, see Droysen, iv. 3, pp. 35-41.

Seckendorf. The British envoy selected for the difficult task was Sir Charles Hotham, a near relative by marriage of the Stanhope family, but endowed with no other obvious qualification. In the spring of 1730 he arrived in Berlin with a formal demand for the hand of the Princess Wilhelmina for the Prince of Wales, and with instructions to express the hope that the Crown Prince might choose the Princess Amelia as his bride. To the intense disgust of Grumbkow, the ally of Seckendorf in the Prussian ministry, the king expressed his gratification at the honour done to his daughter, and his willingness to consider the proposed marriage for his son, provided his own succession in Jülich and Berg was guaranteed as part of the bargain. This unexpected gentleness was attributed to the wiles of the queen and of Knyphausen, the 'Frisian', as Grumbkow venomously called him. Seckendorf received instructions from Vienna to renew his efforts to frustrate a marriage scheme which must inevitably weaken Austrian influence in Berlin. Unfortunately the British envoy played into Seckendorf's hands. In the hope of destroying the influence of Grumbkow, the arch enemy of the queen, Hotham had been furnished with an intercepted letter, which seemed likely to open the king's eyes to his minister's self-seeking and treacherous character. This letter was presented to Frederick William, who flew into a passion at the idea that a foreign power should interfere in his relations to his own servants, stamped the letter under his feet, and turned his back upon the startled and outraged envoy. From this time the quarrel between Britain and Prussia went from bad to worse. Knyphausen, the queen's most efficient partisan, was sent into exile. All the old quarrels with Hanover about Mecklenburg, East Friesland, and the outrages of Prussian recruiting officers, were raked up again. The ill-fated marriage proposals only served to give rise to the bitterest dissension within the Prussian royal family. This led to the attempted flight of the Crown Prince, and to the tragic comedy, which almost came to unrelieved tragedy, of the king's subsequent treatment of his son. An autograph letter from Charles VI was necessary to prevent Frederick William from dealing with the Crown Prince as Peter the Great had dealt with Alexis. It is a repulsive episode, and it is the best-known episode of a rather repellent reign.

After the humiliating failure of his attempt to break off the Austro-Prussian alliance, Walpole had to fall back upon his last expedient, direct negotiation with the emperor. For this his agent was more skilfully or more fortunately selected. Sir Thomas Robinson, afterwards Lord Grantham, is familiar to readers of Macaulay as the jack-boot whom Newcastle sent to lead the House of Commons over the heads of Pitt and Fox. But he was an 'indefatigable' (Frederick the Great's term for him) and by no means a contemptible diplomatist. He had assisted Horace Walpole (the elder) and won his confidence at the French embassy, and he was now sent by Sir Robert to carry the olive branch to Vienna. The olive branch was a substantial one, being nothing less than the offer of a British— and as a corollary a Dutch—guarantee of the Pragmatic Sanction. Walpole must have known that this might involve serious responsibilities in the future, and that in this matter he must part company with France. But he was determined to prevent the outbreak of war, and he was content to solve present problems without overmuch thought of the future. To Charles VI the prospect of a guarantee from the maritime powers—indispensable for the security of his Italian provinces—was a strong inducement. But he could not resist the temptation to give a final and rather reckless proof of his contempt for the Seville treaty. In January 1731 the last Farnese duke of Parma died, and the emperor promptly sent troops to occupy the duchy as an escheated fief of the empire. The 'termagant' queen of Spain declared that this insult could only be wiped out in blood, and clamoured for an immediate declaration of war to enforce the terms of the treaty of Seville. But her clamour had no effect upon Walpole, who refused to fight in the cause of the Spanish Bourbons, and he instructed Robinson to continue his negotiation. A last obstruction was caused by the attempt of George I and the Hanoverian regency to extort from the emperor a favourable settlement of the numerous disputes with Prussia. But Walpole insisted on the postponement of these irrelevant demands, and convinced the king that in case of war Hanover would be the first and the greatest sufferer. On 16th March 1731 the second treaty of Vienna undid the evil results of the first treaty. In return for the guarantee of the

Pragmatic Sanction by the maritime powers, Charles agreed to dissolve the Ostend Company and to sanction the admission of Spanish troops to the Italian fortresses as arranged by the treaty of Seville. Elizabeth Farnese indignantly protested against so lenient a treatment of Austria, but she was compelled to accede to the agreement. The prolonged disturbance in Europe came at last to an end, and Walpole had achieved his one great diplomatic triumph.

The Vienna treaty of 1731 was more than a settlement of past disputes; it was also a defensive alliance of a very binding nature between Austria and the maritime powers. It therefore marks, with the partial alienation of France, a first and very substantial step on the part of Great Britain towards a return to the 'old system' of foreign policy. At the same time it removed the primary cause of the recent rupture with Prussia, and Austria was anxious to bring about the reconciliation of the two powers which, it was hoped at Vienna, would be the strongest supporters of Maria Theresa's succession and of the continued unity of the Austrian dominions. Even the marriage alliance, which Austria had so long vetoed, would now have been welcomed. Seckendorf was instructed to bless what before he had cursed. But Frederick William could not be induced to lay aside his antipathy to his brother-in-law, which had been vastly increased by recent events, and he would hear nothing of the marriages which the British government was still willing to conclude. Wilhelmina was hastily married in 1731 to her cousin, the hereditary prince of Baireuth; and the Crown Prince Frederick, after the cursory consideration of two ladies who afterwards detested him—Maria Theresa and Elizabeth of Russia—was betrothed in 1732 to Elizabeth Charlotte of Brunswick, a niece of Charles VI's wife. The marriage, which took place in the following year, was intended, as it had been originally proposed, to strengthen the ties between Prussia and Austria. Prussian loyalty to the emperor was further demonstrated in 1732, when all its influence was exerted in the Diet to carry through the guarantee of the Pragmatic Sanction against the protests of Bavaria, Saxony, and the Palatinate.[1] But his loyalty was already being sapped

[1] Eugene to Philip Kinsky, 9 January 1732 (quoted by von Arneth, *Prinz Eugen*, iii. 584): 'Il est constant que l'Empereur ne peut que se louer infiniment

by an uneasy sense that at Vienna the British-Hanoverian alliance was more highly esteemed than that of Prussia. And Frederick William's resentment of inadequate appreciation was increased by Charles VI's conduct in the question of the Polish Succession.

The war of the Polish Succession is the last notable episode before 1740 with which Britain and Prussia were concerned. After the death of Augustus II of Saxony, Stanislas Leczinski, the father-in-law of Louis XV, was elected by an overwhelming majority of the Polish nobles. In spite of a previous agreement with Prussia to terminate the connexion between Saxony and Poland, Russia and Austria gave their support to the young Augustus III. For the second time Stanislas was driven from his kingdom by Russian troops, and his Saxon rival was seated on the throne. In this matter Prussia took no part, and Britain, though it encouraged the opposition to the French candidate, had no direct interest. But France and Spain, united in 1733 by a secret treaty which is often called the first Family Compact, seized the Polish Succession dispute as a pretext for attacking Austria, and obtained the support of Sardinia.

The three allies declared war against Charles VI on the ground that he had opposed France in Poland, whereas no Austrian soldier had crossed the Polish frontier. Against this unprovoked attack, for which he was wholly unprepared, Charles VI could only appeal for support to the Empire and to the states which were bound by treaty to assist him, Russia (by the treaty of 1726), Prussia (by the treaty of 1728), and the maritime powers (by the treaty of Vienna, 1731). Russia was far away, and its contingent did not arrive till the war was practically ended. So Charles's fate depended upon the fulfilment of their promises by his other allies. There is a rather startling and uncomfortable contrast between the conduct of the maritime states and that of Prussia. Frederick William had

de la conduite du Roy de Prusse ... s'étant employé entre autres à préparer au consentement à la garantie de la pragmatique sanction les États de l'Empire qui sont en liaison avec lui, avec une chaleur qui n'auroit pû être plus grande s'il seroit agi de l'affaire la plus importante à luy-même.' Eugene continues by expressing the emperor's desire to promote harmony between England and Prussia.

good cause, in view of his past record, to resent the contemptuous way in which the emperor had ignored him and his interests in dealing with the Polish election. His was not a forgiving nature, and his rather sullen disposition was apt to show its resentment by withdrawing into gloomy isolation. But he had a certain dogged loyalty to the Empire, and he punctiliously discharged his obligation by sending the stipulated 10,000 men to serve under Eugene. He even offered to send more if the emperor would repeat his promises as to Berg. Although the refusal rankled, he with his son joined Eugene for some months in 1734, and Frederick had his first lessons in actual warfare under the greatest living master of the art.

The maritime powers, on the other hand, had no grievance. They were bound to admit, as Prussia did, that the unprovoked attack upon Austria constituted a *casus foederis*. All their interests and traditions, especially the British tradition of maintaining the balance of power, urged them to return to the 'old system', and to support Austria. They had for twenty years upheld the Utrecht settlement with the aid of France, and now that France had turned against them that settlement was threatened with complete overthrow. Yet, on condition that their own immediate interests were not imperilled by a French invasion of the Netherlands, they remained resolutely neutral, and allowed Austria to wage a hopeless war against superior forces. Naples, Sicily, and the Milanese with the exception of Mantua, were all lost. In Germany the province of Lorraine was overrun, and the imperial fortress of Philipsburg was reduced by the French. Eugene himself was forced to confess, in August 1735, that the continuance of the war was hopeless without British assistance, and that imminent ruin could only be averted by making a separate treaty with France. It was fortunate for Austria that Fleury, whose hand had been forced by Chauvelin in 1733, had recovered his ascendancy two years later.[1] In his anxiety to avert the military intervention of Russia and the diplomatic intervention of Great Britain, Fleury granted to Charles VI more lenient terms than the course of

---

[1] *Mémoires de Frédéric II* (éd. Boutarie), i. 22: 'Les courtisans de Versailles disaient que Chauvelin avait escamoté la guerre au cardinal, mais que le cardinal lui avait escamoté la paix.'

the war entitled him to expect. By the cession of Lorraine, immediately to Stanislas Leczinski, and eventually to the French crown, and by leaving Naples and Sicily in the hands of Don Carlos, Charles purchased from France three considerable concessions. The duchy of Parma and Piacenza was resigned by Don Carlos to Austria ; the Pragmatic Sanction was guaranteed in the amplest terms by the one great power which had hitherto rejected it ; and tacit approval was given by France to the marriage of Maria Theresa to Francis Stephen of Lorraine, who was to exchange his ancestral duchy for the Grand Duchy of Tuscany, and who ceased to be obnoxious to France as soon as he ceased to hold lands on her frontier.

The divergent conduct of Britain and Prussia in this so-called War of the Polish Succession was not likely to restore friendly relations between the two powers. As a matter of fact they were not restored during the remaining years of Frederick William. All the old squabbles with Hanover served to keep them apart.[1] The Prussian king was absorbed in the prospective fate of Jülich and Berg, in which Britain itself had no very direct interest. The Dutch disliked the Prussian claim, and Britain clung to the Dutch alliance in spite of the failing courage and energy of its maritime twin. Hanover was jealous of all aggrandizement of Prussia, and was in this matter inclined to support the Dutch. But, in spite of Holland and of Hanover, there was in England a strong and a growing desire for closer relations with Prussia, and men looked to a new reign as offering a chance of realizing this desire. Even George II hoped that a nephew would be more conformable than a brother-in-law, and endeavoured by rather grudging and secret doles to the impecunious Crown Prince to establish some claim on the gratitude of the future king.[2]

---

[1] Guy Dickens to Harrington, 12 December 1739 (S. P. For., Prussia, 46): The king of Prussia 'would sooner decline the most advantageous offers on our part than the pleasure of giving our royal master some mortification if he had an opportunity to do it'.

[2] The reports of Guy Dickens to Harrington in 1739–40 leave no doubt that these sums were unconditionally forwarded from England to Frederick. They were disguised in correspondence as books forwarded to a needy student by a benevolent bookseller. One of Frederick's first acts was to

There can be no doubt that Frederick William mismanaged his foreign affairs.   In each decade of his reign the power and importance of Prussia had declined.   Between 1713 and 1720 Prussia had played an active and self-confident part in the northern war, and had gained its prize in the acquisition of Stettin and the control of the mouth of the Oder.   In the next decade Prussia had held the balance between opposing groups of powers, had been eagerly courted by both sides, but had wofully failed, from the Prussian point of view, to profit by its singularly advantageous position.   And in the last decade, 1731-40, Prussia became a comparatively humble and negligible state, to which little attention was paid.   But, if Frederick William was a failure in diplomacy, he was a master of efficient and economical administration at home.   He left behind him a treasury better filled than any other in Europe, and a thoroughly drilled army, whose only defect was that it had so far been more tested on the review-ground than on the battle-field.[1]   And the son, whom he had despised as a useless dilettante, was eager to startle Europe by a lavish use of the resources which the father had been content to hoard.

treat these sums as loans, and to repay the total amount of £12,250, so as to prevent any claim being based upon this assistance.

[1] For Eugene's rather depreciatory estimate of the Prussian troops see von Arneth, *Prinz Eugen*, iii. 202, 551-3.

II

THE AUSTRIAN SUCCESSION WAR,
1740-8

FOR fourteen years, 1726 to 1740, the relations of Great Britain and Prussia had been unfriendly, and at times almost actively hostile. It is true that the actual quarrels had been Hanoverian rather than British, but they were equally fatal to any co-operation between the two states. And, so long as Frederick William lived, reconciliation was impossible. To Walpole, with his hostility to Hanoverian influence and his rooted distrust of Austria, this alienation of a state with which Britain had no cause of quarrel was distasteful, and he welcomed the death of Frederick William and the accession of his son as opening the possibility of improved relations. Several circumstances concurred to make a good understanding with Prussia eminently desirable. Britain was involved in a war with Spain— the so-called 'War of Jenkins's ear'—and it was necessary to provide against the probability, and indeed the practical certainty, that France would be drawn into the war in support of Spain. Austria, the natural ally in such a war, had been alienated by British neutrality in the Polish Succession War, and in addition Austria had been hopelessly weakened and discredited, not only by its losses in that war, but also by the humiliations of its subsequent war against the Turks. Never had Austria stood so low as in the last year of Charles VI. On the other hand, France occupied as commanding a position as in the great days of Louis XIV.[1] It had virtually annexed Lorraine, it had revived the Bourbon power in Italy to balance that of the Habsburgs, and the French ambassador, Villeneuve, had largely dictated the terms of the treaties of Belgrade, which in 1739 had

---

[1] *Mémoires de Frédéric*, i. 24: 'Depuis la paix de Vienne la France était l'arbitre de l'Europe.'

closed the Turkish war. In these circumstances the support of Prussia was desirable and might be invaluable.

Unfortunately the representation of the two states at each other's courts was eminently unsatisfactory. In 1737 the Prussian envoy in London, one of the numerous family of Borcke, was ignominiously dismissed on a charge of seducing British subjects and even soldiers to enter the Prussian service, and, in spite of vigorous protests from Berlin, he was refused a formal audience to take leave of the king.[1] At Berlin Captain Guy Dickens—a useful and not incompetent actor on the diplomatic stage—was a mere *chargé d'affaires*, and had neither the status nor the influence necessary for an important negotiation. And his reports were not reassuring. In his first audience Frederick asked him what support his government would give on the three pressing questions of (1) Jülich and Berg, (2) East Friesland, (3) Mecklenburg; and it was clear that no satisfactory answer could be given.[2] Hanover was opposed to all three Prussian claims; and the Dutch, though they had little interest in Mecklenburg, were resolutely hostile to any increase of Prussian dominions in the west of Germany. Harrington, who still held the seals of the northern department, realized the necessity of sending an envoy of higher rank if he wished to gain Frederick's confidence, and told Dickens that this would be done if Frederick would send an envoy of equal rank.[3]

So matters stood when the death of Charles VI, on the 20th October, suddenly raised the twin questions of the succession to the Austrian dominions and of a new imperial election. Maria Theresa's claim to succeed seemed to be as securely buttressed as such a claim could be, and her appointment of her husband as joint ruler demonstrated her desire and expectation that he should be chosen to follow her father in maintaining the long association—unbroken since 1438—of the imperial office with Austria. But it was certain that in both matters she would meet with opposition. France was unpledged as to the imperial election, and it was a matter of course that she

---

[1] The acrimonious correspondence on this subject is to be found in *S. P. For., Foreign Ministers in England*, 48.

[2] *S. P. For., Prussia*, 47, Dickens to Harrington, 17 August 1740.

[3] *Ibid.*, Harrington to Dickens, 10 October 1740.

should seize the opportunity to break the continuous Habsburg tenure, to which she had been consistently opposed, and especially that she should oppose the election of a prince who might use his authority in Germany to re-claim his lost duchy of Lorraine. And French influence among German princes, based upon propinquity, bribery, and the treaty of Westphalia, was always considerable, and might, in view of the extinction of the male line of Habsburg, be decisive. As to the succession the matter was more complicated. That Bavaria was ready to put forward a claim was known beforehand. That Saxony, in spite of recent pledges, would do the same was probable. Spain and Sardinia could make use of claims, in themselves of little weight, but sufficient to give them a chance of adding to their gains in Italy. But co-operation between rival claimants was obviously difficult and perhaps impossible. And no single claimant was really formidable unless supported by France. Thus Maria Theresa seemed to be reasonably secure, unless French ambition and tradition impelled Fleury to exert his ecclesiastical subtlety to find a pretext for evading the solemn pledge to maintain the Pragmatic Sanction with which he had purchased the reversion of Lorraine. This was the one supreme danger-point on which attention was concentrated both in Vienna and in London.

Rather curiously, in view of British neutrality in the war of 1733–5, there was no vacillation in London as to the policy to be pursued. It is difficult to see, unless the Spanish war made the difference, why British interests demanded that the integrity of the Austrian dominions should be maintained on Charles VI's death, if it was not equally imperative during his life. But consistency was not a conspicuous characteristic of eighteenth-century politicians, and Walpole made no effort in 1740, as he had done in 1733, to oppose the general demand, both in Britain and in Hanover, that treaties should be observed, the 'old system' restored, and Austria maintained to balance the house of Bourbon in Europe. Nor was there any hesitation as to the first step to be taken in carrying out this policy. Both treaty obligations and traditions pointed to Prussia as the state most thoroughly committed to the support of the Pragmatic Sanction. Here was a link which would at last bind the two powers together, and Hanoverian grumbles as to East Friesland or Mecklenburg must be sternly disregarded. George II, eager for the major aim, could not object to the most obvious expedient for obtaining it. Besides, if Prussia should be seduced into an alliance with France, Hanover would be in imminent danger.

As no new envoy had yet been appointed, it was necessary to employ Guy Dickens again, and Harrington instructed him, on the 31st October, to arrange concerted measures with Frederick, 'as His Majesty's engagements for maintaining the indivisibility of the Austrian Succession are the same as those of the king of Prussia'.[1] Before these instructions, prompt as they were, could reach Berlin, they were already obsolete. Frederick's decision was so rapid, and his grasp of the European situation so masterly, as to prove that he must have mapped out his programme before the opportunity came for carrying it out. He was determined that Prussia should no longer be patronized and attached to the 'system' of a greater state, as it had tended to be in the time of his father and grandfather. To the end of his reign the slightest hint of an attempt to guide or dictate his policy excited his passionate indignation. The death of Charles VI gave him the first chance of asserting his absolute freedom from either influence, tradition, or morality. He realized that the weakness of Maria Theresa would be as tempting to others as to himself. France would inevitably be drawn in to assert a dominant share in determining the fate of Austria and the Empire. Britain would, with equal certainty, be forced to oppose France. The two contending powers would infallibly bid against each other for the support of Prussia, and he, acting as his own auctioneer, could lower the hammer whenever one of them was in a position to pay—not merely to offer—a sufficiently tempting price. The one dangerous element in the situation was Russia, whose foreign policy was so swayed by personal motives as to be incalculable. But the death of the Tsaritsa Anne, a firm supporter of the Austrian alliance, was followed by disputes and disorders, which rendered resolute intervention by Russia impossible, and which might end in securing for him Russian support or at least Russian neutrality. In any case, he declared, it was always possible to send an ass

[1] S. P. For., Prussia, 48, Harrington to Dickens, 31 October (o. s.) 1740.

laden with gold into St. Petersburg.[1] Meanwhile he determined to occupy an almost undefended Silesia, and to offer his support to Maria Theresa against all enemies provided she would compensate him for his questionable claims and his indisputable expenditure. If she refused, as she did refuse, then he must trust to the pressure that might be applied either by her allies or by her opponents.

This plan was already fully formed and on the verge of execution when Dickens at last represented to Frederick that the indivisibility of the Austrian Succession was necessary for the balance of power, and that concert should be easy between two powers whose pledges were identical. Frederick replied that if Dickens meant the Pragmatic Sanction, he was not going to support it, had made no promise to do so, and would not be bound by his father's promise. When pressed as to his designs, he grew red in the face, and said no one had a right to make such a demand. Calming down, he added that he was in favour of making the grand duke of Tuscany emperor, but he would never consent to his being king of Bohemia, which was contrary to the Pragmatic Sanction. He then flung out that Britain and France were too inclined ' to bring other princes under our tuition '. When Dickens suggested a guarantee of Jülich and Berg, Frederick replied that it was too late, that he had not much at heart his pretensions towards the Rhine, which would always give umbrage to the Dutch, whereas the maritime powers could have no objection to the expansion of his territories eastward. Dickens further reported that Marshal Schwerin, one of Frederick's two confidants in the scheme, had embroidered his master's text with the contention that if the maritime powers did not support Prussia, the king would be forced to join France, and then where would be the security of Hanover ?[2]

[1] *Politische Correspondenz Friedrichs des Grossen* (i. 90–1) gives a remarkable analysis of the situation, printed from the king's autograph answer to a ministerial memorandum. ' Il ne reste que la Russie seule capable de nous donner de l'ombrage. . . . Si l'Impératrice est morte, les Russiens seront si occupés de l'intérieur de leurs affaires qu'ils n'auront pas le temps de penser aux étrangères ; et, en tout cas, faire entrer un âne chargé d'or à Pétersbourg n'est pas une affaire impossible.' The reference in the last sentence is from Cicero, *Ad Atticum*, i. 16, 12.

[2] *S. P. For.*, *Prussia*, 48, Dickens to Harrington, 6 December 1740.

This report, followed by Frederick's actual invasion and rapid advance in Silesia, destroyed the first illusion of the British ministry. From Holland came the suggestion of a joint demand for the withdrawal of the Prussian troops. But Walpole and his colleagues were wise enough to see that this was likely to do more harm than good. Frederick had already sent his personal friend, Count Truchsess, to London, 'to lull us to sleep', and Harrington responded by sending to Berlin a Scottish peer, Lord Hyndford, who had still to serve his diplomatic apprenticeship. He was instructed to offer his good offices to reconcile Frederick with Maria Theresa, and when 'the Court of Vienna should be induced to do him justice with respect to his rights to part of the duchy of Silesia', Hyndford was to adjust an alliance of Prussia with Austria and the maritime powers, the condition being that Frederick 'upon such satisfaction' should support the Pragmatic Sanction and vote for the grand duke.[1] The necessary collaboration at Vienna was entrusted to Sir Thomas Robinson, and the two envoys were to act in close concord with each other.

It was a sound policy, and Maria Theresa would probably have escaped much subsequent trouble if she had consented to adopt it. But it was obviously unheroic, and it smacked both to Englishmen and Austrians of excessive regard for the security of Hanover. The young queen, with creditable spirit, refused to adopt what seemed to her craven and selfish advice, and very pertinently pointed out to Robinson that a pledge to maintain the Pragmatic Sanction was curiously fulfilled by urging her to break it. So Walpole had to restore the 'old system' by a defensive treaty with Austria,[2] but he failed to induce Prussia to return to the fold which in the days of William III and Anne had included both powers. After staving off the demands of France as long as there was any chance of Austria's giving way, Frederick, already the victor at Mollwitz and the master of the greater part of Silesia, joined, on the 5th June 1741, the coalition which Belleisle had founded in the previous month, by the treaty

---

[1] Harrington's instructions to Hyndford, 10 March (o. s.) 1741, in *S. P. For.*, *Prussia*, 49.

[2] 24 June 1741. Britain was to supply 12,000 mercenary troops and a subsidy of £300,000.

of Nymphenburg, with Spain and Bavaria. The adhesion of Saxony, tempted by the prospect of taking a share in the proposed spoliation of Austria, completed the league which Eugene had declared would be the ruin of Austria if it could ever be formed.[1]

Eugene's forecast would have been literally fulfilled if the coalition had been held together by any stronger cement than the purely selfish interests of its members. While Maria Theresa was in Hungary rousing the loyal spirit of a people who had been the resolute opponents of Habsburg rule, Frederick occupied the capital of Silesia, Upper Austria fell to the combined French and Bavarian forces, and Vienna was only saved by a sudden decision to turn north into Bohemia, the province which conferred on its ruler the right to a vote in the imperial election. At the same time Spain was preparing a formidable force to attack the Habsburg provinces of Italy in conjunction with the king of Sardinia. Perhaps the unkindest and most unexpected blow was that George II, alarmed by the dispatch of a second French army to western Germany, concluded a hasty convention with France by which his electorate was to remain neutral, and George promised to give his vote for Charles Albert of Bavaria. The British ministers, who had not been consulted, disclaimed all responsibility for this act of their electoral master, and declared that it would make no difference to the policy of Great Britain. But it was difficult for Maria Theresa, unfamiliar with the relations between kingdom and electorate, to take these assurances at their face value. And the selfish action of George II contributed to one result which the British ministers were inclined to welcome. The combination of dangers and desertion compelled Maria Theresa to recognize at last that some concession was necessary, and that to escape worse disasters she must buy off either France or Prussia. France, inflated with confidence in itself and in Belleisle, would abate no jot

---

[1] Eugene's famous letter to Charles VI of 6 August 1735 contains this sentence, which is almost prophetic: 'Sollte es Frankreich gelingen . . . Baiern, Sachsen und Preussen zu vereinigen, so ist für die Zukunft nichts gewisser, als dass die Erblande gänzlich zergliedert oder wenigstens völlig verheert und der Schauplatz eines furchtbaren Krieges sein werden'. See von Arneth, *Prinz Eugen*, iii. 475.

of its plan for the final humiliation of the Austrian house. But Frederick was not so obdurate. He had no desire to make France the dictator of Germany, and he was uneasily conscious that the rather inarticulate German patriotism, which it was safer to conciliate than to offend, resented the march of French troops through Germany, and the obvious intention of France to dictate the choice of a German ruler. And it was safer to get the cession of lands in Silesia from the actual wearer of the Bohemian crown than from a foreign power which was only too ready to distribute other people's territories. In addition, there were military reasons for a cessation of arms between Austria and Prussia. Frederick was besieging Neisse, and Neipperg with an Austrian army was advancing to its relief. It is always, as Frederick discovered in 1757, a dangerous thing to conduct a siege and fight a relieving force at the same time, and Frederick was not unwilling to evade the problem. On the other side the loss of Neisse was nothing compared with the loss of Bohemia, and Neipperg's army was urgently needed to oppose the French and Bavarians. Lord Hyndford, instructed to represent both Britain and Austria, was exultant at the prospect of gaining his maiden triumph as a diplomatist. Armed with passports and countersigns, he dashed from one camp to the other, and at last, on the 9th October, he brought Frederick to a secret midnight meeting with Neipperg in the castle of Klein-Schnellendorf. The terms of agreement had already been settled in outline, and Hyndford, after hearing both Frederick and Neipperg, drew up the various clauses of the bargain, and signed it as an assurance of its validity.[1] The procedure was unfamiliar to eighteenth-century diplomacy, and was ridiculed as the work of an amateur by professional masters of the art.[2] And their ridicule was justified by the result.

In adjusting the convention [3] Hyndford acted very much as a conciliator acts in a modern industrial dispute. But an experi-

---

[1] Hyndford tells, with much gusto, the story of the famous interview in a dispatch to Harrington of 14 October 1741 (*S. P. For., Prussia*, 51).

[2] Podewils called it 'a patched up thing contrary to all rule and form'.

[3] The terms of the Convention of Klein-Schnellendorf are given *in extenso* in *Pol. Corr.* i. 371–2 ; in Koch and Schoell, *Hist. abrégée des Traités de Paix*, ii. 303–6 ; and (translated) in Broglie, *Frederick the Great and Maria Theresa*, ii. 282–5.

enced conciliator never quits the room until he has secured the signature of at least one responsible representative of each side, and only appends his own name as an additional guarantee of the authenticity of the agreement. Hyndford entirely neglected this precaution, and it is probable that if he had asked for Frederick's signature it would have been refused. The result was that each party obtained its immediate ends, but neither regarded itself as bound by ulterior promises. Neipperg was allowed to march away without molestation to defend Prague against the French and Bavarians. Frederick was allowed to take Neisse after a sham siege, and he also obtained his first assurance of a cession by Maria Theresa of Lower Silesia as far as the river Neisse. But the promised treaty which was to be concluded by Christmas on the basis of the convention was never considered by Frederick, although Austria innocently took the trouble to draw it up. And the condition of secrecy was impossible of fulfilment. The actual events betrayed collusion, even if Austria had not disclosed it in the hope, not altogether vain, of sowing distrust between France and Prussia. Frederick himself was perfectly cynical in the matter. Within a month from the date of the Convention he made himself secure on the other side by signing, on the 8th November, a secret agreement with Bavaria and Saxony by which the three states guaranteed their respective shares of Maria Theresa's inheritance, Lower Silesia and Breslau to Prussia, Upper Silesia and Moravia to Saxony, and Upper and Lower Austria with Bohemia and Tyrol to Bavaria. When Prague was unexpectedly stormed by Maurice de Saxe on the 25th November, and Neipperg was too late to save it, Frederick deemed it safer to adhere to the side which seemed in a position to 'deliver the goods'. He declared loudly that he had made no bargain with Austria, and resumed hostilities by attacking Moravia. For four weeks he diligently avoided the angry and discomfited Hyndford, though the latter 'haunted him like a ghost', and it was not till Christmas Day, the date on which the still-born treaty should have come to light, that he at last informed the British envoy directly that he had been released from all obligations by the Austrian disclosures, and from all inducement to observe them by the Austrian failure to defend Prague. He admitted that he would have preferred Maria Theresa to keep Moravia and the two Austrias, but she would be too dangerous a neighbour in Bohemia and Upper Silesia. When Hyndford ventured to suggest that the Convention might be published to Frederick's discredit, the king replied that they would only publish their own folly and perhaps would not be believed.[1]

Maria Theresa was even worse off than Hyndford. She had sold her pride and her province, and had gained absolutely nothing by the sacrifice. The fall of Prague, which she had hoped to avert, was followed by two disasters of equal magnitude. In December 1741 a revolution in Russia deposed the infant Tsar, Iwan VI, and overthrew the German gang who, under the regency of the Tsar's mother, had consistently favoured the cause of Maria Theresa. Peter the Great's surviving daughter, Elizabeth, endowed with some of her father's ability and dissoluteness, but devoid of his daemonic energy, was raised to the throne. For the next few months La Chétardie, the French envoy, was omnipotent at the Russian court, and all hope of Russian assistance to Austria came to an end. In January 1742 the long-delayed imperial election took place. The Bohemian vote, which Maria Theresa claimed to give by proxy, was excluded on the ground that Charles Albert was *de facto* king, and the other eight votes were unanimously given for the elector of Bavaria. For the first time for three centuries the imperial dignity, which carried with it the crown of Germany, passed out of the hands of a member of the Habsburg house. The fortune of Maria Theresa had reached its nadir.

And then with dramatic suddenness came the turn of the tide. Neipperg's army was still intact. The Hungarians since September had been arming and training the *insurrectio* or *levée en masse*, which they had voted at the time of Maria Theresa's coronation. Outside the war area other troops had been steadily collected. Steps were being taken to detach Sardinia from the coalition and thus to strengthen the opposition to the Spaniards in

---

[1] *S. P. For.*, *Prussia*, 51, Hyndford to Harrington, 26 December 1741. Frederick lied so successfully that Belleisle, who could not believe that a treaty made by himself could be broken, refused, in spite of the evidence of facts, to believe in the Convention of Klein-Schnellendorf. See Broglie, *u. s.*, ii. 290-1.

Italy. A British fleet was in the Mediterranean. Walpole's long tenure of office came to an end at the beginning of February 1742, and Carteret, the guiding spirit in the new administration, was more enthusiastically pro-Austrian than Walpole had ever been. The most startling events took place in the east of Germany. The new Austrian levies began by recovering Upper Austria, and thus isolated the French and Bavarian forces in Bohemia. While a part of the victorious troops were detached to join Neipperg in Bohemia, the rest threw themselves into Bavaria, defended only by a few isolated garrisons. On the day that Charles VII assumed the imperial crown, the enemy occupied his hereditary capital. The star of Maria Theresa, lately so low, was now in the ascendant, and Frederick began to look back with some longing to the policy of Klein-Schnellendorf. Podewils, by the king's instructions, approached Lord Hyndford, whom he found rather shy after his recent experience. At last the negotiation was set going again. Characteristically Frederick raised his terms and demanded, in addition to Lower Silesia, the town of Glatz with four circles in Bohemia. Maria Theresa indignantly rejected such a demand as preposterous, and declared, with Carteret's backing, that any concession must be paid for, not by neutrality, but by active support. After much haggling, the Bohemian demands were withdrawn, and Frederick agreed to accept Glatz and the two Silesias, with the exception of Teschen and certain other districts. Carteret, on his side, consented to Frederick's neutrality, in the confident expectation that support would ultimately follow.[1] Frederick, in turn, facilitated matters by offering to pay the interest and at due intervals to repay the principal of a loan which Charles VI had obtained from British capitalists on the security of the Silesian revenues. But Maria Theresa, in the unfamiliar excitement of victory, remained as obdurate as ever, and Frederick decided that a little wholesome humiliation was needed to bring her to reason. Hence a sudden incursion into Bohemia, and another Prussian victory at Chotusitz on the 17th May. There the king stopped, making no attempt to extricate the French troops from their almost hopeless position. For his own selfish purpose he

---

[1] *Ibid.*, 53, Carteret to Hyndford, 27 April (o. s.) 1742.

had done enough, and his allies, having served his ends, must look after themselves. Maria Theresa was at last convinced that all other considerations must be postponed to the recovery of Bohemia, and that that could only be secured if Frederick would abandon the cause of France. So Hyndford was consoled for his humiliation of the previous year by being allowed to negotiate—this time in due form—the preliminary treaty of Breslau, which was converted into a final treaty at Berlin. The essential clauses were (1) the cession of the county of Glatz and of the duchy of Silesia, with the exception of certain districts which, with the ducal title, were to be retained by Maria Theresa; (2) the protection of Roman Catholic worship and privileges in the ceded provinces; and (3) the taking over by Frederick of both British and Dutch loans on Silesian security. Hyndford was not ill-rewarded for his share in the transaction. From his own government he asked for and obtained the Order of the Thistle, with which he was invested by the Prussian king. Maria Theresa gave him her portrait set in diamonds, and Frederick made him a thank-offering of 10,000 crowns.[1] This sum Hyndford proposed to convert into a service of plate to be manufactured at Berlin, and Frederick was so pleased with this patronage of Prussian industry that he granted a patent authorizing the earl and his heirs to bear the arms of Silesia in memory of the peace of Breslau.

No sooner had the terms of the treaty been settled than Frederick began to demand the guarantee of the maritime powers, which he thought he had purchased by taking over the Silesian loans, and offered to conclude a defensive alliance with them. To the intense chagrin of Hyndford, the negotiations were taken out of his hands and carried on directly in London with the Prussian envoy, Andrié. To Carteret the Prussian overtures

[1] Frederick was less generous after than before the treaty. On 9 May Hyndford reported that Podewils had offered him 100,000 rix-dollars if he would secure Maria Theresa's acceptance of the Prussian terms (*S. P. For.*, *Prussia*, 53). Hyndford replied that a British peer did not accept bribes, but he evidently thought that Podewils might be gained by similar methods. On 8 September 1742, when the terms of the treaty of Westminster were under discussion, he asked leave to offer him money, and Carteret authorized £1,000. But there is no record that the offer was ever made, and the sum ultimately served to defray the expenses of Hyndford's journey from Berlin to St. Petersburg.

were exactly what he wanted. He was assured in his own mind that France would show such resentment of Frederick's desertion that the latter would be forced in self-defence to join the Anglo-Austrian alliance. So confident was he of this that he rejected the advice of Hyndford and granted the guarantee on the 24th June, on the understanding that the defensive treaty would follow at once. But Frederick, who wanted the guarantee far more than the treaty, was no longer in a hurry, and proceeded to haggle over the terms, especially as he suspected Carteret, with good reason, of a design to prolong the war and to embroil Prussia with France. He issued a declaration that, as Great Britain was about to embark on a war with France, the proposed alliance would not apply to such a war. Carteret replied that Britain had no aggressive policy, that she was only acting as the loyal ally of Maria Theresa, that if France should on that ground declare war Britain would prosecute it. Frederick's declaration, which ' renders the treaty useless and indifferent ', must be withdrawn.[1] A new difficulty was introduced by the raising of old Prussian disputes with Hanover, with which the British ministers had no concern. Frederick will sign the treaty without any reservation, provided the guarantee is extended to cover his claims to Mecklenburg and East Friesland.[2] Carteret replies with unusual self-control that there is no great difficulty about Mecklenburg, but that the Dutch must be consulted about the fate of East Friesland, and also Hanover has rival claims. Ultimately Frederick withdrew his declaration, on an assurance that Britain did not meditate an offensive war, and agreed that the outstanding questions should be settled in a separate agreement with Hanover.[3] At last, on the 28th November 1742, the treaty was signed at Westminster. This was the second triumph of Carteret's foreign policy.

The treaty of Westminster, like so many eighteenth-century treaties, proved a singularly futile document.[4] With great prudence France disappointed the expectation of Carteret and

---

[1] *S. P. For.*, *Prussia*, 55, Carteret to Hyndford, 14 September (o. s.) 1742.
[2] *Ibid.*, Hyndford to Carteret, 29 September 1742 ; *Pol. Corr.* ii. 278.
[3] *Ibid.*, Hyndford to Carteret, 16 November 1742 ; *Pol. Corr.* ii. 290.
[4] It was ominous that Frederick wrote to Podewils on 16 November, ' Je fais cette alliance à contre-cœur', *Pol. Corr.* ii. 295.

deliberately refused to show any active resentment of Frederick's desertion. Thus if war broke out between Britain and France, Prussia was equally bound to both belligerents and could join either side as interest might dictate. But such a war Frederick was anxious to avoid. In order to complete the security of the new acquisitions, he wished for a general peace, and at any rate to put an end to the German war, which might enable Austria at any time to pick a new quarrel with him. The Austrian succession question was virtually settled when the French were expelled from Bohemia and the Spanish attack upon Lombardy was repulsed. All that remained was to pacify Charles VII by restoring his electorate and recognizing his imperial title, and this would deprive his foreign allies of any pretext for continuing the war. France, conscious of the failure of Belleisle's schemes, was not unwilling to come to terms,[1] and if Elizabeth Farnese was more obdurate, she could do nothing single-handed. It was therefore disconcerting to Frederick to learn that Britain had increased her subsidy to Maria Theresa from £300,000 to £500,000, that 6,000 Hanoverian troops were to be added to an increased British contingent, and that the Dutch were to contribute troops to the so-called 'Pragmatic Army' which was to be sent into Germany. Against this entry Frederick vigorously protested, and added, ' I don't care what becomes of the French, but I can't suffer the emperor to be ruined nor dethroned.' Four days later came the significant threat to Hyndford: ' I would have your master remember that Hanover is at a very little distance from me and that I can enter there when I please '.[2] Carteret replied with spirit that Britain had no quarrel with the emperor but with ' the elector of Bavaria prosecuting his private quarrel with a foreign force ', and that ' the great art of France has consisted in this, to lead the several members of the Germanic body into a mistake of the cause of the elector of Bavaria for the cause of the emperor '. Hyndford is to inform Frederick that Hanover will be defended by Britain, if it is attacked out of hatred of Britain, and to remind him that ' the king, my master, may be

---

[1] Frederick says (*Mémoires*, i. 175), ' Les Français étaient les seuls qui désirassent la paix '.

[2] See Hyndford's dispatches to Carteret of 17, 18, and 20 December 1742 in *S. P. For., Prussia*, 55.

a younger elector than the king of Prussia, but he is a much greater king '.[1] Thus within a month of the signing of the defensive treaty the relations between Britain and Prussia were as strained as ever.

These relations became steadily worse in 1743. The whole character of the war was evidently completely changed. The Bourbon coalition, which had been formed to humiliate and partition Austria, was now in its turn on the defensive, while Austria and Britain were organizing a league for the depression of France and Spain. Maria Theresa desired to punish her enemies for the unprovoked rupture of their pre-war pledges, and to obtain compensation for the loss of Silesia by restoring Lorraine to her husband, by recovering Alsace, and by expelling Don Carlos from Naples and Sicily. Carteret was her accomplice, in the hope of depriving the Bourbon powers of the recent gains, which they owed, in his opinion, to Walpole's ill-timed neutrality in the War of the Polish Succession. Between the two rival leagues stood the unfortunate Charles VII, no longer a ' bold Bavarian ', but threatened with the loss of his ancestral dominions and possibly with the necessity of a humiliating surrender of the imperial crown.´ Behind him stood in the background his professed champion, Frederick of Prussia.

The reconciliation of Charles VII with Maria Theresa was the great diplomatic problem of 1743. Great Britain was the obvious mediator in the matter, and negotiations were conducted, partly by the Bavarian minister in London, partly by Frederick, and partly by William of Hesse-Cassel while George II was on the continent in the summer. We are concerned mainly with the negotiations with Prussia, which began in December 1742 with Frederick's suggestion that the emperor should be bought off. Carteret was inclined to entertain the proposal, because there was an obvious gain in detaching Charles VII from France, and also because he wished to keep Frederick passive. Certain conditions were fairly obvious. Charles must recover Bavaria, which might possibly be raised to a kingdom, and his imperial title must be recognized, which Maria Theresa had so far refused to do. On the other hand, the Bavarian claim to the Austrian succession must be withdrawn. If Frederick had been content

[1] *S. P. For.*, *Prussia*, 55, Carteret to Hyndford, 24 December (o. s.) 1742.

with these simple terms he would have held a very strong position. But, in accordance with his usual practice, he put his demands too high, and demanded compensation for the damage done to Bavaria and for the withdrawal of the succession claims. It was made clear from the outset that Maria Theresa would not consent, and that Britain would not ask her to consent, to further infringements of the Pragmatic Sanction; so that compensation could not come from Austria. Therefore Frederick proposed that certain bishoprics should be secularized and certain imperial cities mediatized, and that these should be granted to Bavaria.[1] On this subject negotiations continued for some months. But it was clear that such a proposal, while it might naturally commend itself to two Protestant powers, could not possibly be accepted by a Roman Catholic emperor, nor by Maria Theresa. In the end the scheme leaked out to the public, and Charles VII promptly disavowed it. The more feasible terms adjusted with William of Hesse at Hanau were equally unsuccessful, though at one time it seemed as if Carteret had made up his mind to accept them. But, even if he had done so, it is practically certain that Maria Theresa would have refused to give up Bavaria (always coveted by Austria) until she had secured some other equivalent, and it is very improbable that Carteret would have been willing to put any such pressure upon her as was exerted by his successors in the autumn and winter of 1745. At any rate, whether rightly or wrongly, Frederick attributed the failure to Carteret, and concluded that the British minister had been deliberately wasting time while the Austrian troops made themselves complete masters of Bavaria, and thus prepared the way for a western advance and a junction with the Pragmatic Army. That army, while waiting for the Austrians, was nearly entrapped by the French, and only escaped by cutting its way through at Dettingen (27 June)—a battle which would have sunk into deserved oblivion if it had not been for the personal presence of George II, and for the celebration of his victory by the genius of Handel.

The failure of the negotiations and the obviously aggressive attitude of the present British Government exasperated

---

[1] *Pol. Corr.* ii. 320, 339; *S. P. For.*, *Prussia*, 56, Hyndford to Carteret, 27 February 1743.

Frederick.[1] And before the end of the year two events occurred which added an element of alarm to his exasperation. In order to complete the conversion of Sardinia to the Austrian alliance, Carteret forced upon Maria Theresa the treaty of Worms, which promised definite cessions of territory to Charles Emmanuel. The second article of the treaty guaranteed all the territories of Maria Theresa with express reference to past treaties. As these treaties were all anterior to the treaty of Breslau and no mention was made of that treaty, it appeared to Frederick's suspicious mind that Charles Emmanuel had guaranteed her possession of Silesia, and that this argued evil designs not only on the part of Austria but also on that of Britain. His suspicion would have been all the stronger if he had known that Hyndford, when he signed the Breslau treaty, wrote to his chief of the 'temporary cessions' of Maria Theresa. In December 1743 an alliance was concluded between Austria and Saxony, and this, on account of the geographical position of Saxony, threatened danger to Silesia or even to Brandenburg.[2]

In 1744 the altered character of the war was recognized by the formal declaration of war between England and France in March, and Hyndford was instructed to demand the fulfilment by Prussia of the treaty of Westminster. In a very carefully concocted reply, Frederick declared that if Britain should be attacked he would march in person to its defence at the head of 30,000 men. But he omitted all reference to the electoral dominions, and he added that Britain was so evidently the real aggressor in the present quarrel that the *casus foederis* had not arisen.[3]

[1] *S. P. For.*, *Prussia*, 57, on 16 July 1743, Hyndford reported to Carteret that Frederick 'cannot hide the inveterate hatred which he has against the King and the British nation'.

[2] *Mémoires de Frédéric*, i. 216 : 'Cette alliance avec la Saxe est encore moins innocente ; elle livre aux Autrichiens un passage et des secours pour m'attaquer dans mes propres foyers.'

[3] Hyndford to Carteret, 22 April 1744, in *S. P. For.*, *Prussia*, 59. Frederick's letter to Hyndford is printed in *Pol. Corr.* iii. 104. Three days earlier he sent a summary of its proposed contents to Mardefeld, his envoy at St. Petersburg (*ibid.*, p. 96). On his offer of 30,000 men to defend Great Britain, he sent an interesting commentary to France. ' Outre qu'on a évité soigneusement de faire mention dans cette lettre des pays d'Hanovre, l'offre qui y est d'un secours de 30,000 hommes, en cas que le royaume de la Grande

This provoked vigorous remonstrances from both Hyndford and Carteret against the implied contention that the treaty of Westminster did not include Hanover, and against the actual assertion that Britain had provoked the war. But this controversy, acute as it was, was only conducted by Frederick to blind the British ministers to his real intentions. Weeks before the letters were written on either side, and before the French declaration of war, he had made up his mind to check the aggressive action of Austria and Britain, and to force Maria Theresa once more to defend her own dominions. The outline of his scheme was clearly formulated in his own mind as early as January 1744.[1] He would wait till the Austrian army was far away across the Rhine, and would then throw himself into Bohemia, and conquer the undefended kingdom. This would compel the Austrians to retire eastwards, the French and imperial troops would follow them along the Danube valley and recover Bavaria for Charles VII. If all went well, Frederick hoped to join his allies in the next campaign in an attack upon Vienna, and would then force Maria Theresa to cede Bohemia to the emperor. While he was making his military preparations, he could adjust the terms of co-operation with France, extort from Charles VII cessions in Bohemia which would repay him for his exertions, and protect himself on the side of Russia by arranging a triple alliance between that power, Prussia, and Sweden. In order to provide the emperor with troops, Frederick proposed to form a league of well-disposed German princes for the defence of the Empire and the imperial constitution, and France might, if necessary, be invited to accede to the league as guarantor of the treaty of Westphalia.

This carefully prepared programme was punctually carried out with the exception of two items. He made his treaty with

---

Bretagne devrait être envahi hostilement, quelque spécieuse qu'elle paraisse, est pourtant d'une nature que je suis bien persuadé que la mariée paraîtra trop belle aux Anglais, et qu'ils se garderont bien de m'avoir dans leurs îles à la tête d'une armée de 30,000 hommes' (*ibid.*, p. 106).

[1] The secrecy with which his scheme was prepared is expressed in the statement quoted by Hyndford to Carteret on 1 August 1744, that 'if he imagined his shirt or even his skin knew what he intended to do he would tear them off' (*S. P. For., Prussia*, 60).

France on the 5th June, and later insisted not only that the
Austrians should be harried on their retreat to Bohemia, but also
that a second French army should be sent to threaten or even to
occupy Hanover. The docile and dependent emperor was compelled to mutilate his prospective kingdom by promising to give
three circles in Bohemia to his exacting patron. It was even
suggested that he might have to cut off more slices in order
to buy off Saxony. Frederick obtained the adhesion of the
Palatinate, Hesse, and the emperor to a rather inadequate
League of Frankfort (22 May), and France was admitted by
a secret article (6 June), though this rather militated against the
patriotic pretensions of the League, and William of Hesse
showed some disinclination to associate himself with a state
which proposed to endanger the Protestant succession in Britain
by encouraging a Jacobite rebellion.[1] But Frederick failed
rather badly to obtain adequate security against Russia and to
organize his proposed northern alliance. He had started the
year with confident hopes. He had one of his most trusted
diplomatists, Mardefeld, in St. Petersburg, and Mardefeld had
the cordial co-operation of La Chétardie, the French envoy, who
had returned to Russia in 1743 at the request of the Tsaritsa
when the misconduct of Botta, the Austrian envoy, had alienated
her from Austria and revived her original inclination to France.
With the help of these two envoys Frederick foiled a proposal to
marry Elizabeth's nephew and acknowledged heir, Peter of
Holstein, to a Saxon princess, and secured his betrothal to a
young lady from Anhalt-Zerbst, destined to be famous as
Catharine II, whose mother accompanied her daughter to
St. Petersburg and there played the part of a second agent of
Prussia. Another Holstein prince, Adolf Frederick, had been
forced by Russia upon Sweden as crown prince and heir presumptive in the treaty of Abo, and this prince was married in
1744 to Frederick's sister, Louisa Ulrica. These two Holstein
marriages seemed to offer a substantial basis for the proposed
triple alliance.[2] But Frederick failed to allow for the wiles of

---

[1] See Frederick's remonstrance against this ill-timed intrusion of religious
scruples into politics in *Pol. Corr.* iii. 60-1.

[2] *Mémoires de Frédéric*, i. 209: ' C'était sur ces deux alliances que la
Prusse fondait sa sûreté.'

his arch opponent, Alexis Bestoujew, or for the reckless folly of the presumptuous and incompetent La Chétardie. Bestoujew had raised himself to a dominant position at court by freeing his sensuous and indolent mistress from the drudgery of public business. In opposition to her inclinations, he was a resolute opponent of both Prussia and France, and a supporter of the old alliance of Russia with Austria. There is no doubt that he was in receipt of a regular income from Great Britain, and Frederick, often as he tried, was unable to outbid the British treasury. For fifteen years there was a continuous duel at the Russian court between the Prussian King and the Russian Grand Chancellor, and the latter more than held his own until the general reversal of alliances brought Russia into co-operation with France and made Bestoujew's position no longer tenable. In 1743 Botta had given him a serious shake, but in the next year La Chétardie enabled him to do more than merely recover his lost ground. Unaware that his correspondence was regularly opened and that the secret of his cypher had been discovered, the French envoy indulged in frank and Gallic comments upon Elizabeth's character and mode of life. When sufficient evidence had been collected, Bestoujew laid selected excerpts before the Tsaritsa. Exasperated by the contemptuous language of a man whom she had admitted to unusual intimacy, Elizabeth ordered La Chétardie to be seized by her soldiers and ignominiously expelled from Russia.[1]

Frederick was extremely dismayed by this shrewd blow on the part of his antagonist. The triple alliance was now out of the question, and Russia was the one power of which he stood in some awe.[2] He had laid it down from the outset that the obtaining of a treaty with Russia was an essential condition of

[1] The whole story of La Chétardie's second embassy, of his intrigues to overthrow Bestoujew, and of his ultimate discomfiture, is told, with documentary evidence, in the first volume of the *Recueil des Instructions données aux Ambassadeurs*, &c. (Russie), admirably edited by M. Alfred Rambaud (pp. 427–40).

[2] Frederick 'is more in fear of Russia than he is of God' (Hyndford to Carteret, 18 July 1744, in *S. P. For.*, *Prussia*, 60). Laurence seems to have remembered this phrase when he wrote to Harrington on 15 November 1746, 'it is not the fear of God, but that of Russia, which inspires peaceful thoughts to this Court' (*ibid.*, 62).

his renewal of the war.[1] For a moment he contemplated the postponement or even the abandonment of his projected campaign. But he was gradually reassured as he learned that there was still a party in his favour, that the credit of the two ladies from Zerbst was not wholly destroyed, and that Russian military preparations were so backward that no hostile action need be feared for some time. He decided to continue his programme.[2] When the news came that the Austrians were across the Rhine and engaged in an invasion of Alsace, from which the French vainly tried to distract them by sending Marshal Saxe with Louis XV in person against the Netherlands, Frederick promptly led his troops into Bohemia. He took them through Saxony, and the emperor's request for leave was only made when it was too late to refuse. Prague was taken, and the whole kingdom fell into his hands with startling rapidity. As he anticipated, Charles of Lorraine was promptly ordered to evacuate Alsace, and to return with all possible speed to the recovery of the lost kingdom. Also as he had anticipated, the concentration of Austrian forces in Bohemia resulted in the loss of Bavaria, and Charles VII had one moment of triumph when he was welcomed in his own capital by the plaudits of his loyal subjects. But at this point Frederick's programme began to break down. The French had not forgotten that Klein-Schnellendorf had set Neipperg's army free to attack them, and that Breslau had left them isolated and unaided in Bohemia at the mercy of superior forces. They allowed Charles of Lorraine to retreat and to cross the Rhine without molestation. Traun, the ablest of Austrian generals since Eugene, taught Frederick a lesson in the military art by compelling him to evacuate Bohemia without giving him a chance to fight a pitched battle. He could not take Bohemia from Maria Theresa and transfer it to Charles VII, with the gain of three circles for himself, because he no longer had Bohemia to dispose of. And, to complete the failure of the final part of the programme, Charles VII, disappointing to the end, inopportunely died on the 20th January 1745.

---

[1] *Pol. Corr.* iii. 66: 'Pour exécuter mon projet contre la reine de Hongrie, la première chose est d'être bien ancré avec la Russie.'

[2] For a clear account of Frederick's hesitation and ultimate decision see his interesting letter to Noailles of 28 June 1744 in *Pol. Corr.* iii. 189–93.

E

The treaty of Westminster was already, as we have seen, nearly dead, and Frederick's invasion of Bohemia dealt it the *coup de grâce*. There was no open breach with Prussia, but there could be no alliance so long as Frederick was making war against Britain's ally. Relations were not improved by the fact that the long-expected death of the ruler of East Friesland had taken place at the end of May, and Frederick had promptly sent troops to occupy the province in complete defiance of Hanoverian claims. Hyndford was instructed in August to leave Berlin, where he had long ceased to be a *persona grata*,[1] without taking any formal leave, and to entrust the business of the embassy to a secretary. With singular indiscretion he chose for the purpose a certain Frederic Laurence (or Lorentz), whom he had employed, for £100 a year and free meals at his house, to translate German documents for him. Like most British men of affairs at the time, Hyndford had omitted to learn German. Laurence, in spite of the English-looking version of his name, was not even a British subject, but a native of Lauenburg and a subject of the elector of Hanover. He boasted the command of several languages, and he could write tolerable French. But if his other languages were no better than his English, his linguistic pretensions were not altogether justified. And he had no other qualifications for his job, for which it is true he was quite inadequately paid. Hyndford reckoned that his free meals might be valued at about £100 a year, and concluded that he could live on an income of £200. This might have been possible for a poor hanger-on at the embassy. But for the sole representative of the British Crown—and of Hanover as well—for a man who had to interview ministers and appear at court, it was a preposterous salary. Later, when he had gone to St. Petersburg, Hyndford was induced by Laurence to ask for another £100 for his former dependent, and this was granted. On £300 a year the wretched man had to keep up appearances, maintain a wife and four children, purchase information, and even at times defray the heavy cost of sending his dispatches by

---

[1] *Pol. Corr.* iii. 158. Andrié had complained from London that George II had turned his back on him. Frederick promptly replied (29 May 1744), 'Si le roi d'Angleterre vous tourne le dos, j'en peux faire autant et pis à Hyndford'.

post. For two years Laurence remained at Berlin, sending on scraps of intelligence, mostly borrowed from news-letters, and very rarely answered or acknowledged. At rare intervals there are comments of some shrewdness, probably derived from other people's conversation. At last, in October 1746, Frederick so far took notice of this derelict secretary as to ask for his dismissal, though without formulating any charge against him. Chesterfield, who came into office in place of Harrington at this time, promptly ordered Laurence to proceed to Dresden, where he was wholly superfluous, as the embassy was occupied by that eccentric figure in our eighteenth-century diplomacy, Sir Charles Hanbury Williams, roué and versifier, whose scurrilous lampoons had made London too hot to hold him. By this time Laurence was so heavily in debt that he had difficulty in escaping from Berlin, and had to leave his wife and family behind. At last he borrowed a sum from the Saxon minister [1] which enabled him to satisfy his most persistent creditors and to carry his family after him to Dresden. His subsequent adventures, the storming of his house by a defrauded landlord, Laurence's appeal to his diplomatic privileges, his resentment of Hanbury Williams's contemptuous patronage, and his futile efforts to extort from the Treasury either the payment of his debts, incurred in the public service, or an increased salary, are of no historical importance. At last Newcastle, who succeeded to Chesterfield's office, took refuge from his importunity by resorting to impenetrable silence. But until March 1757 the indomitable man continued to regard himself as a diplomatic agent, and continued to write perfectly futile dispatches, in his quaint Germanized and bombastic English, which probably nobody read, but which fill a volume of the Prussian State Papers. If it was the mission of Ford's Lecturer to purvey amusement rather than instruction, an interesting account could be given of the misadventures of Frederic Laurence. But the story is not altogether to the credit of our Foreign Office.

The departure of Hyndford to St. Petersburg and the leaving

---

[1] Henry Legge, when he went to Berlin in 1748, found it necessary to repay this loan (£95), 'which Mons. Bulow solicited me for in such a manner that I should have thought it a national scandal to have refused the payment' (*Add. MSS.*, 32812, Legge to Newcastle, 22 June 1748).

of Laurence reduced the British embassy at Berlin to an absolute nullity. This was the less important because during the greater part of the time Frederick was absent from his capital on military service, and also because Berlin became less important than Dresden as a centre of diplomacy. One unexpected result of Frederick's rupture of the treaty of Breslau and the consequent transfer of war from Alsace to Bohemia and Silesia was an immense increase of the prominence of Saxony. And Augustus, as king of Poland, was so dependent upon Russia, the power which had placed him upon the throne, that the importance of Russia was increased in the same proportion. The fate of Bohemia and the possible extension of the war into Silesia were largely dependent upon the action of Saxony, and that action would be bold or timorous in precise accordance with the reported balance of parties at St. Petersburg. At the outset Saxony was committed to the Austrian alliance, and this was certain to continue so long as Bestoujew remained in the ascendant. But at the first rumour either that the influence of the grand duke and Catharine and of Catharine's mother was increasing, or that the new vice-chancellor, Woronzow, had been gained over by the grant of the Black Eagle by Frederick or of the rank of a Prince of the Empire by Charles VII, the efforts of Prussia and France to detach Saxony from Austria were redoubled. The task of resisting these efforts devolved in large measure upon the British envoy at Dresden, Thomas Villiers, afterwards earl of Clarendon, who became, for about eighteen months, the most active and prominent of British diplomatists. Whatever direct communications there were between Britain and Prussia during these months passed through the hands of Andrié, the Prussian minister in London.

The reports of Villiers are almost as full of events in Russia as of his interviews with Count Brühl and Father Guarini, the two confidants of the king. He was instructed to act in the closest accord with Hyndford, now at St. Petersburg, whose dispatches passed through Dresden under flying seal so that Villiers could read them. The continued success of Bestoujew ensured the continuance of the Saxon alliance with Austria. Saxon troops joined Traun in the Bohemian campaign, and the danger that Saxony would cut his line of communications was a principal reason that Frederick so hastily evacuated the kingdom. For these services Augustus naturally demanded to be paid. The great enemy from the Saxon point of view was not France, nor Charles VII, but Prussia. Augustus wished Maria Theresa to buy off France and Spain, and to concentrate her forces on the humiliation of Frederick. The compensation which Saxony demanded was the cession of parts of Silesia. That Maria Theresa should assent to the recovery of the province was natural, but it was doubtful whether she would agree to its partition in favour of Saxony.

The Saxon demands, and the obvious determination of Austria and Saxony to humiliate and permanently weaken Prussia, placed the British government in a dilemma. Hitherto Carteret had not overtly departed from the policy of detaching Prussia from Austria and, if possible, of gaining the alliance of Prussia for Britain. His two early triumphs, the treaty of Breslau and the treaty of Westminster, had been gained in pursuance of this policy. It is true that since 1742 further conciliation of Prussia had been abandoned as hopeless, and Frederick's breach of the treaty of Breslau might be held to have released Britain from its obligations. But it was by no means certain that that policy was not still the best in the interests of Britain. It was, however, difficult to resume it in the altered conditions of the war, and George II, imbued with the traditional Hanoverian jealousy of Prussia, was not unwilling to consent to the spoliation of his nephew, which seemed to be the only method of keeping Austria and Saxony united. Carteret, whose position in the ministry had been shaken by the elevation of Henry Pelham to the Treasury in preference to his own candidate, the earl of Bath, was more than ever dependent upon royal favour. The result of these considerations was a decision to support the Saxon demands,[1] which involved the reconquest of Silesia, and to negotiate a quadruple alliance between Britain, the United Provinces, Austria, and Saxony. Hyndford at St. Petersburg was instructed to press for Russian adhesion to the quadruple alliance. With this encouragement, Austria and Saxony, after the recovery of Bohemia, followed up their success by an

---

[1] *S. P. For.*, *Poland*, 62, Carteret to Villiers, 9 October (o. s.) 1744.

irruption in mid-winter into Silesia, which was, however, repulsed by Leopold of Anhalt-Dessau.

This very risky decision to further Maria Theresa's policy
of revenge was the last act of Carteret, who had become Earl
Granville on his mother's death (18 October). The section of
the ministry which had survived Walpole's fall had always
resented Carteret's ascendancy, and shared the view, loudly
voiced by Pitt and the opposition leaders, that he truckled
to the king's Hanoverian interests and aims; and it could
reasonably be contended that his policy had been both costly
and unsuccessful. The aggressive actions against France and
Spain had been perforce abandoned. The Austrian succession
question had been reopened, and Hanover, after repudiating
its neutrality, was as insecure as ever. For a long time there
had been constant intrigues against Carteret, and in November
1744 it was openly asserted that parliament could only be
appeased by the dismissal of the unpopular minister. The king
did his utmost to retain the one man with whom he could
cordially co-operate, but he was unable to resist the pressure
brought to bear upon him, and Carteret was dismissed in the
last week of November. Henry Pelham formed the 'broad-
bottomed' administration, and Harrington resumed the secretaryship which he had resigned to Carteret in 1742. But Carteret's
foreign policy for a time survived him. The quadruple alliance,
which he had planned, was actually signed by Villiers at Warsaw
on the 8th January 1745.[1] Saxony was to continue its assistance
to Austria and was to receive a subsidy of £100,000 from Britain
and of £50,000 (550,000 Dutch florins) from the Dutch. The
precise recompense which Saxony was to obtain at the expense
of the 'common enemy' was left to be settled by a separate
agreement with Austria, which was not concluded till May.

Frederick welcomed with enthusiasm the downfall of Carteret,
whom he had come to regard, since the treaty of Westminster,
as his most dangerous enemy. And he had need of all the
encouragement he could obtain. The death of Charles VII
altered the whole situation in Europe to his disadvantage. The
League of Frankfort was annihilated, and the basis of his alliance

[1] Full powers to sign this treaty had been sent to Villiers by Carteret on
7 September (o. s.) 1744 (*S. P. For.*, *Poland*, 62).

with France was almost destroyed. He realized that, in these altered circumstances, his renewed intervention in the war had been a fatal blunder, and that the whole gain would accrue to his allies. He foresaw that the two Bourbon powers would leave him to fight his own battles, while they profited by his diversion to gain easy successes in the Netherlands and Italy. With his keen and rapid intuition he grasped the fact that his only safety lay in persuading the new British ministers to revert to the earlier policy of forcing or inducing Austria to buy off Prussia in order to offer efficient resistance to its other enemies. On the 27th January, the day after he had received the news of the emperor's death, he sent full instructions to Andrié to open negotiations with Harrington on the basis of the renewal of the treaty of Breslau with modifications in favour of Prussia. These modifications could be raised or lowered as circumstances might dictate. 'C'était l'heure du berger qu'il ne fallait point négliger si on voulait m'avoir.' But he must have 'un bon morceau' and security for the future.[1]

For these negotiations to succeed it was necessary (1) that the British ministers should frankly abandon the anti-Prussian attitude which Carteret had lately adopted, (2) that they should be able to adjust with Frederick such terms as Maria Theresa might be reasonably asked to accept, and (3) that Maria Theresa should be willing to forgo the attractive plan of recovering Silesia and reducing Prussia to a humbler position both in Europe and in Germany. Not one of these conditions was realized at first. George II, though he had failed to keep his minister, was not prepared to abandon his policy, and the king, though he could in extremity be coerced, could not be disregarded, especially in matters concerning Germany. Royal influence, therefore, was against an agreement with Prussia, at any rate until Austria was more likely to consent. The *bon morceau* which Frederick claimed was another obstacle. It would have been unreasonable that Britain should reward him for breaking the treaty of Breslau by securing for him better terms than that treaty had given him. All Frederick's self-confidence was required to enable him to put forward such

---

[1] Frederick to Andrié, 27 January 1745, in *Pol. Corr.* iv. 27, and in *S. P., Foreign Ministers in England*, 48.

a demand at a time when he was threatened with complete isolation. Maria Theresa was confident that she could now redeem the two disasters of her reign by regaining Silesia and by placing her husband upon the vacant imperial throne. Her confidence was increased when her troops reduced the French garrisons in Bavaria, and the young elector, Maximilian Joseph, made peace at Füssen (15 April) on the basis of the restoration of his electorate and the recognition of his father's title. For these concessions he withdrew all claims to the Austrian succession and promised to give his vote for the grand duke of Tuscany. This was a blow to Frederick only second to the death of the emperor, and his appeal for British mediation became more urgent than before. For he realized that the only alternative to his success was to become the subsidized agent of France and to make extremely unpalatable concessions to Saxony.

The death of Charles VII had been as advantageous to Saxony as it had been disastrous to Prussia. During the vacancy the elector was Vicar in the Empire. And, if France continued to strive for the exclusion of the ex-duke of Lorraine, Augustus III, especially after the treaty of Füssen, was the only possible rival who could be put forward for the imperial crown. France had thus a new bribe to offer, and one which Austria could hardly outbid.[1] Dresden became more than ever the diplomatic centre of Germany, and even of Europe.[2] Frederick was extremely reluctant to consent to the elevation of a prince whom he both hated and despised. But he could not afford to break with France so long as his negotiations with Britain were incomplete. He would sooner have a Saxon emperor than lose Silesia. And so he was a half-hearted party to the French negotiations

---

[1] On 3 April Frederick wrote two protests against the offer of the imperial crown to the elector, one to Louis XV, and one to Valory, the French agent who was to carry the offer to Dresden. 'Je crois peut-être qu'en France on peut imaginer qu'on trouvera des avantages dans l'élévation du roi de Pologne à la dignité impériale; pour moi, je vous avoue naturellement que je n'y vois guère encore d'apparence' (*Pol. Corr.* iv. 103).

[2] *Pol. Corr.* iv. 54, Frederick to Noailles, 19 February 1745: 'Le hasard, par une singularité étonnante, a donc mis à présent le destin de l'Allemagne entre les mains du roi de Pologne. Il aurait été bien difficile de prévoir une conjoncture aussi bizarre.'

with Saxony, while at the same time he was urging Andrié to press the British ministers for their own and Maria Theresa's answer to his overtures.

Both negotiations seemed doomed for a time to failure. Augustus and his wife were tempted by the prospect of the imperial title, but the value of the offer was diminished by the doubt as to whether France could give effect to it. On a sober calculation of chances, it appeared that a majority was reasonably assured to the Grand Duke, especially if Maria Theresa could this time procure the admission of the Bohemian vote. But even if the prospect of success had been greater, it is probable that hatred of Prussia would have carried the day against ambition. The imperial crown had brought loss rather than gain to Charles VII, and a substantial acquisition of territory, with the weakening of a too powerful neighbour, was really more tempting than what might, if attainable, prove to be an empty title. Augustus had never forgiven Frederick for compelling him to accept the treaty of Breslau without any gain to balance the aggrandizement of Prussia, and he had a new grievance in the recent trespass of the Prussian forces when they marched through Saxony. His wife, Maria Josepha, deemed herself nearer to the Austrian succession now that Maria Theresa's only surviving sister, the wife of Charles of Lorraine, had died without issue, and clung to the cause of the country of her birth. And always in the background was Russia, whose indispensable favour might be forfeited if Saxony listened to the insidious suggestions of France. And the more secure Maria Theresa felt of the support of Saxony and of Russia the less likely she was to listen to any suggestions of a premature peace, even if Britain had urged them with far more energy and persistency.

The result of the double failure to buy off Saxony and to pacify Austria was that, while France was starting the campaign of Fontenoy and Spain was preparing to overrun the ill-defended plain of Lombardy, Frederick was left single-handed to face the combined attack of Austrian and Saxon forces in Silesia. And in that attack Britain was in a sense a participator, as the Saxon troops were maintained out of the subsidies paid by the maritime powers. Hence the conclusion was obvious that the friendly professions of Harrington were insincere, and that he was only writing 'another volume of Hanau '.[1] Podewils, always inclined to be timorous, was dismayed by the isolation of Prussia, and even Frederick contemplated the transfer of the government and the archives from Berlin to Magdeburg or Cüstrin. But the Prussian king never till 1757 showed higher courage or more brilliant military capacity than in 1745. It was his first experience of purely defensive warfare, which was repugnant to his nature, and he proved himself as great a master as in attack. He was fortunate in having to face only Charles of Lorraine, as Traun, Charles's tutor in the last campaign, was sent westwards to prevent the French army under Maillebois from molesting Frankfort during the imperial election. Frederick allowed the enemy to cross the mountains without molestation, and, once they were on the plain, crushed them in the battle of Hohenfriedberg (4 June), one of his most complete and momentous victories. His natural inclination was to follow up his success by invading Saxony, for which he was fully prepared, and by forcing Augustus to conclude a separate peace. But Saxony professed to be a mere auxiliary of Maria Theresa under the treaty of Warsaw and to be technically at peace with Prussia, and Frederick, though prepared to treat these ridiculous contentions with scorn, hesitated to risk a rupture with Russia by too hasty an act of aggression. Accordingly he waited to see what effect his victory would produce.

The first result of Hohenfriedberg was to put an end to the vacillation of the British ministers. It was clear to them now that the recovery of Silesia was a far more difficult task than had been anticipated, and that, while Austria was absorbed in the attempt, France was making itself master of the Netherlands and threatening the security of the British throne. The lesson of Fontenoy was as clear as that of Hohenfriedberg. The negotiations with Andrié were resumed during the king's summer visit to Germany, and on the 26th August Harrington signed the secret convention of Hanover, by which Britain was pledged to

---

[1] *Pol. Corr.* iv. 126 : 'Toutes ces circonstances me font conjecturer qu'on fera de votre négociation en Angleterre le second tome de celle de Hanau ... le ministère d'Angleterre n'a pas agi rondement ; si son intention était de me procurer une bonne paix, il ne suffirait pas que les Saxons vinssent aussi pour m'attaquer ' (Frederick to Andrié, 20 April 1745).

induce Austria to make peace on the basis of the treaty of Breslau, to guarantee the Prussian possession of Silesia and Glatz, and to procure the insertion of such a guarantee in the final general peace. In return, if Austria agrees to the terms, Frederick will vote for the grand duke, and will guarantee the German dominions of Maria Theresa. As soon as possible after the Convention hostilities are to cease. Britain had returned from the ambitious schemes of 1743 to the sounder policy of 1742.

Although the *bon morceau* was not forthcoming, Frederick was delighted with the news of Andrié's success at Hanover, and was inclined to believe that peace was now in sight. The task of commending the terms of the convention at Dresden and Vienna was entrusted to Villiers and Robinson, as a similar task had been entrusted to Hyndford and Robinson in 1741. They were completely unsuccessful. Saxony, furious at the idea of emerging from the struggle empty-handed, after all the tempting promises that had been made in the early months of the year, insisted upon referring the matter to Austria, as Saxony was only an auxiliary. At Vienna, attention was for a time concentrated upon the imperial election at Frankfort. The success of Traun in forcing Maillebois to retreat from Germany deprived the opponents of Austria of all chance of success. Prussia and the Palatinate, the two surviving members of the League of Frankfort, protested against the validity of the proceedings and withdrew from Frankfort. The Bohemian vote was accepted, and all the electors present chose Francis, the husband of Maria Theresa (13 September). The immediate effect of this triumphant recovery of the imperial dignity by the house of Austria was to stiffen the refusal of the court of Vienna to accept the Hanover terms. Saxony, in spite of the threat of the maritime powers to withdraw their subsidies, was equally resolute, and reverted to its former proposals that Austria should buy off France and Spain by sacrificing the Netherlands and Italy, and then employ its whole forces to crush Prussia.[1] A second great offensive movement was set on foot, and for the second time it was crushed by Frederick, who gained another decisive victory at Soor (30 September 1745). This time the Prussian king was

S. *P. For., Poland*, 66, Villiers to Harrington, 12 and 19 September 1745.

convinced that the desired impression had been made,[1] and he
actually sent his troops into winter quarters.

Villiers took occasion to preach once more the doctrine that
Saxony could only be saved by making peace with Prussia.
But his preaching fell upon deaf ears. Even Father Guarini,
'though moderate upon most points, is most violent on this
question. I believe it would be as hard to engage him to advise
an accommodation with Prussia as to make him change his
religion.'[2] Robinson found Maria Theresa equally obdurate.
British influence was seriously lessened by the Jacobite rising
and Charles Edward's victory at Prestonpans. The news that
Russia would actively resent any attack upon Saxony and was
preparing to send troops for its defence emboldened the two
allies to plan a new attack, no longer on Frederick in Silesia,
but on his electorate of Brandenburg. The double news that
Russia might intervene and that his enemies' hostility was un-
abated convinced Frederick that a purely defensive attitude was
insufficient. Hitherto Saxony had defended its anti-Prussian
measures on the ground that it was not attacking his hereditary
dominions but was only aiding Austria to recover a province
unlawfully torn from her in defiance of the Pragmatic Sanction.
This plea was no longer tenable, and it was necessary to crush
Saxony before Russian aid could arrive. Leopold of Anhalt-
Dessau had long commanded a second Prussian force on the
border of Saxony. Hitherto he had been held in leash, but on
21st November he was released from restraint, and his troops
at once entered Saxony, while Frederick himself crushed the
Austrians in Lausitz. The panic in the electorate was extreme,
and Augustus fled for safety to Prague. Frederick now wrote,
both in person and through Podewils, to Villiers to say that
Saxony could escape further molestation by acceding to the
terms of the convention of Hanover.[3] The pusillanimous ministers who had been left at Dresden were willing to accede to any-

---

[1] *Pol. Corr.* iv. 299, Frederick to Podewils, 6 October 1745: 'Je suis
d'opinion que voilà le dernier venin que la cour de Vienne vomit contre nous,
et qu'elle ne pourra plus résister désormais aux pressantes sollicitations des
Anglais.'

[2] *S. P. For., Poland*, 66, Villiers to Harrington, 6 October 1745.

[3] Frederick's letters to Villiers are in *Pol. Corr.* iv. 355, 362, 371, 381.

thing, and Villiers found it necessary to stiffen their resolution. He was afraid that, if Saxony made a separate peace, Frederick might then proceed to crush Austria and so acquire a dangerous predominance. In order that both powers might make peace simultaneously, it was necessary to give Austria time to come in. Villiers therefore deliberately delayed matters by undertaking to go in person to Prague in order to procure the assent of Augustus to the proposed terms.[1] His conduct was warmly approved by Harrington, and was successful in attaining its object. But the delay was very costly to Saxony. As Frederick had refused an armistice, Leopold of Dessau continued his advance and routed the Saxon forces at Kesselsdorf on the 15th December. On the next day Frederick in person joined the victorious general, and Dresden surrendered on the 17th to the combined Prussian armies. Maria Theresa, seeing that the secession of Saxony was inevitable, that the recovery of Silesia was for the time impossible, and that the continuance of the Prussian war could only result in the complete loss of the Netherlands and of Italy, sent Count Harrach with powers to conclude a treaty. No more time was wasted, and the two treaties were signed at Dresden on Christmas Day, 1745. Saxony was to recover all its conquered territories on payment of an indemnity of a million crowns, and the Electress Maria Josepha was to renounce all eventual claims to Silesia and Glatz. Austria confirmed the cessions made at Breslau, and Frederick, withdrawing the protest he had made at Frankfort, recognized Francis I as emperor.

Thus British diplomacy had for the second time secured to Frederick his original acquisitions, detached Prussia from France, and set Maria Theresa free to defend her distant possessions against the house of Bourbon. In order to complete the return to the policy of 1742 it was necessary to bring about a new alliance with Prussia. The natural agent for such a task was Villiers, to whom Frederick always expressed an apparently sincere gratitude for his share in bringing about the Dresden treaties. The first action of the British ministry in 1746 was to instruct Villiers to proceed from Dresden to Berlin, where the only British representative since October 1744 was the

[1] *S. P. For.*, *Poland*, 66, Villiers to Harrington, 4 December 1745.

ineffective Laurence.[1] There was a brief disturbance in February, when the ministry resigned in a body as a protest against the king's refusal to admit Pitt to office, and George II entrusted the seals once more to his favourite adviser, Lord Granville. Nobody was more startled and alarmed by the news than Frederick, and it was with intense relief that he learned of the resignation of Granville after forty hours' tenure of office, and that the old ministers had returned, with Pitt in a subordinate position. But, in spite of this, Villiers's embassy proved a complete failure. One cause was Frederick's intense and constant suspicion of Hanoverian hostility and of the personal ill will of George II. He never forgave George for taking advantage of Francis's election to protest against the Prussian seizure of East Friesland, and to demand the refusal of imperial investiture. This occurred at the very moment that Great Britain was professedly endeavouring to force the Convention of Hanover upon Saxony and Austria. Any reference to the dual personality of the king and the elector excited Frederick's keenest indignation.[2] He was perpetually on the look-out for hostile Hanoverian influence both at Vienna and St. Petersburg, and did not hesitate to accuse George of secretly intriguing against the avowed policy of his British ministers.[3] But, even if Hanover

[1] Laurence and Villiers both corresponded with Whitehall in 1746 apparently in complete independence of each other. In the letters of Laurence there is not a single reference to Villiers, and the latter only mentions Laurence two or three times. For some unexplained reason Villiers's dispatches from Berlin are included with his previous dispatches from Dresden under ' Poland ', whereas Laurence's correspondence, both from Berlin and later from Dresden until 1751, is equally labelled ' Prussia '. From the Record Office Catalogue no one could gather either that Villiers had ever been at Berlin or that Laurence had ever left it.

[2] *Pol. Corr.* iv. 324 : ' Dois-je regarder le roi d'Angleterre comme une ou comme deux personnes ? '

[3] There are innumerable illustrations of this in Frederick's correspondence. Perhaps the most notable is a letter to Andrié of 19 April 1746, in which he expresses the suspicion that Austria and Russia are planning a reconciliation with France in order to wrest Silesia from her, and that this is furtively encouraged by Hanover. He instructs his minister to inquire whether ' malgré le malin vouloir du roi d'Angleterre, que je savais n'être nullement porté pour moi, la nation anglaise remplirait les engagements pris par la garantie sur notre convention, en m'assistant, quand même le cas devrait

had been out of the question, it would have been difficult to establish any real understanding between London and Berlin. The successive secretaries, Harrington, Chesterfield, and Newcastle, were all partisans of the 'old system', i.e. of the close alliance with Austria. They wanted that system to be reinforced by the adhesion of Prussia, as had been the case under Frederick's grandfather. Frederick, on the other hand, was so profoundly convinced that Austria was his necessary opponent, and that Maria Theresa would never forget or forgive the loss of Silesia, that he could not possibly join an alliance of which Austria was a leading member. He was perfectly willing to make a close alliance with Britain, to send troops to put down the Jacobites, and to aid in the defence of Holland, but only on condition that Britain would accept the Prussian alliance as a substitute for that with Austria. Until the Austro-British alliance was broken he could not venture to risk a complete rupture with France. Villiers, who did not regard Frederick with the same feelings as the Prussian king expressed for him, found his residence at Berlin both irksome and useless. He resented that the negotiations as to the formal guarantee of the treaty of Dresden were entrusted to Andrié in London instead of being conducted in Berlin.[1] In August 1746 he asked and obtained leave to resign his post, and Laurence was once more left as the sole British agent at Berlin. When the latter was removed to Dresden, in November, Britain was wholly unrepresented at the Prussian court, and remained so for more than twelve months.

The tension between London and Berlin, and the more open ill will between Hanover and Berlin, continued to increase. Frederick had a definite grievance against the British government on the subject of the constant capture and confiscation of Prussian ships for carrying contraband goods, in spite of the

arriver que le roi d'Angleterre fasse marcher de son chef ses troupes hanovriennes contre moi' (*Pol. Corr.* v. 63).

[1] *S. P. For.*, *Poland*, 68, Villiers to Harrington, 6 August 1746: 'I must conclude that my staying here can be but of little significance at this juncture, especially as His Majesty has M. Laurence for common occurrences . . . and as the King of Prussia appears more disposed to employ his own minister at the Court he negotiates with than a foreign minister near his own person.'

verbal assurance of their exemption from search which Carteret was said to have given to Andrié. Frederick clamoured loudly for restitution and compensation, but to no avail. With this question was mixed up that of the Silesian loan, which Frederick had again guaranteed by the treaty of Dresden. In spite of the protests that the two things were wholly distinct, Frederick insisted upon detaining the sums due to British merchants as security for his claims against the British government. These quarrels have been so exhaustively dealt with by Sir Ernest Satow, in his monograph on 'Frederick the Great and the Silesian Loan', that it is unnecessary to do more than allude to them here.

Meanwhile, the European war continued between France and Spain on one side and Austria and the maritime powers on the other hand. Lombardy, which had been nearly lost in 1745, was recovered after the treaty of Dresden, when Sardinia, which had been on the verge of desertion, returned to the observance of the treaty of Worms. The death of Philip V (9 July 1746), and the consequent disappearance from the European stage of Elizabeth Farnese, removed all danger of further agression on the part of Spain. But the Austrian successes in Italy were counterbalanced by serious disasters in the Netherlands. The French, under Marshal Saxe, achieved within three years a series of triumphs which Condé, Turenne, and Luxemburg had never surpassed in the days of French military ascendancy. The victories of Fontenoy and Roucoux made them masters of the Austrian Netherlands, and in 1747 it was determined to force peace upon the maritime powers by a direct attack upon the Dutch provinces. The consequent revolution which restored to William IV the powers of the earlier house of Orange brought none of the successes which had followed a similar revolution in 1672. The battle of Lauffelt and the surrender of Cohoorn's great fortress of Bergen-op-Zoom, proved that the Dutch had lost much of the fighting quality which they had displayed in the previous century. Maestricht was not likely to hold out when once it was seriously assailed. To save the Dutch from disasters which would seriously affect the terms of the now rapidly approaching peace, it was determined to appeal to Frederick, whose ancestor, the Great Elector, had been the first prince to rally to the cause of the Republic in the crisis of 1672. The task of negotiating a new alliance with Prussia was entrusted to Henry Legge, the future Chancellor of the Exchequer, who proceeded to Berlin in March 1748 with instructions from Newcastle, who had taken over the northern department from Chesterfield in the previous month.[1]

Legge's mission was no more successful than that of Villiers had been. His first aim, the procuring of Prussian military or diplomatic support for Holland, was rendered unnecessary by the unexpected rapidity with which the preliminaries of peace between France and the maritime powers were signed at Aix-la-Chapelle on the 30th April. The British and Dutch alarm at the imminent fall of Maestricht was balanced by the financial exhaustion of France and by the news that Bestoujew's policy had finally triumphed, and that 30,000 Russians were marching through Germany to take part in the western war. So commanding was Frederick's position, as holding the balance between the contending forces, that both the contracting parties competed with each other for the credit of including in the preliminaries the much-coveted guarantee of Silesia. Hostilities at once ceased, and the Dutch were saved from further molestation. Legge's instructions were now obsolete, but he stayed on in Berlin for several months, at Frederick's own suggestion, to negotiate a defensive alliance with Prussia. There can be no doubt that Frederick genuinely desired such an alliance, partly because he was grateful to the maritime powers for insisting, in spite of the opposition of Kaunitz, on the inclusion in the preliminaries of the guarantee of Silesia, and partly because he desired security on the side of Russia, and believed that British bribes would disarm the hostility of Chancellor Bestoujew.[2]

---

[1] George II's consent to Legge's mission was extorted with difficulty. In the previous year Henry Pelham wrote to Horatio Walpole, a consistent advocate of the Prussian alliance, ' You would have him court Prussia, rather than be necessitated to take a bad peace: he had rather take any peace from France, than court Prussia to carry on the war' (Coxe, *Memoirs of Lord Walpole*, ii. 195).

[2] *Pol. Corr.* vi. 113, 125; *S. P. For.*, *Prussia*, 64, Legge to Newcastle, 14 May 1748: ' There is no power on earth the King of Prussia respects more than Russia.' Legge continues that nothing would do more to detach him

For a short time all seemed to go well. Hanoverian disputes were thrust into the background,[1] and Frederick instructed Michell, who had taken Andrié's place in London, to cease worrying Newcastle about English piracies, as circumstances had changed.[2] On the 11th May Legge reported an interview at Potsdam, where Frederick admitted that 'to be the ally of France was to be her slave', whereas he was bound to the maritime powers, and especially to Britain, by interest, religion, and blood. But six weeks later Legge began to perceive that the obstacle which wrecked the negotiation with Villiers had not been removed. He pointed out that we might make terms with Prussia, but what were we to do about Austria? How far would it be safe to leave any of our friends behind? These matters must be decided by His Majesty.[3] The inevitable answer came, ominously from Hanover, on the 17th July. The foundation of our system, says Newcastle, has always been the union of the maritime powers with the Emperor and the Empire. If the king of Prussia has really good intentions, he should join this union. 'Everything that comes short of this, though it may seem specious at first, will fail in its execution.' The Dutch will never 'concur upon an exclusive plan of a separate union between the maritime powers and the king of Prussia'.[4] Legge was invited to Hanover to imbibe the true doctrine, and on his return to Berlin he intimated that Britain desired a close union between Prussia and the allies of Britain, and 'that any union short of that would be too partial and incomplete to answer the real interest of either of the courts'.

Frederick treated this answer as a rebuff, refused to talk politics with Legge, and instructed Michell to prosecute his

from France than security from St. Petersburg. On 24 May Frederick wrote to Finckenstein, Mardefeld's successor at the Russian court, 'tant que je m'entendrai et serai d'accord avec l'Angleterre, je n'aurai rien à appréhender de la Russie' (*Pol. Corr.* vi. 123).

[1] *Add. MSS.*, 32812, Legge to Newcastle, 12 May 1748: 'I am glad to find none of those electoral disputes which might have given great trouble subsisting.'

[2] *Pol. Corr.* vi. 114, Frederick to Michell, 18 May 1748.

[3] *S. P. For.*, *Prussia*, 64, Legge to Newcastle, 22 June 1748.

[4] *Ibid.*, 64. This important letter from Newcastle is also in *Add. MS.* 32813, f. 58.

demands for the compensation of Prussian traders.[1] The 'old system' stood in the way of an Anglo-Prussian alliance. Newcastle refused to admit that Austria cherished any hostile designs against Prussia, and insisted that any such enmity must always be subordinated to Austrian hostility to France. He little foresaw that subsequent events would justify Frederick's suspicions, and that Maria Theresa and Kaunitz would shock all British traditions by adopting a wholly revolutionary policy. Legge remained at Berlin until the final conclusion of the general peace at Aix-la-Chapelle (18th October), but his mission had really ended in August. In his last letter from Berlin he admits that Prussia 'cannot be gained to the true system', and that 'nothing remains, in my humble opinion, but to take timely precautions against any ill intentions the King of Prussia may have, to hold him fast to the confirmation of the Pragmatic Sanction, and to the payment of all the Silesian debt'.

ADDITIONAL NOTES

A. LORD HYNDFORD AT BERLIN

John Carmichael, third earl of Hyndford in the Scottish peerage, was a novice in diplomacy when, at the age of forty, he was sent on his important embassy to Berlin. It was not unnatural that he should make blunders in his new career. (1) Although he boasted that he had in his pay a valet in Valory's household, he failed to discover that Frederick had made a treaty with France in June 1741, and Harrington had to inform him of this vital fact. (2) His drafting of the Convention of Klein-Schnellendorf was, as has been shown in the text, wholly irregular, and his omission to obtain a Prussian signature facilitated Frederick's repudiation of the agreement. (3) He cyphered a letter from Frederick, thus giving away the secret of the cypher, and compelling the Foreign Office to send him a new one. (4) He exultingly bribed Schmettau, a general in Frederick's confidence, whereas Carteret, immediately on coming into office, discovered that Hyndford was duped, and that Schmettau's pretended revelations were dictated by Frederick. (5) In May 1742, when the

---

[1] *Pol. Corr.* vi. 194, Frederick to Michell, 5 August 1748.

British government was eagerly pressing Maria Theresa to buy off Prussia by ceding Silesia, Hyndford endangered the success of the negotiation by a personal quarrel with Frederick. A woman, alleged to be of bad character, was arrested at the suit of her creditors in the British embassy. Hyndford, *fier comme un Écossais*, insisted on the immunity of his household, and demanded an ample apology from the Prussian court. Frederick, sooner than wreck the negotiations, conceded the demand, but wrote a letter to Hyndford in terms which have rarely been used by a sovereign to the representative of a friendly court. ' Il me semble, Milord, que vous associez un peu mal à propos l'honneur d'une banqueroutière avec l'honneur du Roi votre maître, et le nom d'une personne prostituée avec le nom auguste d'un souverain ' (*Pol. Corr.* ii, 152). Frederick was so indignant that he suspected Hyndford, as the nominee of the late ministers, of trying to thwart the policy of the present government, and thought of asking for his recall. Later, however, the king was reconciled with the envoy, and agreed, somewhat unwillingly, to invest him with the Order of the Thistle. (6) Hyndford made a serious blunder in recommending Laurence as a suitable British representative after his own departure from Berlin. Apart from any question of character and capacity—and apparently Laurence possessed neither— the mere fact that he was a Hanoverian was a disqualification. Frederick regarded all Hanoverians as enemies of Prussia, and when he insisted upon Laurence's removal he specially asked that only Englishmen should be appointed in future.

After leaving Berlin, Hyndford was employed at St. Petersburg, where he succeeded the volatile and irascible Lord Tyrawley, from 1744 to 1749. In 1752 he was sent by Newcastle on a special mission to Vienna, in order to induce the Austrian Court to carry out the Barrier Treaty in the recovered Netherlands, and also to approve the efforts of the British ministry to procure the election of the Archduke Joseph as king of the Romans during his father's lifetime. This closed his diplomatic career. Hyndford's dispatches during his three missions may be studied in Foreign State Papers in the Record Office, and those of the first two (1742–9) in the Hyndford Papers in the British Museum. The Record Office has the originals of Hyndford's own letters, while the British Museum has those of the letters which Hyndford received. For some unexplained reason the British Museum did not acquire Hyndford's papers relating to his third mission, to Vienna in 1752. These, which I have been allowed to consult, have remained in the possession of the Carmichael family at Carmichael House, Thankerton. They do not include many documents which cannot be found, either originals or copies, in the Record Office or in the Newcastle Papers in the British Museum, but there are among them a number of autograph letters, from Newcastle, Hanbury Williams, and others, which ought to be associated with the other Hyndford Papers in the British Museum.

B. THE VACANCY IN THE EMPIRE, 1745

The choice of a successor to Charles VII was a matter in which Great Britain was vitally interested, and in which the elector of Hanover had a direct voice. The Newcastle Papers (*Add. MSS.*, 32804) contain an interesting correspondence between Newcastle and Chesterfield (then at the Hague) which illustrates, not only the divergent views in the British ministry, but also the difficulty of inducing a German sovereign to pay any attention to British wishes in what he considered to be an entirely German business. On the 23rd February 1745 Chesterfield wrote to advocate the support of Augustus of Saxony, ' The maritime powers, who have surely some right to advise the Queen of Hungary, should talk to her in a pretty fair tone. . . . To me, it is the plainest point in the world that if the Great Duke be set up for Emperor, everything will be in greater confusion than ever. He is despised by the whole world, and hated in the Empire, where I dare say he would have but three votes, including Bohemia, should that vote be admitted. . . . Whereas, by setting up the Elector of Saxony, you snatch him from France, that is now holding out her arms to him, and I think you have a secure majority in the Electoral College. The Archduke [Joseph] should be King of the Romans: and, if Saxony refuses, then he should be Emperor.'

Newcastle replied on the 22nd February (o.s.) that he and his colleagues have little say in the matter of the imperial election. ' We are always told that His Majesty understands that best himself, that he must go his own way, that that, being the business of the Electors, must be left to them, and neither the interposition of England, nor Holland, in that matter, is at all tasted.' Newcastle expressed his conviction that, at all costs, Saxony must be secured. If neither the grand duke nor the archduke can secure election, he is then ready to support the elector of Saxony. But he refused to follow Chesterfield in an actual preference of Saxony. ' It is for the general interest of Europe that the imperial crown should be fixed in the house of Austria. A weak Emperor will be, and sooner or later must be, a French Emperor.' He continues that if the elector was emperor and the archduke king of the Romans, there would be constant bickerings between Dresden and Vienna. And what would Prussia be doing in such a case? It is clear that Newcastle inclines towards buying off Prussia with the renewal of the treaty of Breslau.

On the 9th March Chesterfield replies that, ' You cannot gain the King of Prussia without enraging the Queen of Hungary, and probably losing the elector of Saxony, and in consequence Russia.' 'Whatever may be said in the English Council,' Hanover will declare for the grand duke. ' This comes from Lord Granville's quiver.' On the next day Chesterfield returned to the attack. ' The King of Poland is setting himself up at auction.' If Austria won't buy him, France will. Hanover is the only keen supporter of the grand duke, who, if he survives Maria Theresa, will have no territory but Tuscany. On the 5th March (o. s.) Newcastle announced that the Hanoverian agents, ' unknown to all the King's English ministers,' have signed a pledge of the Hanover vote to the Duke of Lorraine.

C. THE HOUSE OF BRUNSWICK WOLFENBÜTTEL

This house, the elder branch of the Welfs, is so closely associated with Prussia, and especially with the relations of Prussia to Great Britain, in the eighteenth century, that some knowledge of its history is essential. Lewis Rudolf, who died in 1735, was succeeded by his cousin and son-in-law, Ferdinand Albert II. Besides the daughter who married his successor, Lewis Rudolf had two other daughters : (1) Elizabeth Charlotte, the wife of Charles VI and mother of Maria Theresa ; and (2) Charlotte, who married the ill-fated Alexis of Russia, and was the mother of Peter II (Tsar 1727–30).

Ferdinand Albert II, who died in the year of his succession to the duchy, was the father of a numerous family. (1) His eldest son Charles succeeded him and married a sister of Frederick the Great. (2) Another son, Antony Ulric, married Anne of Mecklenburg (great-niece of Peter the Great), and was the father of the unfortunate infant Tsar, who was placed on the Russian throne in 1740 and deposed by Elizabeth in the next year. (3) Elizabeth Charlotte was married to Frederick, then Crown Prince of Prussia, in 1733, after the English marriage scheme had broken down. (4) Another daughter, Louisa Amelia, married Frederick's brother, Augustus William, and was the mother of Frederick's successor, Frederick William II. (5) Ferdinand (d. 1792) was the famous general who commanded the British forces in the Seven Years' War and won, among others, the victory at Minden. (6) Albert was killed in the Prussian service at Soor. (7) Frederick was killed, also in the Prussian service, at Hochkirch.

Charles, who held the duchy for forty-five years (1735–80), and who was doubly the brother-in-law of Frederick the Great, was the chief agent in bringing Britain and Prussia together on the eve of the Seven Years' War. His son and successor, Charles William Frederick, married a sister of George III, and their daughter Caroline was the notorious wife of George IV.

D. THE HOLSTEIN MARRIAGES

(See pp. 16 and 47)

The house of Holstein-Gottorp was one of the numerous German families which through fortunate marriages rose to unexpected prominence in the eighteenth century. It traced its descent from Adolf, a younger brother of Christian III of Denmark. Adolf held the county of Holstein, an imperial fief, and the duchy of Sleswick, a Danish fief, on rather anomalous conditions, from the Danish crown, with which the two provinces (indissolubly associated with each other) had been united since 1460. In the seventeenth century the house of Holstein was connected by two marriages with Sweden, the traditional rival of Denmark in the north. Adolf's grandson, Frederick III, married his daughter to the warrior king, Charles X (of Zweibrücken), and Charles's victories enabled the duke of Holstein to free his provinces from all but nominal dependence upon Denmark. Frederick's grandson, Frederick IV, married Hedwig Sophia, the elder sister of Charles XII, and was killed at Clissow in 1702, fighting in the cause of his brother-in-law. During the minority of his son, Charles Frederick, Holstein and Sleswick were administered by Frederick's younger brother, Christian Augustus. The close alliance of the regent with Charles XII led Denmark, disappointed of Bremen and Verden, to seek compensation in the occupation of Sleswick and Holstein, which the Danish crown still claimed. By the treaty of 1720 Holstein was restored but Sleswick retained. Meanwhile the young Christian Frederick had been passed over for the Swedish crown, to which he had a claim by primogeniture, in favour of his mother's younger sister, Ulrica Eleanor, and her husband, Frederick of Hesse Cassel. Peter the Great took up his cause for a time (see p. 16), and arranged a marriage for him with his own elder daughter, Anna, who died in 1738. Their son, Charles Peter Ulrich, was recognized by his aunt Elizabeth as her heir to the Russian throne, which he ascended on her death in 1762. During his minority Holstein was administered by his father's first cousin, Adolf Frederick, for whom Elizabeth obtained recognition as successor to the Swedish throne by the treaty of Abo in 1743. This prince married Frederick the Great's sister, Louisa Ulrica, in 1744, and became king of Sweden in 1751 on the death of Frederick of Hesse-Cassel. Peter III, when he became Tsar in 1762, became the ally of Frederick the Great, and prepared with his help to wrest Sleswick from the Danes. This project, in which Russia had no interest, was one of the causes of the revolution which overthrew Peter in the year of his accession, and his widow and successor, Catharine II, in the name of her son, the Grand Duke Paul, sold Holstein and the claim to Sleswick to Denmark in 1767. This treaty was confirmed by Paul, on his coming of age in 1773, and thus Danish support was secured by Russia during its troubled relations with the Triple Alliance (1788-91).

E. The Foreign Secretaries of Frederick

At the accession of Frederick the conduct of foreign affairs under the crown was shared between three ministers, Adrian Bernhard von Borcke, Heinrich von Podewils, a nephew of Grumbkow, and Heinrich von Thulemeier. Thulemeier died suddenly on the 4th August 1740. Borcke, according to Guy Dickens, was blind and dying, so when the Austrian succession question arose Podewils was practically single-handed. In February 1741 a younger Borcke, Caspar William, was recalled from the Prussian embassy at Vienna to take Thulemeier's place, and on the 25th May in the same year the elder Borcke died. Podewils and Caspar von Borcke were partners, with Podewils distinctly the predominant partner, until Borcke's death on the 8th March 1747. Axel von Mardefeld, previously Frederick's trusted envoy at St. Petersburg, was now associated with Podewils until his death on the 8th December 1748, when the vacant post was conferred upon Count Carl Wilhelm Finck von Finckenstein. Podewils died during the Seven Years' War, on the 29th July 1750, and Finckenstein carried on alone till the end of the war. On the 5th April 1763 Ewald Friedrich von Hertzberg was associated with Finckenstein, and these two continued in office till the end of the reign.

The evidence is conclusive that these men exercised no personal influence upon Frederick's policy and were merely the mouthpiece of his imperious will. Very rarely did Podewils venture on a humble suggestion, and was usually soundly trounced for his pains. Finckenstein, who clung to office for fifty years, never ran such a risk during Frederick's lifetime. Hertzberg was the only minister who seems to have had views of his own which did not coincide with those of his master, but he had to conceal them from the king, and it was only under his successor that he attempted to direct the foreign policy of Prussia—with very imperfect success.

Throughout his reign Frederick corresponded directly with his agents in foreign courts, and often gave them directions which were not communicated to his ministers. Only when his mind was made up on a certain line of action did he employ the latter to draft the necessary documents. The man who really knew most about Frederick's mind was his mysterious private secretary, August Wilhelm Eichel, who served him with unfailing industry and loyalty from May 1741 till he died in February 1768, and who was with the king through all the greatest crises of his reign. Hanbury Williams writes to Newcastle, on the 22nd July 1750, that the king's real confidant is Eichel, 'who is so carefully watched that a person may be at this court seven years without once seeing him' (*S. P. For.*, *Poland*, 71). M. Richard Waddington quotes an interesting memorandum given to Nivernais in 1755 by the French Foreign Office. 'M. Eichel est inconnu et inaccessible à tout le monde; il travaille tous les jours avec le roi de Prusse et expédie toutes les affaires. Il a sous lui plusieurs secrétaires, aussi invisibles que lui. Il est le seul qui connaisse les affaires que traite sa Majesté Prussienne, à l'exclusion des autres ministres' (*Louis XV et le Renversement des Alliances*, pp. 355-6). Andrew Mitchell, almost the only foreign minister whom Frederick really trusted, seems to have been the only one who was allowed to have intercourse with Eichel, and even to use him to impress his own views on the king. Eichel had two successors, Ludwig Ernst Heinrich Cöper (1768-82) and Theodor Stephan Laspeyres during the last four years of the reign, but neither seems to have possessed the ability of their predecessor.

III

THE DIPLOMATIC REVOLUTION. THE ORIGIN OF THE SEVEN YEARS' WAR IN EUROPE. THE ANGLO-PRUSSIAN ALLIANCE.

THE treaty of Aix-la-Chapelle seemed to leave the 'old system' in Europe, which had been revived during the war, absolutely intact. It is true that the war had left behind it, as is not unusual, some mutual dissatisfaction within each of the allied groups. Austria owed a substantial debt to Great Britain, but sought to diminish its obligations by harping on the sacrifices that British influence and interests had compelled it to make to Prussia, to Sardinia, and finally to Don Philip. On the other hand, the maritime powers complained that Austria had thrown the main burden of the war upon them, that it had contributed to the conquest of the Netherlands, and to the threatened conquest of Holland, first by its neglect to carry out the Barrier Treaty, then by the Silesian campaigns of 1745, and later by its obstinate absorption in the Italian war. The reluctance of Maria Theresa to renew the Barrier, except at the price of ruinous commercial concessions, was another cause of friction. Between the maritime powers, too, there was a growing rift. The Dutch had been as sluggish as ever in the late war; over and over again influential statesmen had to be diverted to the Hague in order to induce them to fulfil their engagements; and even in their own defence they had shown little energy or efficiency. The revolution which had restored the house of Orange had also revived the anti-Orange party in the Republic, and that party was hostile to Britain, partly by tradition, and partly on account of William IV's close connexion with Britain through his wife. Equally obvious, on the other side, was the dissatisfaction between France and Prussia. Three times Frederick had cynically deserted his ally to gain his own ends. Once, it is true, he had repented, but on the other two occasions his withdrawal from the war had been extremely disastrous to the enemies of Maria Theresa. In 1742 it had restored Bohemia to her, and in 1746 it had restored Lombardy. And Frederick, on his side, resented the patronizing and somewhat dictatorial tone of France, as if Prussia existed for her benefit. He expressed his genuine opinion, with some exaggeration, when he told Legge that to be the ally of France was to be her slave.

But all these differences were mere lovers' quarrels as compared with the overwhelming pressure of motives which seemed to bind the two sets of allies to their separate unions. France and Austria were apparently as hostile as ever. Their interests clashed in the Netherlands, in Italy, in Germany, in Turkey, and in Poland. The election of Francis had established in the Empire the rule of the ex-duke of Lorraine, to whom France must always be hateful as the despoiler of his patrimony. Britain and France were divided by traditional enmity in Europe, and also by that colonial rivalry which had come to the surface in the recent war and had been left without any attempt at settlement in the peace. The two tender points at which France could most easily injure Britain were the Netherlands and Hanover, and the Dutch, though they might have little interest in Hanover, had every reason to dread French aggression in the Netherlands. Thus, in opposition to France, the maritime powers seemed bound to co-operate with each other and to regard Austria as their natural, and indeed inevitable, ally. On the other hand, France had been weakened by the loss of Spain. During the reign of Ferdinand VI the Family Compact was in abeyance, and Britain, in spite of Gibraltar and Minorca, was able to establish not unfriendly relations with Madrid. All attempts on the part of France to gain over Russia had been foiled by the resolution of Bestoujew and by the relations which France continued to maintain with Sweden, Poland, and Turkey. France was now so isolated that it was forced to cling to the Prussian alliance, and could not afford to quarrel with Frederick for his infidelities. For precisely similar reasons Frederick found it necessary to adhere to the French alliance, especially in view of Austria's ill-disguised determination to seize the first opportunity for the recovery of Silesia.

This system, however, which seemed to nearly all observers to be the natural and necessary balance of Europe, was hopelessly shattered at the end of eight years. Its destruction is known as the diplomatic revolution, and one very vital result of that revolution was the earliest close co-operation between Britain and Prussia. The first statesman to foresee the approach of the revolution, and to realize that this co-operation must follow, was Frederick the Great. As long ago as 1742, just after the treaty of Breslau, Hyndford reported that the Prussian king 'seems to apprehend that sooner or later the house of Austria will endeavour to reconquer Silesia, and for that purpose they would hereafter leave the maritime powers and join with France'.[1] By 1748 this apprehension had grown in his mind into an assurance, and he felt it necessary to insure against it.[2] Hence his offers to Legge of a Prussian alliance, which constitute the first deliberate attempt to alter the existing balance of Europe. If his offers had been accepted, France would have been driven into the arms of Austria, already partially prepared to receive her, and the diplomatic revolution would have taken place eight years earlier than it did. But Newcastle was a man of shorter views than Frederick, and George II was in no way inclined to amicable relations with his nephew. Frederick's offer, as we saw, was rejected, and the 'old system' survived its first assault.

Frederick's anticipation of a coming alliance between Britain and Prussia is the more remarkable because during the next few years the relations between the two powers were almost as strained as they had been in 1730. The old Hanoverian quarrel

[1] *S. P. For., Prussia*, 54, Hyndford to Carteret, 4 August 1742.

[2] Frederick's forecast is so striking that it deserves to be recorded in his own words. On 7 May 1748 he, by his own account, assured Legge 'qu'il pouvait compter que, dès que la paix générale serait faite, la cour de Vienne commencerait à chipoter avec celle de Versailles, et qu'alors l'Angleterre pourrait compter sur moi comme sur son allié le plus fidèle' (*Pol. Corr.* vi. 102). On 3 June he wrote to Podewils : 'Le système de l'Europe y est déjà changé effectivement en sa plus grande partie, que je me trouverai dans peu sur un bon pied avec la Grande-Bretagne' (*ibid.*, p. 130). On 7 June he wrote to his representative in Paris, Le Chambrier : 'Il n'est point à douter que, dès que la paix sera constatée, les Autrichiens ne fassent alors de leur mieux pour se rapatrier en quelque manière avec la France' (*ibid.*, p. 133).

about East Friesland was revived by George II's unremitting efforts to force Frederick to a trial of his claims to the duchy before the *Reichshofrath*. At no time, since the first five years of George I, was Hanoverian influence so supreme in Whitehall as in the last years of Henry Pelham, when Newcastle was scheming to secure the succession to his brother's office. The king's principal advisers were the brothers Münchhausen, one president of the council at Hanover, the other the agent of the Hanoverian council in London.[1] They succeeded in securing British influence and British money for Hanoverian objects in a way that Bothmer and Bernstorff would have admired and envied. The conspicuous illustration is George II's scheme to secure the continued association of the imperial office with Austria by the election of the Archduke Joseph as king of the Romans. The court of Vienna was not even consulted until after the project had been mooted,[2] and regarded with something not unlike resentment the patronizing intrusiveness of its meddlesome ally. But for three years George paraded his loyalty to the ungrateful house of Austria and induced Newcastle to take an active part in a negotiation which a few years earlier the king had held to be no concern of British ministers.[3] With a reckless profusion, which excited the alarm of his more cautious brother, the compliant duke pledged Britain to pay lavish subsidies in time of peace to secure the votes of greedy German electors. No subsidies during the war had been so indefensible or so justly unpopular. Frederick regarded this British activity in Germany with mingled anger and contempt. As the ally of France, he could not support a scheme of which France naturally disapproved, and it was not formally communicated to him until after it was thought that an adequate majority had been secured. It did not tend to conciliate him that the communication was made by a remarkably ill-chosen envoy. Sir Charles Hanbury

---

[1] On the two brothers, Gerlach Adolf, the president, and Philip Adolf, the London baron, see A. W. Ward, *Great Britain and Hanover*, pp. 165–70.

[2] Newcastle to Pelham, 2 June (n. s.) 1750: 'I then told his Majesty that he had made an emperor ; that if he could make a king of the Romans too, it would be the greatest honour to him in the world. He replied, "And that of my own proposing, without being asked"' (Coxe, *Henry Pelham*, ii. 340).

[3] See above, p. 69.

Williams, one of Newcastle's ' very pretty young men ',[1] was sent in 1750 to the Berlin embassy, which had been vacant since Legge's departure in November 1748. He possessed neither tact nor discretion, and his reckless tongue so exasperated Frederick that the king and his ministers refused to hold any converse with him.[2] Only five months after his arrival—a great part of which time he spent at Warsaw—Frederick formally demanded his recall, which Newcastle was compelled to grant as his continuance in Berlin was clearly useless. When Williams reported, in January 1751, the contemptuous rejection of 'the design which the youngest Elector of the Empire was carrying on by subsidiary treaties and other clandestine negotiations ',[3] George II was so infuriated that he ordered the envoy to leave Berlin at once. No successor was appointed until 1756. As during this time Prussia had no agent in London except a Swiss named Michell, who was not even a secretary of legation, diplomatic relations between London and Berlin were almost completely broken off.

Besides these German disputes, from which Newcastle would have done well to hold aloof, there were two direct causes of quarrel between Frederick and Great Britain. Berlin became during these years a centre of Jacobite intrigues,[4] and it was

[1] Newcastle applies this term to Williams and Joseph Yorke in a letter to his brother of 2 June 1750. Coxe, *Henry Pelham*, ii. 339.

[2] The only definite charge which Williams could discover, and which was revealed to him by the French envoy, was that he had said 'it was better to be a monkey in the island of Borneo than to be a minister at Berlin'. *S. P. For., Poland*, 71, Williams to Newcastle, 27 February 1751. For some inexplicable reason, except that he was at Dresden both before and after he was at Berlin, Williams's Prussian correspondence is bound and calendared under 'Poland'.

[3] *Ibid.*, Williams to Newcastle, 28 January 1751. In a document forwarded with this letter, Frederick stated his objections more strongly : ' Ces ouvertures sont faites, après s'être arrangé avec la plus part des autres Électeurs, et après que le plus cadet du Collège électoral eût mis des voyes illicites et prohibées par la Bulle d'Or, et contraires au serment qu'elle exige, en usage pour assurer une grande partie des suffrages au candidat qu'il proposait, voyes qui ravaloient trop la majesté du Corps germanique, et qui sappoient par ses fondements les constitutions les plus sacrées de l'Empire.'

[4] Newcastle to Hardwicke, 21 September 1753 : 'The King of Prussia is now avowedly the principal, if not the sole, support of the Pretender and the Jacobite cause' (Coxe, *Henry Pelham*, ii. 492).

confidently rumoured that Charles Edward himself had taken up his residence in the Prussian capital. These stories were doubtless encouraged by the favour shown openly by Frederick to the two famous brothers, George Keith, the Earl Marischal, and James Keith, the soldier who in 1747 had quitted the Russian service to become a field-marshal in the Prussian army. Both had been proscribed for their share in the rising of 1715, and both had since lived in exile. The British king naturally regarded it as a deadly insult that in 1751 Frederick sent Lord Marischal as his envoy to Paris, where he was cordially received by the French government.[1] But the most embittered quarrel of all was about the Prussian ships and the Silesian loan. There can be no doubt that in some cases British men-of-war had acted unjustifiably in their search for contraband of war,[2] and the British interpretation of international law in the matter of contraband and neutral traders was not popular among continental powers. And Frederick did two things which exasperated opinion in this country. He set up a court of his own to investigate Prussian complaints and to assess the damages due to his subjects. And when his demands were rejected as inadmissible, he calmly detained the interest and the instalment of principal due to the creditors of the Silesian loan as security for his ultimate satisfaction. This was a gross breach of his treaty obligations, and was wholly unfair to the creditors, who had no responsibility for the conduct of British cruisers. The quarrel was the more irreconcilable because, as Newcastle wailed, the sum at stake was too small to justify a war, yet the honour of the British state forbade any concession.

While the relations between Britain and Prussia were so envenomed, a second and more considerable attack upon the old system had come from the quarter to which Frederick's forecast had pointed. The one great exception to the general rule of

---

[1] *Ibid.*, ii. 404. Newcastle suggested that Michell should be dismissed from London as a protest.

[2] *S. P. For., Prussia*, 64 : Legge to Newcastle (14 September 1748) speaks of the conduct of British cruisers as 'unjustifiable', and as 'little short of downright piracy'. He adds that this has been a great weapon in the hands of the French party. See, on the whole subject, Sir Ernest Satow, *Frederick the Great and the Silesian Loan.*

'as you were before the war' in the treaty of Aix-la-Chapelle had been the confirmation of the aggrandizement of Prussia. This really supplied the chief impulse towards a diplomatic revolution. Two great personages at Vienna, Maria Theresa and Kaunitz, came to the momentous conclusions (1) that Prussia was really a more formidable enemy to Austria than France, and (2) that Prussia could not be reduced to harmlessness unless Austria could obtain the assistance of France. Their view was stoutly contested by the emperor himself, imbued with the Lorrainer's enmity to France,[1] and by the older advisers of Maria Theresa, who clung to the cherished traditions of the Habsburg past. But in spite of this opposition the empress queen, who loved her husband more than she respected his opinion, determined to give as much effect as possible to the proposed revolutionary policy, and Kaunitz went in person to France in 1750 to obtain at least the severance of France from Prussia. At Versailles he found the forces of routine as strongly entrenched as at Vienna, and no sovereign with the will or the capacity to overcome them. After two years the Austrian diplomatist abandoned the task as hopeless. For the second time the assailant of the old system was repulsed. But such assaults, though they fail at the time, often have a sapping effect which ultimately weakens the structure against which they are directed.

The next links in the chain of events leading to the reversal of alliances are so familiar that it is needless to do more than allude to them. The quarrels about boundary between British and French settlers in America brought the two countries to the verge of a war which, with the best will in the world, could hardly have been avoided. And the indefensible actions of Newcastle's feeble and vacillating ministry rendered it impossible for France, whose government was quite as feeble and more pacific, to stop short of the verge. As the war approached, British ministers became nervous as to the protection of those two vulnerable points, the Netherlands and Hanover. Prussia was the enemy of Britain and the ally of France. It was not easy, after all that had happened, to prove that France was the

---

[1] Hanbury Williams (from Dresden) to Newcastle (15 July 1753) says of the emperor, 'France is as odious to him as Prussia is to the Empress Queen' (Coxe, *Henry Pelham*, ii. 469).

aggressor, at any rate not on the high seas. And if Frederick deemed himself bound either by treaty or by interest to support France in a war that seemed to be forced upon her, his army would be fatal to Hanover and dangerous to the Netherlands. There were three obvious ways of guarding against the danger. (1) It was notorious that Elizabeth of Russia and her grand chancellor were bitterly hostile to Frederick the Great, and also, though less bitterly, hostile to France. It was also known that Russia was as dangerous to East Prussia as Prussia was to Hanover,[1] and that Frederick would not willingly commit himself to a western war unless he was secure from attack from the east. In order to repress Prussia George had in 1750 acceded to the treaty of the two empresses concluded in 1746, though he had rejected the secret article by which they pledged themselves to deprive Frederick of Silesia if he should again resort to war. Since then a subsidy treaty which should place a considerable Russian force at the disposal of Great Britain had been favourably considered at St. Petersburg. But the Russian demands for money were excessive, and Guy Dickens, who had been envoy in St. Petersburg since 1749, had not sufficient weight to carry it through. As the matter was now pressing, that pretty young man, Hanbury Williams, who had failed at Berlin, was hurriedly sent to try his luck in Russia, in the hope that he would be more successful in commending himself to a female ruler. (2) A second and equally obvious expedient was to appeal to our old ally, Austria, to strengthen its forces in the Netherlands. A well-equipped army there would not only protect these all-important provinces; it would also render it impossible for France to send an army against Hanover without running the risk of having its communications cut or of an attack on its flank. (3) It was now highly expedient that those subsidies which had been vainly expended to secure an election which nobody but George II and Newcastle wanted, and which had never taken place, should be diverted to princes who had troops instead of votes to dispose of, and in this way an army could be built up for employment wherever the paymaster needed it.

These three expedients were all resorted to simultaneously.

---

[1] Newcastle to Hardwicke, 6 September 1751: 'Prussia can only be kept in awe by Russia' (Coxe, *Henry Pelham*, ii. 406).

G

Two of them were apparently successful. The impetuous Hanbury Williams, inspired by a personal grudge against Frederick, and endowed with qualities which made some appeal to the Tsaritsa Elizabeth, succeeded in getting the long-delayed treaty with Russia (30 September 1755), although it cost him far more time and trouble to obtain its ratification, and though it contained in a secret clause a prohibition of separate negotiations with the 'common enemy' which was destined to give him considerable trouble later, when the question arose as to who the common enemy was. The treaty was for four years, and during that period Russia was to maintain 55,000 men on the borders of Livonia, together with a fleet on the coast of that province. The treaty bore the signature of Frederick's old enemy, Bestoujew. Three months earlier a start had been made with new subsidy treaties by an agreement with that sturdy Protestant, William of Hesse-Cassel, who was to furnish 8,000 men and increase them to 12,000 when required. But, to the astonishment and alarm of both London and Hanover, the Austrian alliance, the pivot of the whole system, failed to meet the demand upon it. Maria and Kaunitz realized that if, in existing circumstances, they supplied Great Britain with the desired backing in the Netherlands, they must abandon all their dreams of ever gaining the alliance of France, and this they were not prepared to do. As they could not reasonably offer a direct refusal, they evaded the demand by attaching to their consent such burdensome conditions that the maritime powers could not possibly accept them. George II and Newcastle realized, with equal astonishment and indignation, that after all they had done and had gratuitously offered to do, Austria had failed them in their hour of need. The corner-stone of the 'old system' had fallen away.[1]

The British government was in dire perplexity in the autumn of 1755. War with France might break out at any moment, and they were without any assurance of adequate support.

[1] Holderness, in a letter to Andrew Mitchell of 10 October 1755, sums up the causes of the rupture with Austria. 'The true state of the case is this: our object is France; theirs is Prussia. . . . Nor will they give us their assistance against the one, unless we make an enemy of the other, and help them to recover what they lost in the last war' (*Add. MSS.*, 6832).

8,000 or even 12,000 stout Hessians might be a useful contingent, but they could hardly be regarded as an army. Besides, they might be needed for the defence of Britain. The Russian treaty was not ratified; it would take a long time for so dilatory a government to collect troops and equipment in Livonia, and Livonia was a long way off. Obviously, Hanover could not be protected as things stood. It was, therefore, with the feelings with which a drowning man clutches at an unexpected life-buoy that the distracted ministers learned that their most dangerous foe might become their most efficient helper. In April Frederick had offered to France a Prussian occupation of Hanover in order to force George II to keep the peace.[1] In June France, confidently assured of the Prussian alliance—the treaty of 1741 did not expire till the following year—intimated that an envoy of exceptional rank, the duc de Nivernais, was about to proceed to Berlin to arrange for a renewal of the treaty and for co-operation in the approaching war. In August came an unexpected overture from Great Britain. Duke Charles of Brunswick, the brother-in-law of Frederick, was the recipient of subsidies from France, but had begun to seek a reconciliation with George II in the hope of marrying one of his daughters to the young Prince of Wales, the future George III. Holderness, who had held the northern secretaryship since Newcastle's promotion to the first lordship of the Treasury, and who continued to hold it until Bute's admission to the cabinet, seized the opportunity to suggest a bargain with Prussia by which the continuance of peace in Germany might be secured. The duke hastened to transmit a full report of this conversation to his brother-in-law,[2] and to express his willingness to act as mediator in bringing about so patriotic an agreement.

Frederick was exultant to find himself once more, as in 1741, the arbiter courted by both sides in a vital quarrel of great states. But there was one essential difference between his present and his past position. In 1741 his aim had been aggrandizement, in 1755 it was security. In 1741 he found that Great Britain either could not or would not extort the demanded concessions from Austria, so that he was forced into the French

---

[1] *Pol. Corr.* xi. 106-7, Frederick to Knyphausen, 5 April 1755.
[2] *Ibid.*, xi. 251-2.

alliance. In 1755 he realized that France wanted his assistance in war, which meant insecurity, whereas Britain wanted his aid in excluding the war from Germany, and could offer him, so he thought, the invaluable boon of safety on the side of Russia, the only enemy which he really dreaded. There was no real hesitation about his decision. He only waited till he had received full assurances as to Hanbury Williams's treaty with Russia, and then sent full powers to his London agent, Michell— promoted for the purpose to the rank of secretary of legation— to sign the convention which had already been submitted to him in draft. He only insisted on one alteration, the substitution of ' Germany ' for ' the Empire ', in order to gratify France and to limit his own obligations by excluding the Austrian Netherlands, which might be regarded as still in theory belonging to the Empire as the Burgundian circle. With fatal over-confidence France had delayed the sending of Nivernais until it was too late, and the envoy only arrived in Berlin to learn in his first business conference that the convention of Westminster had been signed on the 16th January 1756. The contracting parties agreed to guarantee their respective possessions and to maintain peace in Germany during the approaching war by joint opposition to the entry of foreign armies. This agreement constitutes the second stage in the diplomatic revolution.

In concluding with such notable rapidity the convention with Britain, Frederick made what proved to be two gross miscalculations. In the first place he believed that British influence at St. Petersburg would be strong enough to hold Russia to the September agreement, although the circumstances in which it had been concluded had undergone a complete change, and the ' common enemy' had become the friend of one of the parties. Hanbury Williams and Bestoujew were profoundly disconcerted when they learned that Russian aid was to be secured, not against the detested king of Prussia, but against France and in concert with Prussia. For months the British envoy, with the secret aid of the grand chancellor, conducted a difficult, and to himself a rather distasteful, struggle against the vice-chancellor, Woronzow, and the numerous partisans of the Austrian alliance. The struggle was watched with the keenest interest in London and in Berlin, where it was realized that the momentous issue of continental peace or war turned upon the result. At one moment Frederick, who had no confidence in Williams's judgement, urged the sending of a new envoy to St. Petersburg,[1] but in the end he concurred in his retention, on the ground that his relations with the chancellor and with the Grand Duke Peter and Catharine held out some prospect of success. But in January 1757 Williams had to confess his defeat when Russia finally adhered to Austria and France. Elizabeth might have some affection for Britain and still more for British subsidies, but her hatred of Frederick was infinitely stronger, and she had often shown a personal inclination to France. Bestoujew found himself ousted from all real control of affairs, and neither the health nor the reason of the British envoy recovered from the long strain of 1756.

Frederick's second miscalculation was his belief that he could reconcile the convention of Westminster with his obligations to France, and that he could convince his old ally that the neutrality of Hanover was really advantageous to France—as it probably was. But the Prussian king, himself the touchiest of rulers, ought to have made more allowance for the sensitive pride of what was still regarded as the first monarchy in Europe. From the French point of view it was not a question whether it was desirable or undesirable to attack Hanover, but whether it was tolerable that a client state—so they regarded Prussia—should presume to dictate to France what it should or should not be allowed to do. And Frederick's conduct was the more intolerable in that France had paid him the compliment of sending the duc de Nivernais, and he had not even waited to hear what this distinguished envoy had to say. In spite of these obvious considerations, which Frederick had partially foreseen, the king calmly assumed that he had done nothing to alienate France, and expressed to Nivernais his willingness, and even his desire, to renew the French treaty which was about to expire. And the envoy, who believed that the Prussian alliance was still

[1] *S. P. For.*, *Prussia*, Mitchell to Holderness, 3 June 1756 (printed in Bisset, *Memoirs of Sir Andrew Mitchell*, i. 181), 7 June (printed in *Pol. Corr.* xii. 385-6), 22 June (printed in Bisset, i. 183-8). Compare *Pol. Corr.* xii. 427, where Finckenstein reports to Frederick that Mitchell had agreed, 'en haussant ses épaules, que le chevalier Williams avait beaucoup d'esprit et peu de jugement, et ajouta qu'il en avait déjà marqué son petit sentiment à sa cour'.

imperatively needed against the hostility of Austria, waited for some months in Berlin for instructions to renew the treaty, although he had actually received from home leave to terminate his mission. The decision at Versailles to reject the Prussian offer was come to while the first indignation at the Anglo-Prussian agreement was in full force, and that decision involved another which was much more far-reaching. Unless France was prepared for complete isolation in Europe, it must terminate its secular quarrel with Austria. In the autumn of 1755 the Austrian overtures for a close alliance with France, after being in abeyance for three years, had been renewed, and the Austrian envoy, Starhemberg, had submitted tempting offers as to the Netherlands, at first in secret conferences with the Abbé Bernis and Madame de Pompadour, and later to carefully selected ministers of the crown. Nothing so far had come of these negotiations because France had no quarrel with Prussia, and Prussian co-operation was, for immediate purposes, more valuable than that of Austria. But what France regarded as treacherous desertion and insolent dictation on the part of Prussia altered the whole situation, and gave to the Austrian ambassador an advantage which he pressed to the uttermost. Still, in spite of the impetus thus given to his schemes, Starhemberg failed to attain his real object. Open war had now been declared between France and Britain, and the first enterprise of France, the attack on Minorca, had been crowned with startling success. In view of the incompetence and discomfiture of the British ministry, distracted by constant changes and personal jealousies, it was preposterous to expect that France should jeopardize its prospects of victory over its immediate enemy by embarking on a continental war to promote the interests and the vengeance of Austria. No desire to punish Frederick and no gains in the Netherlands could induce France to adopt so suicidal a policy. And so Starhemberg had to be content with the lesser gain, the severance of France from Prussia, which would have satisfied Kaunitz in 1752. On the 1st May 1756 the first of the successive treaties of Versailles was signed by Starhemberg for Austria, and by Rouillé, the foreign minister, and Bernis on behalf of France. Austria undertook to remain neutral in the Franco-British war, and France was to abstain from all attacks on the

Netherlands or other territories of Maria Theresa. Each power was to aid the other against attack with 24,000 men. The treaty of Versailles, which was the direct result of the convention of Westminster,[1] marks the completion of the third and final stage of the diplomatic revolution.

The first six months of 1756 were a period of great perturbation in both London and Berlin. At the outset both courts were jubilant at the conclusion of the convention of Westminster. Frederick believed himself safe in Silesia. Austria might be hostile, but would never risk a war unless it could obtain the help of Russia or of France. He was confident that Russia would be gained by British influence and British gold, and he now held, in opposition to his previous forecasts, that France and Austria could never come together.[2] In his most sanguine moments he saw Prussia acting as mediator between France and Britain and thus playing the greatest part possible in time of peace.[3] In London the convention was welcomed with enthusiasm. Even the opposition, as Michell reported to Frederick, could find no fault with it.[4] The long-dreaded alliance between France and Prussia had to all appearance been broken off. Hanover was secured without any of the costly subsidies

---

[1] Frederick summed up the situation in words which are worth quoting: 'Le traité de neutralité signé entre la Prusse et l'Angleterre est l'époque du revirement du système qui s'est fait en Europe. Les évènements qu'on prévoit ne sont que des suites des impressions différentes que ce traité a fait sur les différentes cours.' *S. P. For.*, *Prussia*, 65, Mitchell to Holderness, 9 July 1756, forwarding a copy of a *Mémoire raisonné sur la situation présente de l'Allemagne*, with the observation that it shows the 'hand of the master'. The *Mémoire* is printed from Frederick's autograph draft in *Pol. Corr.* xii. 472–5. It was forwarded by Eichel to Finckenstein for communication to Mitchell on 28 June.

[2] *Pol. Corr.* xii. 127, Frederick to Klinggräffen (at Vienna): 'Vous savez que leurs intérêts sont trop opposés les uns contre les autres que jamais ils sauraient être mêlés ensemble.' Frederick was always able to believe what he wished to believe.

[3] *Ibid.*, xii. 125, Frederick to his brother, the prince of Prussia, 19 February 1756: 'Cette année-ci, que je compte avoir gagnée, me vaut autant que cinq des précédentes, et, si dans la suite je puis servir de médiateur aux puissances belligérantes, j'aurai fait à la Prusse le plus grand rôle qu'elle puisse représenter en temps de paix.'

[4] *Ibid.*, xii. 75, Michell to Frederick, 20 January 1756.

which Pitt had so bitterly denounced in the previous year. The Hessian troops, which had been hired for the defence of Hanover, were now brought over to defend England against a French invasion, and, in spite of Pitt's protests, Hanoverians were added to them. The recent causes of quarrel between Britain and Prussia were sedulously removed. Frederick undertook to pay off the Silesian loan, and he accepted the sum of £20,000 as compensation for the injuries to Prussian shipping. In order to secure cordial co-operation between the two states it was necessary to resume that normal diplomatic intercourse which had been interrupted since 1751. Prussia already had a representative in London in the person of Abraham Michell, a Swiss from Neufchâtel, as were so many of Frederick's agents. He had resided in England in an inferior capacity since 1741, had recently been accredited as *chargé d'affaires*, and in that capacity had signed the convention of the 16th January. Although his first experiences in England had been unfortunate,[1] he was a man of real capacity and had an intimate knowledge of British politics and politicians. Somebody had now to be found to act as British minister in Berlin. Chesterfield suggested to Newcastle, 'some inferior person, a sort of counterpart to Michell, who should not presume to be meddling.'[2] In the end Newcastle and Holderness entrusted the important post to a man who played a really great part in the relations between Great Britain and Prussia. Andrew Mitchell, who had reached the age of forty-eight, belonged to an Aberdonian family, but was born and educated in Edinburgh, where his father was minister of St. Giles's. He sat in Parliament for the Elgin Burghs, and, like most of the Scottish members, was a loyal supporter of the government. Mitchell was a man of solid rather than showy accomplishments, with a large circle of acquaintance among both politicians and men of letters. At Berlin, where he spent the greater part of his remaining years, and where he died in 1771, he became a familiar and a prominent

---

[1] Michell had been arrested in 1741 on a charge of criminal assault on the wife of a London citizen, and Andrié, his employer and fellow countryman, had to exert his diplomatist's privileges to secure his release (*S. P. For.*, *Foreign Ministers in England*, 48).

[2] Chesterfield to Newcastle, 20 January 1756 (*Add. MSS.*, 32862).

figure. Podewils, after a first interview, described him to the king as 'franc et sincère, assez uni et ouvert et plein de bonne volonté. Il parle assez bien, mais un français très fort prononcé à l'anglaise.'[1] Mitchell's sturdy honesty and outspokenness, combined with a real appreciation of Frederick's better qualities, enabled him to gain a strong hold upon the Prussian king, and it was largely due to him that the subsequent alliance worked as smoothly as it did.[2]

As the weeks passed by, the original exultation of the unfamiliar allies gave way to disillusion. One piece of bad news was followed by another. France refused Frederick's offer of a renewal of the treaty of 1741, which was thus allowed to lapse, and the basis of the old system was destroyed by the reconciliation of Austria and France. With the old system perished the union of the maritime powers. Not only did the Dutch refuse the request to send troops for the defence of England, but the anti-Orange party triumphed over the regent Anne, the daughter of George II, by agreeing with France that, if the Barrier was respected, the United Provinces would observe complete neutrality in the war. Any possibility of the restoration of the old alliance was destroyed by the measures taken by Britain to prevent the Dutch from extending their carrying trade for the benefit of France.[3] In Sweden, where the queen was Frederick's sister, a conspiracy to free the crown from the dominant oligarchy was discovered, its leaders were executed,

---

[1] *Pol. Corr.* xii. 319, Podewils to Frederick, 9 May 1756.

[2] Mitchell's dispatches are in the Record Office, but there is also a complete collection of his correspondence in the Mitchell Papers in the British Museum. These have been largely resorted to by historians, and a selection of letters and dispatches both to and from Mitchell has been printed in Andrew Bisset's *Memoirs of Sir Andrew Mitchell* (2 vols., London, 1850). Unfortunately, Mr. Bisset was not equipped for his task by an adequate knowledge of the history of the time, and, largely in consequence of this, some of his transcripts are faulty and defective. The selection of documents also might be much improved. But to the general reader the book may be commended as of considerable value.

[3] Newcastle to Bentinck, 6 July 1756 (*Add. MSS.*, 32866): 'We cannot suffer without ruin to ourselves that the whole trade of France should be carried on for them.' The 'rule of 1756' forbade a neutral power to carry on in time of war a trade which it was not allowed to conduct in time of peace.

and the prerogatives of the crown were further restricted. In Germany Frederick was not beloved, and it was probable that, in case of a rupture with Austria, all the Roman Catholic and perhaps some of the Protestant states would support the enemies of Prussia. And finally Russia rewarded the frantic exertions of Hanbury Williams with a declaration intimating that the treaty of the previous September had been concluded against Prussia and would not be enforced against any other power. It had become clear that the convention of Westminster had produced disastrous instead of beneficial results, and that insecurity had increased instead of being removed. In face of the gloomy outlook it was necessary for the threatened states to draw closer together. Holderness went so far as to draw up the heads of a new defensive treaty and to forward them to Mitchell at Berlin.[1] But nothing came of the project. Frederick was not prepared to have his hands too closely tied, and it was feared in Britain that the news of a close alliance with Prussia would complete the exasperation of Russia and would drive Elizabeth finally into the arms of Austria.

Although there was great depression at Whitehall in the summer of 1756, and some depression at Berlin, there was still a not unreasonable prospect of continental peace. This brings me to the most important and the most controversial part of my lecture. The diplomatic revolution is so closely associated with the Seven Years' War in Europe that they have come to be regarded as cause and effect. The most recent historian of the period regards the aggressive second treaty of Versailles as the necessary result of the first treaty, and Sir Adolphus Ward has accepted this conclusion.[2] I confess that a study of the evidence leaves me quite unable to accept this dogma. The

---

[1] *Add. MSS.*, 6832, Holderness to Mitchell, 4 June 1756.

[2] Waddington, *Louis XV et le Renversement des Alliances*, p. 366 : 'Il est certain que, s'il y eut faute commise en signant l'acte de 1756, elle fut fort aggravée par les traités postérieurs ; mais il est impossible d'admettre que les seconds ne furent pas le résultat logique du premier.' A. W. Ward, *Great Britain and Hanover*, p. 181 : 'It was the action of Frederick II in agreeing to the British treaty which stung the supine and pacifically disposed government of Louis XV into taking the first step that made the second inevitable.'

matter is so important for my subject that it requires a very careful analysis. In the first place, as already stated, the Austrian scheme by which French co-operation against Prussia was to be purchased by lavish concessions in the Netherlands had not been accepted by France. In its place was a strictly defensive treaty by which France was only pledged to limited assistance if Austria should be attacked. There is nothing in this treaty which was inconsistent with the convention of Westminster, and it is significant that Frederick was far less excited or alarmed by the news of its conclusion than the ministers in London were. It is true that the negotiations were not broken off, that Madame de Pompadour was inclined to favour the anti-Prussian scheme, and that Louis XV was tempted by the prospect of gains in the Netherlands for himself and his son-in-law, Don Philip. But the majority of the French ministers were against it, and they could employ two arguments of overwhelming strength. (1) It was certain that a continental war would fatally distract French energy and resources from the maritime and colonial struggle which had begun so successfully. (2) It was not in accordance either with French interests or with French traditions to destroy the recently created balance in Germany and to restore the ascendency of Austria by unduly weakening Prussia. The ill-feeling against Prussia excited by the Westminster agreement was sure to die down, if Frederick abstained from rekindling it by any further action. (3) It had always been the policy of France to oppose the advance of Russia as dangerous to French influence in the three client states of Sweden, Poland, and Turkey. That policy would have to be abandoned if France entered into an offensive alliance with Austria, and thus became at any rate indirectly associated with Russia in assailing the king of Prussia. A Russian attack upon Frederick's main provinces must be conducted through Poland, and a Russian occupation of Poland was in the highest degree repugnant to France. This difficulty actually proved, in the course of the war, to be a serious source of weakness to the coalition. In addition to these arguments it was certain that, though the Austrian party were for the moment in the ascendant in Russia, and though Elizabeth displayed a personal animosity against Frederick which he professed himself unable to understand, there were always possibilities of regaining a hold upon Russia. Russian policy was so completely dominated by personal considerations as against substantial interests, that its continuance in a certain direction was never assured. Bestoujew was still in office, the Tsaritsa was in bad health, her heir, Peter of Holstein, was notoriously pro-Prussian, and commercial intercourse gave Britain a strong hold upon Russia. Elizabeth might die; a revolution might deprive her of the crown which she owed to a revolution; or a court intrigue might destroy the credit of Woronzow and restore the ascendency of Bestoujew. Hanbury Williams in his dispatches, and British ministers in their communications to Berlin, undoubtedly exaggerated the favourable aspects of the Russian situation, but Frederick himself admitted that it was not hopeless when he advocated the retention of Hanbury Williams at St. Petersburg. And finally it must be remembered that Russia, even after further cause of offence had been given, did not join the hostile league against Prussia until the very end of the year. Frederick later chose to assert—or possibly was led to believe—that Austria and Russia had concluded an offensive alliance, that they had agreed upon military measures against him, and had only postponed them till the following spring in order to have time to complete their preparations. But the assertion is demonstrably untrue, it was known by many at the time to be untrue,[1] and Frederick, if he believed it, was lamentably misinformed. The simple fact is that there was a reasonable chance, if not of gaining Russia, at any rate of securing its neutrality, if Frederick abstained from giving any further provocation. There is also one other vital point to be borne in mind. Even if Austria and Russia had gone further than they had done, and had agreed upon a partition of the Prussian dominions, it is certain that Austria had determined to take no active step in such a direction until it had secured the complicity and support of France. And so far it had failed to do so. Any wantonly aggressive act on the part

---

[1] *S. P. For.*, *Prussia*, 66, Holderness to Mitchell, 10 August 1756. Holderness maintains that Frederick is wrong in asserting a definite agreement between Austria and Russia. Bestoujew certainly knows nothing of such a treaty, and, however much his credit may have declined, the Tsaritsa would never take such a step without informing the grand chancellor.

of Austria would forfeit even the limited aid which France was pledged to give by the treaty of Versailles.

The situation in the summer of 1756 is as clear as anything can be in a period of such confused and conflicting diplomatic effort. The avoidance or postponement of a continental war—and postponement, in spite of Machiavelli's famous dictum, may often lead to avoidance—rested with Frederick the Great. And what was Frederick's own position ? He had no very secure alliance with Britain, where ministers like Newcastle and Hardwicke were eager to avoid anything which might render impossible a return to the old relations with Austria.[1] He was pledged to aid in keeping Germany in peace and neutrality, and especially in the protection of Hanover. He could only fulfil this obligation by scrupulously avoiding any aggressive action and by throwing the onus of disturbing the peace upon his enemies. It is true he might run some risks in doing so, but an opposite course involved not only risks but the certainty of dangers which no ruler has a right to bring upon his state. The inevitable sequence of events was clear. If he further infuriated France, he would drive her to adopt the schemes of Austria. Austria would at once close with Russia, and a triple alliance would be formed of the three greatest powers on the Continent. The combination of France and Russia, hitherto rivals at Stockholm, would bring in Sweden on the northern frontier of Prussia, and Saxony, hitherto afraid to commit itself, would be emboldened to declare its ill-concealed hostility. And Frederick ran the risk, not only of exasperating his enemies but of losing his friends. If he broke the convention of Westminster and involved Germany in war, he would release Great Britain and Hanover from their obligations. The old Hanoverian jealousy would be revived, and Prussia might find itself absolutely isolated in Europe.

Prussian hero-worship of Frederick, which Carlyle adopted

---

[1] Newcastle to Mitchell, 9 July 1756: 'Though I am for taking measures with the King of Prussia, it is upon a supposition of his entire separation from France, and if the court of Vienna gives His Prussian Majesty no disturbance, we should avoid doing anything that may make their return to their old allies (now happily joined with Prussia) impossible' (*Add. MSS.*, 6832). This letter is very faultily transcribed by Bisset, i. 189-91.

and expounded to this country, has created a legend of his
infallibility both as a general and as a statesman. It is, however,
a simple historical fact that he was apt to make gross and reckless
blunders in both capacities, though his astounding recoveries
from the results of his blunders have tended to obscure the faults
which rendered these superhuman efforts necessary. And so
it is that Frederick's emergence from the Seven Years' War
with undiminished territories and with vastly increased reputation
has blinded posterity to the extraordinary recklessness of his
decision to attack Bohemia in the autumn of 1756, and to
prelude his invasion by the occupation of Saxony. Of course
he used the old plea that aggression is often the only defence
of the weaker power, that he could not afford, after the experience of 1744, to enter Bohemia leaving a hostile and fully
armed Saxony in his rear, and that the archives of Dresden
contained ample evidence of the hostile designs of his enemies.
The only valid plea is the military contention, which he could
put forward with incontestable authority. But this very fact
that military reasons compelled him to deal first with Saxony
makes his political defence the more difficult. For Saxony had
close relations both with France and with Russia, the two
powers which he should have tried to conciliate. The dauphine,
the prospective future queen of France, was the daughter of
Augustus, and would naturally do her utmost to urge her father-
in-law to avenge the wrongs of her parents, and especially the
insults offered to her mother. Russia had placed Augustus on
the throne of Poland, and Frederick's invasion of Saxony in
1745, though then thoroughly provoked, had helped to bring
about Elizabeth's alliance with Maria Theresa in the following
year. One of Frederick's greatest securities was the difficulty
of bringing France and Russia into co-operation, and he did
his best to destroy this security by giving the two powers a
common grievance. The outbreak of the Seven Years' War in
Europe—as distinct from the colonial and maritime war between
Britain and France—and the formation of the great coalition
against Prussia which was completed by the second treaty of
Versailles on the 1st May 1757, were not due to the convention
of Westminster, nor to the first treaty of Versailles, but to
Frederick's invasion of Saxony in 1756. The evidence of

hostility in the archives of Dresden is wholly irrelevant. Nobody doubted that Austria and Russia were hostile to Frederick. The sole question at issue is whether they were prepared at the time to translate their hostility into overt action. It must not be forgotten that Hertzberg, who compiled the *Mémoire raisonné* which was to justify Frederick's conduct to the world, is himself one of the severest critics of the invasion of Saxony.

I cannot dwell upon Frederick's motives—still a subject of controversy—nor upon his failure, owing to the unexpected resistance of the Saxon army, to gain all that he had hoped to gain by surprising his enemies. He had to postpone his invasion of Bohemia until the next year—thus giving Austria ample notice—and he had to withdraw his advanced troops, which had already entered the kingdom. This withdrawal, which was interpreted in St. Petersburg as a retreat, gave the final impulse to Elizabeth to accede to the first treaty of Versailles (30 December 1756) and to conclude an offensive alliance with Austria (January 1757).[1] The point which I am compelled to press is that Frederick's action was a complete breach of his obligations to Britain. The attack upon Saxony rendered inevitable the intrusion of French and Russian troops into Germany. It exposed Hanover to the certainty of a French attack.[2] Nor was this all. The necessity of protecting his central territories against the enemies whom he had wantonly provoked made him unable to give efficient assistance in the defence of Hanover. He could not even defend his Rhenish provinces, and had to withdraw his garrison from the fortress of Wesel, the ' key of Hanover '. In fact Frederick had deliberately torn up the convention of Westminster, of which he had made such an ostentatious parade. It is difficult to believe that, if Britain had then possessed a competent and energetic ministry,

[1] Williams to Holderness, 9 December (*Add. MSS.*, 6824), states that the Prussian retreat from Bohemia, and the assurance that France will send troops both to aid Austria and to attack Cleve, make Russia regard Prussia as less formidable than they had reckoned, and therefore it has been decided to accede to the treaty of Versailles.

[2] Holderness to Mitchell, 6 August 1756, most secret and confidential (*Add. MSS.*, 6832) : ' The moment a rupture happens between the King of Prussia and the Empress-Queen, France will take that opportunity of attacking the King [George II] in Germany.'

which dared to speak its mind openly and fearlessly, Frederick
would have ventured as he did to risk the alienation of his only
ally. And it is certainly not difficult to find excuses for the
attitude of the Hanoverian ministers in 1757, though they were
loudly blamed by Andrew Mitchell at the time and have found
few defenders among British or German historians.

It was not that the British ministers failed either to see the
danger of Frederick's aggressive action or to urge him to abstain
from carrying it out. Holderness's successive dispatches are
filled with instructions to Mitchell to dissuade the Prussian king
from endangering the common cause. But it is impossible to
read these exhortations without feeling that they are timorous
and half-hearted, and one is not surprised to find that Frederick
paid no attention to them. All that he conceded to Mitchell's
remonstrances was that he undertook, before taking any hostile
step, to inquire at Vienna as to the aim of the military preparations
—an inquiry which gave Kaunitz the opportunity of drafting a
delightfully evasive reply—and also to postpone his attack until
the end of August, so that France could not do anything in
Germany until the next year. But he never took the British
king or ministers into his confidence nor consulted them as to
his plans ; and it was not till the very last moment that he
betrayed his design to begin his attack in Saxony. And if the
attitude of British ministers was pitiful before the event, it was
still more pitiful afterwards. They dared not quarrel with
Frederick, who, if he involved them in dangers, seemed also to
be the only power that could extricate them. Their chief fear
was lest George II, a blunt Hanoverian who never loved his
nephew, and who wholly disapproved of the Saxon adventure,
should blurt out what was in his mind.[1] When Frederick was
besieging the Saxon army at Pirna, and defeated the relieving
force at Lobositz, they wrote cringing letters of congratulation.
And yet they had little assurance that Frederick would really

[1] Vol. clxxxi of the *Newcastle Papers* (*Add. MSS.*, 32866) contains a
memorandum drawn up by Newcastle on 12 September 1756 for a meeting
with the king on the next day : ' To beg the King not to publish, either at
Vienna or Ratisbon, any disavowal of the King of Prussia's conduct in
attacking the Queen of Hungary or taking possession of Saxony, To observe
a perfect silence upon it,'

save them. As Holderness put it, if he was defeated they were ruined, and if he was victorious it would be of little use to them against France.[1] Newcastle came to the tardy conclusion that the conduct of the state in such difficult times was too much for him, and that he must shift the burden on to stronger shoulders.[2] In November 1756, deserted by Fox and unable to gain the help of Pitt, he actually did resign. And then followed a ministerial interregnum of eight months, for the so-called ministry of Devonshire and Pitt, without either royal or parliamentary support, never had the stability necessary for grappling with the problems before them. During these months the only element of continuity in foreign policy was supplied by the indefatigable Holderness, who stuck to the northern department and for a time held both seals, and it was his resignation which ultimately forced the king to accept the Pitt-Newcastle coalition, the most famous and successful coalition in our past history.

During this interregnum difficulties of all kinds accumulated, and the Anglo-Prussian alliance was on the verge of dissolution. Frederick bitterly complained that ' it was his misfortune to have allied himself with England in her decadence and to have been used as no ally of England ever was '.[3] The trouble arose in the winter of 1756–7, partly from the supineness of Britain in delaying the return of the mercenary troops to the Continent, and in failing to choose a general for the army which was very tardily collected to defend western Germany, but still more from the

---

[1] In the same volume are notes of a Cabinet meeting on 9 September, when Holderness argued, ' if the King of Prussia is not successful and we have no means at hand, the King is undone in Germany: if he is, and can force the Empress into a separate peace, how will our ends be served unless we engage him in some measures against France?'

[2] See Newcastle's despondent letter to Hardwicke on 28 August 1756 (*Add. MSS.*, 32866). ' The appearance of an immediate war in Germany by the King of Prussia's attacking the Empress-Queen, the little prospect of an adequate force for the defence of Hanover and the immense expense in doing it upon any foot, the necessity of keeping the King's German forces here, the constant expectation of some attempt from France, the ill-humour in the nation, the present state of the royal family and the administration, and what is to be feared with regard to the temper of the House of Commons,' &c. The conclusion is that he must resign.

[3] *S. P. For., Prussia*, 69, Mitchell to Holderness, 11 July 1757. The dispatch is printed in Bisset, i. 144–6, and in *Pol. Corr.* xv. 236–7.

actual ill will of Hanover. The electorate desired safety, but disliked owing its safety to Prussia. While Britain tacitly acquiesced in the invasion of Saxony as the act of a superior being, Hanover made no attempt to conceal its disapproval. When the suggestion came from Vienna that Hanover might have its neutrality recognized as in 1741, it was eagerly welcomed by the brothers Münchhausen and their colleagues, and was not frowned upon by George II. But the Austrian offer had to be homologated by France, which was to conduct the threatened attack, and France and Austria did not quite see eye to eye in the matter. Although France had broken off relations with Prussia after the attack upon Saxony, it had not yet signed the second treaty of Versailles. So, while Austria wished for Hanoverian neutrality in order that France might have all its forces free to attack Prussia, France, whose first enemy was Great Britain, had its own reasons for molesting Hanover and for occupying it as an asset in future negotiations. For this reason France, though it did not reject its ally's proposal, insisted that it should be accompanied by conditions as to the transit and support of French troops which rendered the offer of neutrality far less attractive. The recent experience of Saxony showed what a professed *transitus innoxius* might mean, and George II, who had to reckon with British as well as with Hanoverian opinion, rejected what Holderness called an 'insidious, insolent, and impracticable' proposal. But the incident did not tend to increase Frederick's confidence in his ally. Hanover remained discontented,[1] and Cumberland had to be appointed to command the western army, as it was feared that the Hanoverians would refuse to obey another general.

Nor were relations improved by the campaign of 1757. Frederick left the west of Germany to look after itself, and

---

[1] Mitchell, who shared the strong British prejudices against Hanover, and who had become devoted to the cause of Frederick, records his impressions of the electorate in February 1757 in a private letter to Holderness. 'When I arrived at Hanover, I was greatly surprised by the language held there. If I had not known I was in the King's country, I should have imagined we had been at war with Prussia' (*Add. MSS.*, 6831, Mitchell to Holderness, 8 February 1757). Holderness had to beg him to moderate his language about Hanoverian ministers in his office letters.

concentrated his attention on the invasion of Bohemia. A very hard-won victory before Prague (6 May) enabled him to lay siege to the capital, but his subsequent defeat at Kolin (18 June) compelled him to abandon the siege and to retreat to Silesia. A subsequent attempt to force a battle in Lausitz was unsuccessful. Meanwhile the French had carried all before them in the west. In April they commenced the occupation of Gelderland, Cleve, and the other western provinces of Prussia, including the fortress of Wesel, 'la clef et le principal boulevard de l'électorat d'Hanovre'.[1] In July they overran Hesse-Cassel, and d'Estrées defeated Cumberland at Hastenbeck (26 July). After his defeat Cumberland steadily retreated before Richelieu, d'Estrées's successor, who conquered the greater part of Hanover and Brunswick. Finally Cumberland, cut off in the duchy of Bremen, exercised the powers conferred upon him by his father, and averted a complete surrender by accepting the humiliating convention of Kloster-Zeven, by which his army was to be dispersed. This left the French free to attack Magdeburg and so to carry the war into Frederick's central provinces. Disasters elsewhere seemed to foreshadow a speedy and complete victory for the hostile powers. An expedition against Louisbourg, the capital of Cape Breton, which had been taken in the previous war and restored at the peace, was a humiliating failure. So was an attack on Rochefort on the French coast, the earliest of Pitt's side-shows, which diverted forces that might have been invaluable in Germany. Worst of all, from Frederick's point of view, the Russians had at last begun to move. They occupied Memel, which Frederick had hoped to be covered by a British fleet, they defeated Marshal Lehwaldt at Gross-Jägersdorf (30 August), and East Prussia lay at their mercy, when they mysteriously withdrew. But the welcome respite was only temporary. Apraxin, the general, was the accomplice of the anti-Austrian party, and his treachery was discovered. The seizure of his papers was followed by the final overthrow of Bestoujew, the discredit of the grand duke and his wife, and the annihilation of the party by whose help Hanbury Williams had hoped to paralyse the military efforts of Russia. The result was to stiffen the determination of Elizabeth, and Fermor, Apraxin's successor, was

[1] *Pol. Corr.*, xiv. 119.

ordered to have everything ready for an early advance against Prussia at the beginning of 1758.

It is necessary to remember these things in order to appreciate the magnitude of the task which confronted Pitt at the outset of his administration, and the lamentable legacy which he inherited from past incompetence. So far as Europe was concerned, two things were imperatively necessary: the collapse in western Germany must be made good by the repudiation of the convention of Kloster-Zeven, and a similar collapse must be averted in the future by coming to a full and clear understanding with Prussia. The two things are closely associated because, if the convention was carried out, the ruin of Prussia was inevitable. Not even Frederick's courage and capacity could have resisted in 1758 the simultaneous attack from different sides of France, Russia, Austria, Sweden, and the army of the Empire. Andrew Mitchell can hardly be described as an optimist, and he was so eager to shame Britain into greater and more loyal exertions in Germany that he may have used his gloomiest colours, but it is difficult to deny that his description of Frederick's position at this time is well founded. ' What will posterity say of an administration that made the Treaty of Westminster for the safety of Hanover, and suffered the Hanoverian ministers to say openly that they have no treaty with the King of Prussia, nay, have suffered them to betray that prince who has risked his all to save them, and whose misfortunes are due to his generosity and good faith? The King of Prussia has now against him the Russian army and fleet, 20,000 Swedes, an army of the Empire supported by 30,000 French, and the great Austrian army of 100,000, and, as if he had not enemies enough, the convention to save Hanover from winter quarters will let loose 60 or 80 thousand more French. What prospect can you have, my dear Lord, to exist till next year, far less to continue the war?'[1]

The most pressing need was to get rid of the so-called convention of the 8th September. The story of its repudiation is complicated and not very edifying. It is a stock illustration of continental historians when they wish to demonstrate the perfidiousness of Albion. Technically the convention was a

[1] *Add. MSS.*, 6831, Mitchell to Holderness, 28 August 1757.

Hanoverian act, for which British ministers disclaimed all responsibility. But this only brings out the essential difficulty of
conducting two separate governments under a single head. The
Hessian troops were not hired by Hanover, but under a contract
made by Great Britain, yet their fate had been determined by
Cumberland acting under authority from the elector of Hanover.
Also the British ministers could not abstain from intervention,
because the whole of their policy with regard to Prussia and
Germany hinged on the observance or rejection of the convention. Ultimately the matter came before a Cabinet conference
on the 7th October, at which Sir John Ligonier, as interim
commander-in-chief, and Baron Münchhausen, as representing
Hanover, were present. The minute, carefully drafted by Pitt,
admitted that the convention was an affair of the electorate, but
added that, if the Hanoverian ministry should decide to reject
it, the pay and charge of what was called ' the army of observation' should be undertaken by Great Britain.[1] Thus, very
adroitly, the pecuniary interest of George II, always a very
powerful motive, was enlisted on the side of repudiation. The
king was in a very difficult position, from which he did not
extricate himself with either credit or dignity. Alarmed by
the unanimous condemnation of British opinion, he threw the
whole blame upon his son, and declared that his instructions
had been disobeyed. Cumberland, with notable loyalty and self-
restraint, abstained from all public defence and resigned his
offices. But this did not advance matters. If the convention
had been a civil agreement requiring ratification, procedure
would have been simple. But it was a military act, a virtual
armistice, concluded by a general in the field, and was certainly
valid without ratification. In fact steps had been taken at once

---

[1] *S. P. For., Prussia*, 70, Holderness to Mitchell, 10 October 1757.
Holderness transmitted the minute of the conference with a rather verbose
but illuminating commentary: ' His Majesty has in the most gracious manner
communicated the transaction to his English servants who, though they
did not dare to presume to offer their humble advice to the King in regard
to the affairs of his Electorate, yet they thought it their duty to lay at His
Majesty's feet their opinion as to the support England ought to give to the
King, if His Majesty should be advised, by his Electoral servants, no
longer to understand a convention made under the circumstances of that of the
10th September, and already broken by the enemy, to be binding on the King.'

to carry out its provisions, and only a lucky dispute as to details postponed their completion. The French government, which equally disapproved of the convention as too lenient, acted quite correctly in accepting it with a declaration as to the interpretation of its terms. There was another difficulty. The Hanoverian ministers, to whom the matter had been referred, did not desire repudiation. They had all along craved for neutrality, and they infinitely preferred the convention to the occupation of Hanover by the troops of a hostile power. And it is by no means certain that George II, in spite of his blustering efforts to conciliate British opinion, did not in his heart agree with them.[1] For some weeks the convention remained in suspense, neither carried out nor rejected. This indecision was at last terminated by the news of Frederick's brilliant victory at Rossbach (5 November) over the imperial forces and the second French army under Soubise. The prospect that Prussia might now be able to come to the aid of Hanover removed the hesitation of George II and his electoral advisers. On the two pretexts, that no term was fixed for the suspension of hostilities and that the French interpretation of the convention was not justified by its terms, the agreement was formally denounced. Ferdinand of Brunswick, Frederick's brother-in-law and a general in his service, was invited to take command of the army in place of Cumberland, and at once proceeded to take measures for the expulsion of the French from Hanover.

Frederick's two great winter victories, Rossbach and Leuthen, not only saved him from the ruin which had seemed so imminent in the autumn, but also, by kindling enthusiasm for him in Britain, immensely facilitated Pitt's second task, the settlement of the future relations between Britain and Prussia. The alliance had passed through two crises, the negotiations as to Hanoverian neutrality at the beginning of the year and Kloster-Zeven in the autumn, and had been strengthened by neither. It rested upon

---

[1] Holderness seems to have thought so. In a private letter to Mitchell on 16 September (*Add. MSS.*, 6832) he says: 'What a scene is this, when the only service one can render to the King is to thwart the execution of his favourite measure. The Electoral ministers may involve this kingdom in the ruin they have drawn upon the King's electoral territories, but at least they cannot, they shall not, involve us in perfidy.'

no substantial foundations. With the French in Westphalia and the Russians about to re-enter East Prussia, the treaty of Westminster became obsolete. The suggested new treaty which was to take its place had been dropped. There were perpetual recriminations as to how all the present difficulties had been brought about. On the British side it was contended that Frederick's aggression, carried out against British wishes and advice, was the cause of the German war.[1] Frederick maintained that he was involved in all the existing dangers because of his undertaking to defend Hanover, that his enemies had determined to punish him for making the treaty of Westminster, and that Britain was bound to assist him because his loyalty to Britain had provoked the hostile coalition. Both sides complained that the other was not fulfilling its obligations. Britain said that Frederick had failed to carry out his promise to defend Hanover, and had selfishly left his western allies at the mercy of the French. Frederick loudly complained that the promised fleet had never been sent to his aid, that Russia and Sweden were allowed a free hand in the Baltic, that Britain had carefully abstained from sending any of its own troops to Germany, and that fair words were a poor substitute for deeds. Mitchell, who sympathized with Frederick, transmitted these complaints with an expressed or implied approval which exasperated his employers.[2] The source of trouble was that Britain and Prussia,

---

[1] The British point of view is clearly expressed by Newcastle in a letter to Mitchell of 12 October 1756 (*Add. MSS.*, 6832): ‘It will not be sufficient for His Prussian Majesty to allege that his whole force is employed against the Queen of Hungary. That was his own choice and his own doing. The obligation of joining with the King to hinder the entry of the French troops into Germany remains still, and it cannot be expected that the whole burthen of that should be singly upon the King.’ The same dispute occurs in Frederick's controversy with Bute and Grenville in the last year of the war. Frederick's contention is given in a dispatch from Mitchell of 31 August 1757. ‘The treaty he had made with the King had been the occasion of this war, the adherence to that treaty had drawn upon him the whole power and resentment of France’ (*Pol. Corr.* xv. 314–16 ; Bisset, i. 270–2).

[2] Mitchell's gloomy letters must have been exasperating. ‘I think the situation of the King of Prussia's affairs is desperate ... nothing less than a miracle or an absolute submission to France can save him’ (31 August 1757). ‘The English till now were envied and hated on the continent, at present they are despised. The late expedition against France [Rochefort]

like Austria and France, looked at the war from different points of view. Britain was at war with France, and wanted Prussia to fight against the French. To Prussia the enemy was Austria, and not France, which Frederick would have conciliated if he could. This divergence of view made each power suspect the other. In Britain, and still more in Hanover, there were incessant rumours that Frederick was about to come to terms with France, and Frederick himself was always asserting that influential people in Britain were hankering after the 'old' system and the Austrian alliance.

It was not, therefore, a very easy matter to put Anglo-Prussian relations on a friendly footing, especially as Pitt had to work with colleagues, like Newcastle, who were responsible for past misunderstandings, and had to commend his measures to Parliament, which, in spite of the present popularity of the Prussian king, had been taught by Pitt himself to regard any war in Germany with patriotic suspicion. Fortunately, two changes had taken place since 1756. (1) Frederick was no longer a dictator. Hitherto he had haughtily refused to accept any aid in money, and had countered the offer by suggesting that he should pay a subsidy to Britain. But after Kolin he admitted that the curtailment of his revenues by the loss of his western provinces and by the imminent loss of East Prussia would render it impossible for him to carry on the war without pecuniary assistance.[1] Britain could not refuse ; all haggling as to the amount ceased after Kloster-Zeven, and Frederick's demand of four million crowns ($£250,000$) was agreed to, though British ministers were never tired of dilating on the unprecedented amount of the grant. (2) Pitt was not so submissive a negotiator as Newcastle had been in the previous year. He had no hesitation about the subsidy or its amount, but trouble arose when

makes them to be considered as triflers incapable of acting for themselves or assisting their allies' (1 November). 'I think our affairs on the continent are absolutely and irretrievably ruined.' These extracts are from his private letters to Holderness; but on 28 November he said in an official letter : ' During the whole campaign England has done nothing, the strength of the nation was melted away in faction.' Holderness remonstrated strongly against ' such unguarded not to say indecent expressions' (21 December 1757).

[1] S. P. For., Prussia, 69, Mitchell to Holderness, 29 June 1757 (printed in Pol. Corr. xv. 194).

the terms of the subsidy treaty came up for discussion. Pitt demanded that British opinion must be pacified, and the treaty of Westminster fulfilled, by the sending of Prussian reinforcements to the west. Frederick in turn demanded the sending of the Baltic fleet and of British troops.[1] Neither would nor indeed could give way: Frederick because he had no troops to spare without fatally weakening his own inadequate army, especially after the new Russian advance had begun in February; and Pitt because he had to commend his measures to the House of Commons, which might grant money but would certainly not grant men. Curiously enough, both blamed their representatives for the failure to come to terms. Pitt, whose past relations with Mitchell in the House of Commons had not been cordial, was annoyed by his pessimism, which was said to have impelled Cumberland to conclude the convention of Kloster-Zeven, resented his persistent depreciation of British efforts, and held that he had encouraged Frederick to believe that his demands were so reasonable that they must be accepted. Frederick, on his side, declared that Michell spoke with the voice of Pitt.[2] In the end, after a struggle in the Cabinet, Pitt insisted that Mitchell should be recalled, and it was decided to send Joseph Yorke, a son of Lord Hardwicke and another of Newcastle's 'pretty young men', to obtain Frederick's consent to a draft treaty. Frederick at the same time determined to supersede Michell by sending to London the Baron von Knyphausen, one of his most eminent diplomatists, who was now unemployed on account of the rupture with France, where he had succeeded to Lord Marischal in the Prussian embassy. Both changes proved to be unnecessary, as Pitt and Frederick had at last agreed to the mutual withdrawal of their extreme demands. It was decided

[1] Holderness tells Mitchell, 21 December 1757, that the sending of English troops abroad is impossible. 'The system in Parliament will not support it; the spirit and bent of the nation is against it'. (*Add. MSS.*, 6832). The Baltic fleet was not refused on any principle, but because it was unsafe unless one of the northern powers could be gained over, and because there was so much for the fleet to do elsewhere.

[2] *Pol. Corr.* xvi. 253, Frederick's autograph postscript to Michell, 18 February 1758: 'Vos relations sont d'un secrétaire du sieur Pitt et non d'un envoyé du Roi; je suis excessivement mécontent de vous.' Also in Schäfer, ii. 1, p. 534.

to trust to each other's honour rather than drive a hard and fast bargain as to the actual method of fulfilling their obligations. The subsidy treaty was signed on the 11th April 1758, and it contained the all-important clause that neither party should carry on separate negotiations.

The alliance was now as complete as it ever became. The peccant envoys were forgiven. Knyphausen, who had arrived in time to sign the treaty, was left in London, but Michell remained as his colleague. Yorke, who behaved extremely well, made a short visit to Frederick's camp in company with Mitchell, found that his principal task, the adjustment of the treaty, was already accomplished, discovered what had been all along obvious, that Frederick would resent any change in the representation of Britain, and cheerfully acquiesced in his own return to the Hague, where he remained for many years.[1] With the decision to leave Mitchell at his post, the Anglo-Prussian alliance passed its last danger-point before the final quarrel began.

[1] The whole story of Yorke's excursion is told with some malice by Mitchell in a 'Narrative of Major-General Yorke's Mission to the King of Prussia' in *Add. MSS.*, 6867 (*Mitchell Papers*, vol. 64). Extracts from the 'Narrative' are given in Bisset, i. 165–7. There are also numerous letters referring to the episode both in the Record Office and in the British Museum. The general impression left by these documents is that Mitchell's friends were always in a majority, that Yorke was never intended to stay in Prussia, and that if Pitt had finally procured Mitchell's recall, Lord Hyndford would have been sent in his place.

IV

THE QUARREL

THE alliance between Great Britain and Prussia rested upon two foundations: (1) the treaty or convention of Westminster, signed on the 16th January 1756, and (2) the annual subsidy treaty, the result of the decision to repudiate the convention of Kloster-Zeven, which had been concluded by Pitt in April 1758, and had since been renewed as a matter of course in the successive Decembers of 1758, 1759, and 1760. It was due to expire, if not again renewed, on the 12th December 1761. On the whole the alliance had worked well, and both parties could look back to its past record with some complacency. It is true that Frederick had resented the constant refusal of the British government to send a naval contingent to the Baltic,[1] where it might have arrested the invasion of Pomerania by the Swedes, and would have facilitated the defence of his great Baltic stronghold, Colberg. But he could not deny that the army paid by Britain and commanded by Ferdinand of Brunswick had, by its successful resistance to the French in Hanover, Westphalia, and Hesse, covered the western frontier of his central provinces against what should have been, by all past reputation and estimates, his most formidable foe; and had thus enabled him to offer that dogged resistance to the Austrians, Russians, and other enemies, which would otherwise have been wholly impossible. On the other hand the German war had fatally distracted the energies and attention of France, and had contributed to enable Britain to gain an unparalleled series of triumphs on the sea, in America, in Africa, and in the East and West Indies. And,

---

[1] According to Thiébault, Andrew Mitchell fell into disfavour on account of the British obstinacy on this point. One day he met some friendly officers who suggested that it was the court dinner-time. 'No ships, no dinner,' replied the British envoy, and Frederick, on hearing of the answer, resumed his friendly relations with Mitchell.

although English traditions were hostile to a German war, and especially to a war in defence of the unpopular electorate, the victories of Ferdinand had roused a feeling of elation in Britain, and Frederick's prolonged struggle against overwhelming odds, together with his assumed championship of Protestant interests, made him a popular personage. A favourite signboard on public-houses opened during the war was ' The Protestant Hero ' or ' The King of Prussia '.

In spite of all this, the alliance was, from the technical point of view, extremely defective. Its aims were obscure and indefinite. The avowed object of the treaty of Westminster was to exclude foreign armies from northern Germany, and this had obviously not been achieved. It was only an assumption that it further involved the duty to expel them. The nearest approach to a normal binding alliance was the fourth clause of the subsidy treaty, which provided that the two powers were to ' negotiate no treaty of peace, truce, neutrality, nor any other convention or agreement whatever, but in concert and by mutual consent '. But this was only an annual treaty and not binding in the letter, though perhaps in the spirit, of the agreement even for the duration of the war.[1] And it was certain that the inevitable growth of war-weariness would fasten upon the German war as the least vital to British interests, and as a war in which victories, however gratifying, were won by a preponderantly foreign army commanded by a foreign general, and thus contrasted strikingly with the triumphs at sea and overseas which were genuine British successes. Finally, Frederick's disasters in 1761 seemed to point to his inevitable ruin, and vulgar minds in high places had an instinctive desire to free themselves from obligations which might involve British sacrifices in order to extricate an unsuccessful ally.

The men who had worked the alliance and made it successful deserve a word of notice. George II, in whose reign it was made, had too vivid a recollection of past friction to be more than lukewarm, and he did not live to see the alliance tested by

---

[1] It is clear that, if the difficulty had been foreseen, it would have been averted by making the necessary change. In the press of war activities Pitt never thought of it, and it would have been difficult for Prussia to suggest that a change was necessary.

serious Prussian defeats. The real pillars of the alliance were Frederick himself and William Pitt, two men who differed profoundly in character, but each of whom could appreciate the elements of greatness in the other. Frederick is a far less attractive figure in history than Pitt, but they are not unequal in stubborn courage, supreme self-confidence, and genuine devotion to the interests of their respective states. Behind them were the humble instruments who guided the wheels of inter-state relations. Finckenstein, since the death of Podewils the sole Prussian Secretary of State, who held office continuously for the abnormal period of half a century, counts for little, as he never aspired to be more than the mouthpiece of his sovereign, and later events proved that he was no enthusiastic adherent of the English alliance if any alternative was available. But there was a principal clerk in the Prussian foreign office, Ewald Hertzberg, a consummate master of diplomatic and genea-logical history, who was destined to emerge into prominence as the negotiator of the treaty of Hubertsburg, who became subsequently a colleague of Finckenstein, and when freed from royal dictation succeeded in restoring for a brief period a close co-operation between Britain and Prussia. In London Frederick was represented by two men of some note. The Baron von Knyphausen, a tall and distinguished-looking Prussian, was the son of the minister of Frederick William I who had been driven from office in 1730 as a punishment for his obstinate advocacy of the double marriage treaty,[1] and had thus an hereditary associa-tion with the Hanoverian-British dynasty. He had been sent by Frederick in 1758 to adjust the terms of the subsidy treaty, and had succeeded in gaining the confidence of Pitt. With him was associated a humble but equally efficient colleague, Louis Abraham Michell, who had been attached to the embassy in England since 1741, had been left in sole charge during the period of estrange-ment from 1748 to 1756, had played an active part in concluding the treaty of Westminster, and had been rewarded by being raised to the rank of secretary of legation. The two envoys always acted together. They interviewed ministers together, they sent joint reports to the king, and almost all his letters are addressed to them both as if they had been a firm. How they

[1] See above, pp. 21–2.

divided their tasks between themselves is a mystery, but it may be assumed that Knyphausen performed the social duties of the embassy, while Michell undertook most of the clerical drudgery. The latter was one of the few foreigners in the eighteenth century who understood the British constitution and the workings of the party system, which often puzzled and exasperated Frederick. On the British side some credit should be given to Holderness, who has been unduly depreciated by historians. He may have been lacking in originality, but he was a capable and industrious man of business, while his calmness of temper and his prudence were no mean equipment for a man who had to deal with so impetuous and irascible a ruler as the king of Prussia. It was a misfortune for the alliance that Holderness had to go out of office in 1761 to make room for Bute, who had none of his experience or self-control. But unquestionably the most important of the minor agents in the alliance was Andrew Mitchell, the British envoy at Berlin since 1756, the most prominent and not the least able of those rather numerous Scotsmen who during the latter half of the eighteenth century played an active and influential part in the diplomatic service of the country. Mitchell's letters and dispatches are an invaluable authority for the history of the Seven Years' War, and have been largely drawn upon, not only by Carlyle, but also by continental historians. He accompanied Frederick on his campaigns until 1761, when ill-health rendered this impossible, and thus acquired, for a civilian, an exceptional knowledge of military movements. The editors of that great compilation, the *Politische Correspondenz Friedrichs des Grossen*, have paid Mitchell the singular compliment of printing those dispatches which describe his intercourse with Frederick in the same type as they give to the king's letters, and almost *in extenso*. No other foreign reports are printed at all, and the excerpts from the dispatches of Prussian envoys are in very minute type. So completely had Mitchell gained the confidence of Frederick that the rather timid Prussian ministers often appealed.for his advocacy as more likely to be efficacious than their own.

In 1761 the alliance was still intact. It had survived so far the vicissitudes of war, but it had still to pass the far more severe test of negotiations for peace. There had been some slight

friction in the recent winter, when the British ministers had offered
to attempt the relief of Prussia by detaching France from the
hostile coalition, and promised, if a separate peace was made
with France, not only to continue the subsidy, but also to pay
an additional contribution in order to enable Frederick to take
into his service the Hanoverian and other mercenary troops that
would perforce be released from their contract with Britain.[1]
Frederick had for some time been urging Britain to come to terms
with France, but in the answer which his envoys returned to this
proposal they rather awkwardly and ungraciously suggested
that his assent was a concession to Britain. This was eagerly
resented by the section in the Cabinet which was inclined to
depreciate the Prussian alliance, and Mitchell was ordered to
remonstrate with some warmth on this point. More serious was
the ill feeling caused by Frederick's rather greedy estimate of
the extra subsidy necessary to enable him to take over the
German troops. He asked for five million crowns, which, added
to the subsidy just renewed, would raise the British contribution
to nine million crowns, a sum which even Mitchell admitted to
be preposterous. But the proposal which gave rise to these
discussions came to nothing, as overtures for peace came from
the hostile powers.

On the 26th March 1761 the five allied powers, Austria, Russia,
France, Sweden, and Saxony-Poland, demanded a congress at
Augsburg of all belligerents and their allies to adjust a general
peace. At the same time Choiseul proposed a separate negotiation with England on the ground that 'the nature of the objects
which gave rise to war between France and England was totally
distinct from the quarrels of Germany'. Although the several
plenipotentiaries were appointed, the congress of Augsburg
never met, and only gave rise to a not uninteresting wrangle as

---

[1] How startling this proposal to continue the support of Prussia after
terminating the French war appeared to politicians of the old school is
shown by a private letter from Holderness to Mitchell of 12 December 1761:
'I will make but one remark upon the dispatch of to-day. I little thought
I should see an English minister have courage and credit enough to support
a war on the continent as auxiliary, when the English quarrel with France
was at an end. That miracle now appears in favour of the king of Prussia'
(*Add. MSS.*, 6832).

to whether the Emperor was or was not a belligerent and therefore entitled to be represented in that capacity at the congress. But the negotiations in London and in Paris made no inconsiderable progress. With the rival proposals as to the distribution of overseas dominions and the vexed question of the Newfoundland fisheries, Frederick had no concern, but there was one matter in which he was very vitally interested. Ever since 1757 French troops had been in occupation of the Rhenish provinces of Prussia, and had deprived him of the power of getting either money or men from these territories. If France were now to withdraw from the war, Frederick felt himself entitled to demand through his ally that his western dominions should be restored to himself, and neither handed over to Austria nor even simply evacuated, as in the latter case Austria could easily occupy them with troops from the Netherlands. Pitt took the same view of the obligation of England, and on this point he was at the time backed by his colleagues, including Bute, who had succeeded Holderness as secretary for the northern department and was thus directly associated with Prussian affairs. In an ultimatum to France of the 24th July the British government explicitly demanded the complete evacuation and restoration of all occupied territories in Germany, including Hesse, Brunswick, Hanover, with Wesel and other Prussian dominions; and Pitt treated the French contention that the Prussian provinces, being held and ruled in the name of Maria Theresa, could not be surrendered without her consent, with the same scorn as he showed to the French attempt to claim redress for alleged grievances of Spain.[1] As Pitt was obdurate, and as Choiseul was only manœuvring to obtain Spanish support by a new Family Compact (actually concluded on the 25th August), the negotiations were broken off in September, and on the 10th October Frederick instructed Knyphausen and Michell to thank Pitt for his zeal in upholding the interests of Prussia.[2] Five days before this letter was written Pitt had retired from office, and the first fatal blow had been dealt to the Anglo-Prussian alliance.

[1] *S. P. For., Prussia*, 77: Bute writes to Mitchell (9 October 1761) that the French conditions are 'so unreasonable and so totally inadmissible . . . as to those which relate to the King of Prussia in particular' that Stanley has been recalled from Paris. [2] *Pol. Corr.* xxi. 18.

I propose to deal at some length with the quarrel between Frederick and the British government, which he identified from this time onwards with Bute, partly because it is in itself an interesting episode, which has hardly been adequately examined by English historians, partly because it influenced for a quarter of a century our own history and that of Europe, but chiefly because it is likely to receive considerable attention in the future. It has been for some time the fashion, and is likely in coming years to be still more the fashion, to find excuses for Bute against Frederick's wholesale denunciations, or rather to accept Bute's defence of himself, as there is nothing material to add to it. And it is quite true that neither party to the quarrel was absolutely righteous and just, that Frederick became unreasonable when once his suspicions were roused, and that Bute's contentions on certain points are not lacking in force. But, on the whole, after a careful survey of the evidence, the impression left on my mind is that the episode is one of the least creditable in the history of English diplomacy.

It must be remembered that when the rupture began Great Britain was in a triumphant and almost unassailable position; and her maritime power was so strong that, as Frederick pointed out, even if Spain joined the hostile powers, the only result would be to enlarge the area of her conquests and to render her naval ascendancy incontestable.[1] On the other hand, the position of Frederick was wellnigh hopeless. His outlying territories, both in the east and in the west, were lost, and his grip upon Saxony, his one security for the recovery of the occupied provinces, had been fatally loosened by the loss of Dresden. Worst of all, the valued province of Silesia seemed likely to be wrested from his grasp. Its strongest fortress, Schweidnitz, was closely besieged by Laudon, the most strenuous and successful of the Austrian generals. Pomerania was threatened by both Russians and Swedes, and the siege of Colberg was being ruthlessly pressed. Berlin was no longer secure, and the Prussian court and ministry had been removed to Magdeburg. Frederick's military forces, depleted by five years of warfare, were largely composed of raw recruits, who

---

[1] S. P. For., Prussia, 79, Frederick's autograph letter to George III, 22 January 1762. The letter is printed in Pol. Corr. xxi. 194.

could neither fight nor march as efficiently as the armies with which he had begun the war. He himself was ill and exhausted, and even his indomitable spirit confessed that ultimate defeat was almost inevitable. His only hope was that his enemies might be distracted by what we should now call ' side-shows '. The Turks might be induced to invade Hungary ; the Tartars of the Crimea might be bribed to attack Russia from the south ; the Danes, as the constant rivals of the Swedes, might free themselves from French influence, and supply that naval aid in the Baltic which he had vainly solicited from Britain ; and finally a rising in Poland, provoked by the hardships imposed by the Russian occupation, might compel the advanced forces of Russia to retire from Pomerania. All these threads were in his hands in the autumn of 1761. But if these schemes failed, and even if the most promising of them, the Turkish diversion, could not be brought about, it was clear that no British subsidies, even if they were more lavish than in the past, would avail to save Prussia.[1] And at the beginning of October came the news that Laudon, using human bodies as fascines to bridge the trenches, had forced Zastrow to surrender Schweidnitz, *un évènement presque incroyable.*[2] It requires little effort of imagination to grasp the depressing effect in these circumstances of the news that the loyalty of his one ally was beginning to weaken.

Bute's point of view is clear and undisputed. He desired to put an end to the war as soon as possible, and so to obviate all popular pressure for Pitt's return to office. He had had no long association with Prussia, and he imperfectly appreciated Frederick's services to the common cause. To his limited vision the obstinate insistence upon the integrity of the Prussian dominions as an essential condition of any treaty was not justified by the military situation in Germany, and was an irritating obstacle to the conclusion of general peace. He could not dictate terms to Prussia, but he could use the subsidy as a means of putting pressure upon Frederick, and in the meantime he could free himself from the irksome necessity of obtaining Prussia's consent to a separate treaty with France. And he was confident that, if France and Britain came to terms, Frederick

[1] *Pol. Corr.* xxi. 42, 69, 112. [2] *Ibid.,* pp. 6, 9.

would have to make peace by sacrificing some fragments of his territories to Austria and Russia.[1] The first obvious step was to refuse to include clause 4 in any renewal of the subsidy treaty. Frederick, assuming renewal as a matter of course, had sent full powers to his envoys in London. Although Bute had given a pledge that the recent ministerial changes involved no alteration of foreign policy,[2] he met the Prussian overtures with the demand that clause 4 should be omitted. Frederick, to whom it was referred, growled but assented, on the understanding (1) that any treaty with France should stipulate for the restitution of the Rhenish provinces, and (2) that if Britain withdrew military assistance in virtue of a French treaty, pecuniary aid should be given to him in addition to the subsidy. Both of these principles had been accepted in 1761, though there had been some haggling as to the precise sum to be paid, and Frederick was entitled by Bute's assurance to assume that they would be maintained. But, by the time this answer reached Bute, the latter's attitude was changed. The rupture with Spain, which Pitt had proposed to anticipate, was not averted by the servility of his successors, and in December Spanish insolence convinced Bute and Newcastle that war was inevitable. This involved, not only an extension of maritime operations, but in all probability the provision of assistance to Portugal.[3] Bute now

[1] It is only fair to Bute to say that Pitt had asked the Prussian envoys in 1761 what cessions Frederick was prepared to make, and this had provoked a strong protest from the Prussian king, addressed to Pitt himself, in which he declared that he would not surrender any of the territories which Britain had guaranteed (*Pol. Corr.* xx. 480, 507-9). Also Andrew Mitchell, who cannot be accused of being a partisan of Bute, held that cessions on Frederick's part were inevitable. 'I fear this obstinacy for the entire conservation of Silesia will soon or late be the ruin of the house of Brandenburg' (*S. P. For.*, *Prussia*, 77, Mitchell to Bute, 13 May 1761). And Knyphausen and Michell, as appears in the text, held the same view.

[2] *S. P. For.*, *Prussia*, 78, Bute to Mitchell, 9 October 1761. See also Frederick's grateful acknowledgement in *Pol. Corr.* xxi. 59.

[3] The Spanish declaration of war against Portugal, because that power refused to join the Bourbon states against Britain, was so flagitious an act as to excite the moral reprobation of Frederick. It is always interesting when Satan rebukes sin: 'Si ces procédés gagnent faveur, le droit du plus fort pourrait bien se rétablir dans notre Europe, depuis que la balance des pouvoirs y est si prodigieusement détraquée'. Frederick to Ferdinand of Brunswick, 5 February 1762, *Pol. Corr.* xxi. 230.

proposed to drop the subsidy treaty altogether, and merely to ask Parliament for a grant of such sum as might be necessary. Although this placed him altogether in the hands of the British ministers, Frederick again found it necessary to consent,[1] assuming that the grant would be a double one, to include the old subsidy of four million German crowns (£670,000) with the further payment to be made in the event of a separate peace with France. Colberg fell at last, on the 1st January 1762, and Prussian fortunes sank lower than ever. The subsidy treaty had expired on the 12th December, but the subsidy itself, with this unsettled eventual addition, was still held out to Frederick.

The misfortunes of Prussia, and the consequent ease with which the English proposals had been accepted, impelled Bute to tighten his grip. On the 8th January he wrote a momentous letter to Mitchell at Magdeburg, the substance of which was shortly afterwards communicated to Knyphausen and Michell. With regard to money, the subsidy treaty was not to be renewed, but Parliament was to be asked at a convenient time to grant the amount of the old subsidy. No allusion was made to the eventual extra payment which had figured so prominently in past correspondence. Then Bute went on to state that Frederick's recent reverses, combined with the increased obligations of Britain, must impel him to make a speedy treaty with Austria, and to 'suit its terms to the means that may be in his power of enforcing his demands by the sword'. And in the meantime the British government, the paymaster, desires to be informed (1) as to his military resources and plans, and (2) as to the terms on which he will purchase peace from his opponents. Mitchell was instructed to convey this in person to Frederick's camp at Breslau, or, if his health would not allow him to do this, somebody must be sent to take his place.[2] Mitchell, who knew Frederick better than Bute did, foresaw the effect which would be produced on his irascible temper by the suggestion that, while one ally was securing gains in every quarter of the globe, the other, after far greater sacrifices, was to be compelled to make humiliating cessions. He excused himself from the

---

[1] Frederick to Knyphausen and Michell, 17 January 1762, *Pol. Corr.* xxi. 186. See also p. 192.

[2] *S. P. For., Prussia,* 79, Bute to Mitchell, 8 January 1762.

journey to Breslau on the ground of health, and made his communication to the king through Finckenstein. But he could not have foreseen that Frederick, at the time he received it, would be further exasperated by the presumption of his envoys in London, who not only forwarded Bute's advice, but actually urged that he should follow it in order to disprove the current report that he was an inveterate opponent of peace.[1] The indignation provoked by the British suggestions and demands of January was never obliterated from Frederick's mind, and it coloured all his subsequent estimates of Bute's words and actions. His only consolation was that the Spanish quarrel must impede a separate peace between France and Britain, and that the mere defence of Hanover would compel the latter power to continue the continental war for another year.[2]

This, however, would not have saved Frederick, nor would the dilatory Turks, nor the greedy Tartars, nor the hesitating Danes, nor the unruly and untrustworthy Poles. At the moment of deepest depression, the news came to Breslau on the 19th January 1762 that Elizabeth of Russia, his most inveterate opponent, more resolute in her enmity even than Maria Theresa, had died a fortnight earlier. What might result was as yet uncertain. The new Tsar, Peter of Holstein, had been, until the war broke off their intercourse, an admirer and a correspondent of Frederick. He was not likely to maintain the close alliance with Austria: indeed, the recall of the Russian troops from the front was already intimated. But he might, in deference to Russian opinion, insist upon the retention of East Prussia, or at least on its occupation until the final conclusion of the war.[3] On the other hand, there was a possibility that he would magnanimously restore Russian conquests, and he might even be induced to join Frederick against Austria,

---

[1] *Pol. Corr.* xxi. 223. Frederick's characteristic outburst is, as usual, in an autograph postscript: 'Apprenez mieux votre devoir, et sachez qu'il ne vous convient en aucune façon de me donner conseils aussi ineptes, aussi impertinents que ceux dont vous vous avisez. Pour moi, je vous conseille fort pour de bonnes raisons de n'y plus revenir, ou vous pourriez fort vous en repentir.'

[2] *Ibid.*, pp. 192, 324.

[3] See, for the various possibilities, Frederick's careful instructions to Goltz (7 February 1762) in *Pol. Corr.* xxi. 234.

if only he could be induced to abandon or postpone his well-known desire to enforce his claims to Sleswick against the Danes. Frederick had good reason to congratulate himself that his desperate plans of the last few months had not been carried out.[1] If he had become the close ally of Turkey, if the Tartars or Poles had attacked the Russians at his instigation, worst of all, if the Danes had been induced to join in the defence or recovery of Colberg, his chances of gaining the favour of Peter III would have been infinitesimally small. With characteristic promptitude he shifted his policy to suit the new circumstances. He must now divert the Tartar attack from Russia to Hungary, he must convince the Porte that Austria and not Russia was the natural enemy, and he must drop all communications with Denmark and with Polish malcontents. To conciliate Peter, he ordered the release of all Russian prisoners, and issued special instructions to spare the principality of Zerbst, belonging to the brother of the new Tsaritsa, which had hitherto been racked by Prussian requisitions. At the same time he selected a young officer, Bernhard Wilhelm von der Goltz, raised him to the rank of colonel, and sent him to St. Petersburg to explore the situation there and to make the best of it.

The need of opening relations with Russia made Frederick for the moment more dependent upon England and compelled him to postpone any open resentment of Bute's attitude. The British government was not at war with Russia and had never broken off diplomatic relations with St. Petersburg. Thus Frederick had to request Mitchell to transmit his first messages to the Tsar to Robert Keith, a cadet of the Earl Marischal's family, who had been British envoy at the Russian court since 1758, and who for a few weeks had to represent the interests of Prussia as well as of his own country. And it was from Mitchell alone that Frederick could obtain a safe conduct to enable Goltz to proceed to Russia. To Mitchell also Frederick confided a confidential injunction to Keith not to risk a major gain by being too ready to frown upon Peter's anti-Danish policy, however much it might run counter to the traditions of the British Foreign Office.

[1] *Pol. Corr.* xxi. 274: 'Si j'avais pu deviner cet évènement, je n'aurais pris les mesures que la nécessité de ma situation me força de prendre alors.'

But the ultimate result of the Russian negotiations was to weaken the connexion with Britain. As Goltz, spurred on by Frederick, gained one concession after another from the willing and almost fascinated Tsar ; as Frederick was able, first, to make peace with Russia (5 May 1762) and recover all his eastern provinces, secondly, to make peace with Sweden (22 May), where the pro-French party was soundly beaten, and thirdly, to make an actual alliance (19 June) whereby Russian troops under Czernicheff, previously combined with the Austrian army, actually joined the Prussians in the great attempt to recover Schweidnitz, Frederick's political, and also his financial, dependence upon British aid steadily diminished. He was at last free to speak his mind. The subsidy treaty had gone, and the subsidy itself had ceased to be of primary importance. Frederick saw his way to meet the expenses of one more campaign, and he was now confident that it would be the last. The current textbook explanation of the quarrel is that Bute and his colleagues alienated Frederick by withholding the subsidy at the time of his dire necessity. This is not wholly accurate. The subsidy was never absolutely refused by Britain until after Frederick had repudiated it because the conditions ultimately attached to it were intolerable to him. Long after the actual subsidy treaty had lapsed Bute continued, both to Knyphausen and Michell and through the agency of Mitchell, to dangle the prospect of the parliamentary grant before Frederick, in the confident expectation that the desire to gain it would make him more amenable to British wishes. This explains the otherwise cryptic phrase employed by Frederick in his memoirs, where he says of Bute, 'Cet Anglais croyait que l'argent fait tout, et qu'il n'y avait d'argent qu'en Angleterre'.[1] As Mitchell warned Bute on the 25th March, nothing could be more maddening to Frederick than to be treated as a mere mercenary or stipendiary prince, like Hesse or Brunswick, whose services and subjects were for hire.[2] And on the 9th April Bute took a new line. He declared

---

[1] *Mémoires* (ed. Boutaric), ii. 222.
[2] *S. P. For.*, *Prussia*, 79, Mitchell to Bute, 25 March 1762 : 'The knowledge I have of the king of Prussia's temper, and even of his caprices, induces me to write with this freedom, as I believe nothing would more disgust that monarch than if he should be treated as a pecuniary dependent.

to Mitchell that the subsidy was to be paid ' for peace and not for war ', and therefore he must know what use is to be made of the money before it can be·given.[1] This was a preposterous afterthought, as if the subsidy had not always been for military expenditure, and as if the continance of the war was not necessary to induce the hostile powers to make peace. But it was enough to exhaust Frederick's patience. On the 23rd April he instructed his ministers in London ' not to say another word to Bute about the subsidy '.[2] And Mitchell reported that, in three successive interviews, on the 29th April and following days, Frederick gave him no opportunity of speaking of the subsidy, and that it was impossible for him to force a conversation on the subject.[3] Mitchell did not know that before these interviews took place Frederick had received intelligence which made dependence upon Britain more hateful than ever.

The disputes about the subsidy were unquestionably the origin and a prominent cause of the alienation of Frederick, but they by no means stand alone. If they did, it would be difficult to deny that Bute's defence, based mainly upon the altered conditions of the two powers since the 5th January, has some cogency. In his elaborate apologia of the 26th May, written just before he quitted the Secretaryship to become First Lord of the Treasury in place of Newcastle, he sums up the situation with unusual force. ' We have a very powerful additional enemy to contend with : his Prussian Majesty has a new and very powerful friend. The weight of Spain is thrown into our opposite scale ; that of Russia, and of Sweden too, is taken off his. The king of Prussia had Pomerania and Brandenburg to defend besides Saxony and Silesia. The two former are no longer in danger.

He may for a time seem to dissemble; but he will not easily forget; and the first opportunity that offers, he will not fail to take his revenge, even at the expense of his real interest.' This important letter is printed in full in Bisset, ii. 276-80.

[1] S. P. For., Prussia, 79, Bute to Mitchell, 9 April 1762.
[2] Pol. Corr. xxi. 384. As late as September Knyphausen and Michell reported that the British ministers were prepared to offer the same subsidy as was to be paid by France to Austria under the treaty of Versailles. Frederick replied that, if Bute made the offer, he would not accept it. Ibid., xxii. 234.
[3] S. P. For., Prussia, 80, Mitchell to Bute, 2 May 1762. Pol. Corr. xxi. 406.

We had on our part a most expensive land war in Germany: we must now provide for another in Portugal '.[1] In view of these circumstances it was easy to argue that Parliament was not likely to admit the necessity of giving money to Frederick. And as a matter of fact Frederick could not assert that he needed it.

But already the subsidy question had been dwarfed in Frederick's eyes by a discovery of Bute's past relations with Russia. To Frederick the death of Elizabeth and the accession of Peter had meant salvation in the place of imminent ruin: it had further held out the intoxicating prospect of a triumph over the enemies who had combined to crush him. It is necessary to read Frederick's letters during the spring of 1762 to realize the immensity of the change to him. He was even optimist enough to hope that it would impel the British government to make a strenuous effort for victory in the common cause.[2] But Bute regarded the course of events in Russia from a wholly different angle. Every gain to Prussia made it more and more improbable that Frederick would accept what Bute considered to be the only possible conditions upon which Austria could agree to peace. It must also be remembered that Bute was a comparative novice in continental politics, and that he had little knowledge of Peter III and his predilections. His undisguised desire was to utilize the altered attitude of Russia to hasten the conclusion of peace and to avoid anything that would tend to prolong the war. He was afraid that Austria, deserted by Russia, would be driven into closer relations than ever with France, whereas the British Foreign Office always cherished the desire that the treaty of Versailles should break down, and that the 'old system' should be revived by the return of Austria to its former ally. It was in this spirit that Bute determined to guide the British embassy at St. Petersburg. He distrusted Keith as being, like Mitchell, rather too loyal to the Prussian alliance, and therefore

---

[1] *S. P. For.*, *Prussia*, 80, Bute to Mitchell, 26 May 1762. The letter, which deserves careful study, is printed in full by Bisset (ii. 294–302), who is inclined to take it at its face value. Adolphus, who also prints it (*History of England under George III*, vol. i, App., pp. 584–9), incorporates the substance in his text (pp. 79–80).

[2] *Pol. Corr.* xxi. 209, 246.

determined to give him a colleague in the person of Wroughton, who had been British Consul at St. Petersburg since 1760, had gone home on leave in 1761, and had gained Bute's favour by insinuations against Keith.[1] Wroughton, who boasted the favours of the new Tsaritsa's lady-in-waiting, was to carry the instructions for Keith and himself, and was to urge the Tsar to advise Frederick to accept reasonable terms rather than encourage him to continue the war.[2] At the same time, on the 6th February Bute had an interview with Galitzin, for several years Russian envoy in London, who was about to return to St. Petersburg as Vice-Chancellor, and who was known, or at any rate supposed, to be hostile to Prussia and an advocate of the Austro-Russian alliance.[3] Galitzin, as in duty bound, reported the matter to the Tsar, and Peter, in his infatuation for his idol, transmitted the report through Goltz to Frederick, who received it on the 23rd March.

Galitzin's report may be briefly summarized. After explaining Wroughton's mission and the British desire for friendly relations with Russia, Bute went on to state that it depended upon the Tsar whether peace should or should not be restored to Europe. It appeared to the British government to be a necessary condition of peace that Prussia, on account of its dilapidated condition, should make considerable cessions of territory, should, in fact, purchase peace at its own expense. Therefore six weeks ago Mitchell had been instructed to urge the king of Prussia to think seriously of peace, and to state that war could not be continued for ever to please him. To this no answer had been as yet received, nor was any favourable answer probable so long as Frederick was buoyed up by chimerical hopes of Russian assistance. These hopes appear to Bute to be chimerical because he cannot believe that the Tsar would ever prefer the king of Prussia to his natural allies, or put the interests of Frederick before those of the court of Vienna.

---

[1] For the ill-feeling between Wroughton and Keith see *Grenville Papers*, i. 421.

[2] See Schäfer, *Geschichte des Siebenjährigen Krieges*, ii. 2, p. 462. He quotes a dispatch from Hellen, Prussian envoy at the Hague, who got his information from Sir Joseph Yorke.

[3] *S. P. For.*, *Prussia*, 80, Mitchell to Bute, 2 April 1762.

The British government does not therefore desire the withdrawal of the Russian troops, which would prolong war instead of hastening peace. What it really wishes is to save Prussia from ruin by forcing Frederick to make reasonable sacrifices.[1] Although Goltz, after transmitting the report, added that Peter had refused to receive Wroughton, and in an interview with Keith had spoken strongly of the discredit which Britain would incur if Prussia was left in the lurch,[2] Frederick's intense indignation was in no way mitigated. He felt as a drowning man might feel if a soi-disant friend, himself securely seated in a boat, should endeavour to snatch away the life-buoy just as he was about to clutch it. He vented his first uncontrollable rage in an outburst against his unfortunate ministers in London, whose only fault was that they had failed to discover Bute's attempted intrigue with Russia. In an autograph postscript, without any explanation, he burst out upon them, 'I believe, Sirs, that you are the paid servants of Bute. It is clear that you are not Prussians. Your father, Knyphausen, took money from France and England, and was exiled for it. He must have bequeathed this habit to you as a heritage'.[3] But his permanent wrath was reserved for Bute, who is henceforward an arch-criminal for whom no epithets and no punishment could be too bad. He never doubted the truth of Galitzin's report, and the latter's bias in favour of Austria seemed a reasonable guarantee of its truth. And it is almost certain that Bute did speak to the alleged effect, though the points may have become more brutal when con-

---

[1] The extract from Galitzin's report is printed in full in *Pol. Corr.* xxi. 311, and in Schäfer, ii. 2, App., pp. 745-6. See also on the instructions to Wroughton, *S. P. For., Prussia,* 79, Bute to Mitchell, 6 February 1762; Adolphus, i. 576.

[2] Schäfer, ii. 2, p. 465, quoting from Goltz's report. Keith was not unnaturally surprised by the coolness of Peter III and the aloofness of Goltz. 'The Emperor is less cordial since he conceived the unhappy jealousy of our court.' 'Baron Goltz has been but once in my house for five weeks.' Letter from Keith to Mitchell (9 April), forwarded by Mitchell to Bute (21 April) in *S. P. For., Prussia,* 80.

[3] *Pol. Corr.* xxi. 317 (25 March 1762); Schäfer, ii. 2, App., p. 747. The latter also gives the not undignified replies, for once separate, of Knyphausen and Michell. Frederick, who must have realized the unfairness of his outburst, never offered any apology, but never reverted to the charge.

densed in the reporter's summary. Bute's own defence, in his manifesto of the 26th May, is in the highest degree halting and unconvincing. He admitted the interview and the date and the occasion, but his words had been misinterpreted or misrepresented. He could not have urged the leaving of the Russian troops or the preference of Austria to Prussia, because during the interview he was guided by his original instructions to Keith, in which satisfaction was expressed that the Russian troops were to 'advance no further' (which was not inconsistent with their remaining with the Austrians), while Keith was instructed to execute the instructions of the king of Prussia, which were certainly not pro-Austrian. The real answer would have been to produce the instructions carried by Wroughton, to which Bute makes no allusion. Even Mitchell, in communicating Bute's letter to Finckenstein, admitted ruefully that the defence on this point was 'tiré par les cheveux'.[1] When the story became known, Bute's reputation for honesty and straightforwardness was lost, and his fellow countrymen rather unfairly had to share the discredit.

Frederick received Galitzin's disclosure on the 23rd March. On the very same day Knyphausen and Michell wrote from London their discovery that the British government had opened secret negotiations with Austria, and that they had met with an ignominious rebuff from Kaunitz.[2] Frederick eagerly welcomed new evidence of ill faith, and, though his envoys said nothing of the sort, jumped to the conclusion that the basis of negotiation was the cession of Prussian territories, which were being bargained away behind his back. If this had been true, it would have been unpardonable, but it had no foundation at all. Frederick had simply fitted into one puzzle pieces which belonged to another. Because Bute had told him and had told the Tsar that Frederick must purchase peace by cessions, therefore Bute must be seeking to buy peace from Austria by

---

[1] Finckenstein's interesting report to Frederick on 9 June is printed by Schäfer in ii. 2, App., pp. 749–51. Keith to Mitchell, 23 August 1762, says: 'The account which Prince Galitzin transmitted before he left London of a conversation with Lord B—— was certainly and literally true' (*Add. MSS.*, 6825).

[2] *Pol. Corr.* xxi. 311–12, 353–5.

Prussian sacrifices. On this main point the defence is absolute, though in other respects the action of the British ministry was open to criticism. The facts are simple. The Family Compact between France and Spain had been concluded without the assent of Austria. This was a breach of the treaty of Versailles. Also the Compact itself was distasteful to Austria, because the two branches of the house of Bourbon had in two successive wars combined to weaken or destroy Austrian power in Italy. What could be more obvious to the British Foreign Office, always hankering for the return of Austria to the true fold, than to explore the possibility of using this weapon to sever Austria from France? It is true that a restoration of the Austrian alliance meant the dropping of Prussia, and so nothing in the meantime could be disclosed to Frederick. The negotiation began in January. At the same time that Bute instructed Mitchell to urge upon Frederick the necessity of making peace with Austria, he authorized Joseph Yorke to sound the Austrian minister at the Hague on the possibility of joint action in Italy against France and Spain in order to oust the Bourbons from some of their recent gains. Probably nothing would have come of the overtures anyhow, but any chance of success was destroyed by the altered policy of Russia. Kaunitz could not possibly risk the alienation of France, and the scheme was practically stillborn. Bute told the whole story to Mitchell for communication to Frederick on the 26th March, and defended the previous secrecy on the ground that Prussia had no interest in Italy, and that the recovery of lost Italian provinces might induce Maria Theresa to abandon Silesia. He was furious because Mitchell did not at once proceed in person to lay the documents before Frederick, and threatened the ambassador with disgrace.[1] In consequence of this, Mitchell, in spite of continued ill-health, had to make his way to the camp at Breslau, where he had his first interview with Frederick on the 29th April. He began by presenting a précis of Bute's letter to Yorke of the 12th January, and was taken aback when Frederick, after a hasty glance, said ' it was a *pièce supposée* and did not agree with the accounts he had from other quarters, from whence he was informed that my court had proposed to the court of Vienna considerable cessions

[1] *S. P. For., Prussia*, 80, Bute to Mitchell, 26 and 30 April 1762.

of his, the king of Prussia's, territories'. This was, in fact, untrue, as Frederick derived the information from his own suspicious temper, and Mitchell replied warmly that the alleged intelligence was absolutely and demonstrably false. Frederick then turned abruptly to the Galitzin disclosures, of which Mitchell had no knowledge whatever, and he could only reply that the British ministers would be able to refute the calumny as soon as it was made known to them.[1] Five days later Frederick wrote a carefully drafted letter to George III, in which he formally accepted the authenticity of the papers with regard to the Austrian negotiations, but not obscurely hinted his continued adhesion to his original suspicions.[2] It was Mitchell's report and Frederick's letter to the king which extorted Bute's elaborate defence of the 26th May.

While Frederick was cherishing his three grievances with regard to the subsidy, the negotiations with Austria, and the obnoxious suggestions of Bute to Russia, the British ministers were not content with a mere defence of their conduct. They also put forward charges against Frederick, especially with regard to his negotiations with Russia and Sweden, and also with reference to the conduct of the Prussian ministers in London. This side of the quarrel has received less attention than the other, partly because the British complaints were less fundamental than those of Frederick, and also because they had less lasting consequences. After all, it was on the Prussian side that the ill feeling endured. Bute and his successors, after the war was over, were quite ready to be reconciled with Prussia and even to renew the alliance, provided no more attractive substitute was available. But at the time, especially in the hands of irritating controversialists like Bute and Grenville, the British

[1] *S. P. For.*, *Prussia*, 80, Mitchell to Bute, 3 May 1762. Mitchell's report is printed in *Pol. Corr.* xxi. 403-6.

[2] *S. P. For.*, *Prussia*, 80, Frederick to George III, 2 May 1762. This letter is printed in full in *Pol. Corr.* xxi. 413-14; also in Schäfer, ii. 2, App., p. 748. The offensive words are, 'Je ne saurois cependant dissimuler à Votre Majesté que l'usage ordinaire des alliés n'est pas d'entamer des négociations à l'insu de leurs confédérés et de traiter de leurs intérêts sans les consulter'. As this was a virtual giving of the lie to the British king, it was not unnatural for Bute to declare, on 26 May, that a continuance of controversy on the Austrian negotiations was neither dignified nor possible.

counter-charges were as acrimonious in their tone as Frederick's charges, and they undoubtedly helped to embitter the quarrel. With regard to Russia Frederick knew that he was partially at fault, and this made him the more resentful of criticism. It was through British channels that he had opened his momentous intercourse with the Russian court, and when Goltz went to St. Petersburg it was understood that he and Keith were to act in complete concord with each other. Yet when Frederick was pressed to disclose his instructions to Goltz he would only give evasive replies. Even Mitchell complained of the ' reserved and unfriendly behaviour of the Prussian king', though he urged Bute not to show resentment, on the ground that Frederick was not in a position to refuse any Russian demands and could plead necessity as his excuse.[1] Bute, however, refused to dissemble, and maintained that Frederick's reserve was indefensible. The real explanation was suspected from the first, and was disclosed in the course of March. Britain wholly disapproved of aggressive action against Denmark, whereas Frederick was willing to pay any price for Russian support. In the end, to the intense irritation of Bute, he agreed to guarantee Sleswick to the Tsar, on condition of a similar guarantee of Silesia to Prussia.[2] This, as Bute pointed out, was to extend the war instead of making peace.[3]

Frederick pleaded that as Britain was not at war with Russia her interests were unaffected, and also that, as all Goltz's negotiations were conducted in concert with Keith, Britain was in touch with the whole matter. Both pleas were insincere. He knew that Britain was keenly interested in the Danish question, and for that very reason had instructed Goltz to say nothing to

---

[1] *S. P. For., Prussia*, 80, Mitchell to Bute, 25 March 1762 ; Bisset, ii. 279.

[2] Mitchell on 25 March rallies Finckenstein on the disclosure of the secret. 'Après cette Déclaration [i. e. that Peter would restore all conquests], M. de Goltz, *sans doute selon ses Instructions*, proposa à Sa Majesté Impériale de garantir la Silésie au Roy de Prusse, ce que l'Empereur a paru disposé à faire, pourvu qu'en revanche S. M. Prussienne voudroit garantir le Duché de Sleswic à l'Empereur de Russie. Voilà le secret de l'Eglise découvert; pourquoi ne l'avoir pas communiqué plus tôt!' Copy of Mitchell's letter to Finckenstein, forwarded to Bute with above dispatch.

[3] *S. P. For., Prussia*, 80, Bute to Mitchell, 9 April 1762.

Keith about it,[1] and in the end he ordered him to drop all communication with the British envoy, worthy and honest man though he be.[2] It is a good illustration of his duplicity that when Keith wrote to congratulate him on the Russian treaty he replied that it was 'entirely due to you'.[3] The treaty with Sweden was also denounced by Grenville, who had succeeded Bute in the northern Secretaryship, partly on the ground that Britain had never been consulted, and partly because no allusion was made to the Anglo-French war, so that Sweden, a notoriously pro-French power, was free to take any part it liked against Britain.[4] To this Frederick's answer is crushing. (1) Sweden was not at war with Britain, and therefore British consent was not needed; (2) he did communicate his intention to make peace on the basis of the treaty of 1720, and he forwarded the treaty the moment it was concluded; and (3) Sweden was pledged not to assist any enemy of Prussia, and therefore was bound to give no aid to France.[5]

Far more substantial were the complaints as to the conduct of the Prussian envoys, and to these Frederick had no reply to make except untruthful denials. As soon as he had made up his mind to dispense with the subsidy, and to put no restraint upon his wrath against Bute, he instructed Knyphausen and Michell to speak 'rondement et sans détour' and no longer timidly and gently to the British ministers.[6] This explains the truculence of their manners. Three weeks later, on the 11th May, he informed them that, so long as Bute remained in office, relations with Britain were practically at an end, and that he only left them in London for three reasons, (1) to avoid encouraging the enemy by the disclosure of an open rupture; (2) to act as spies, and (3) to *souffler le feu* against the ministry.[7] Over and over

---

[1] *Pol. Corr.* xxi. 235 (7 February 1762); p. 307 (20 March).

[2] *Ibid.*, p. 388 (23 April). See Keith's account of Goltz's reserve in his letter to Mitchell, 2 April 1762, in *Add. MSS.*, 6825.

[3] *Ibid.*, p. 462 (22 May).

[4] *S. P. For.*, *Prussia*, 80, Grenville to Mitchell, 29 June 1762.

[5] *Ibid.*, Mitchell to Grenville, 21 July, enclosing Finckenstein's reply to Grenville's dispatch of 29 June.

[6] *Pol. Corr.* xxi. 384 (23 April).

[7] *Ibid.*, xxi. 426.

again he ordered them to concert measures with the opposition, to supply them with information, arguments, and even catch-words, and to spare no effort to procure the overthrow of Bute and his colleagues.[1] Such conduct on the part of foreign envoys would be resented as intolerable at any period and in any country, and it says something for the self-restraint of the British government that it was content to go no farther than formal complaints, which Frederick disregarded.

Hitherto the quarrel had been between Frederick on the one hand and Bute and his colleagues on the other. In his first outburst of rage on receiving the disclosures of Galitzin, the Prussian king drew a distinction between Bute and Bedford, 'the sole authors of this outrage', and the nation, with Pitt at its head, 'which would be as indignant as I am if it knew the truth'. And he continued with a forecast which was only falsified by his own future action: 'these clouds will clear away, and England will return not only to its old sentiments with regard to myself but also to those ties of alliance which will enable us to hold the balance of power in Europe.'[2] For many months he still entertained confident hopes that a wave of public reprobation would compel George III to dismiss his ministers and to recall Pitt to office.[3] As has been seen, he ordered his envoys to co-operate in the good work. The final blow to his belief in English loyalty was dealt in the course of 1762–3, when the ministry negotiated a peace with France in which Prussian interests were sacrificed, and the House of Commons, instead of censuring their flagitious conduct, approved the treaty by an overwhelming majority. He had reckoned without George III, or Henry Fox, or the fascinating simplicity of political corruption in the eighteenth century.

In 1762 there was a general desire to terminate the war. The English ministers indeed showed an eager haste for peace which tended to defeat their own aims, as it encouraged the rival powers to raise their terms. France, though more discreet and reticent, was almost equally keen and hurried, partly because public opinion was now openly hostile to the war, but mainly because

---

[1] *Ibid.*, xxi. 480, 547 ; xxii. 21, 117, 207, 215.
[2] *Ibid.*, xxi. 321, Frederick to Goltz, 27 March 1761.
[3] *Ibid.*, xxi. 503, 506, 547 ; xxii. 207.

there was some fear as to the stability of the Bute administration, and Choiseul declared that he would rather serve in the galleys than renew negotiations with Pitt.[1]   Austria was thoroughly exhausted, its financial position was hopeless, all prospect of substantial gain was removed when Russia transferred its strength to the opposite side, and there was no small alarm lest Frederick's continued intrigues at Constantinople might bring the Turks into the field against Austria, if the war went on.   Spain alone, eager to conquer Portugal and blindly confident in the strength of its West Indian defences, frowned upon all overtures for peace. But Spain was not concerned with the Prussian problems, and its attitude rapidly changed when the advance upon Lisbon was repulsed and Havannah, its most valuable transatlantic possession, surrendered to the British attack.   Frederick watched the progress of negotiation, not without interest and even anxiety, but with a firm refusal to participate.   He was guided by two well-defined resolutions : the first overtures to him must come from Austria, and the quarrel with Austria must be settled by the two powers concerned, without any external mediation, and least of all that of Great Britain.

The main negotiations were, as in the previous year, conducted between Britain and France.   Ever since the fall of Pitt the two governments had been in indirect touch with each other through the Sardinian envoys in London and Paris.   In the spring of 1762, Egremont and Choiseul were in direct correspondence, the initiation as regards overtures for peace resting with the former.   It was decided to carry through the initial agreements by mutual exchange of proposals and counter-proposals, and not to appoint ambassadors until a final settlement was in sight. From the not very pleasing story of the negotiations it is only necessary to extract those which relate to the disposal of the western provinces of Prussia, Cleve, Mark, Ravensberg, Gelderland, and Wesel.   The British ministers made an ostentatious parade of communicating the relative documents to Frederick, although they held that the obligation to do so had expired with the subsidy treaty.   But their purpose was merely to point the

---

[1] ' J'aimerais mieux aller ramer aux galères que d'avoir rien de pacifique à démêler avec Mr. Pitt.'   Choiseul to Bailli de Solar, 13 May 1762, in *Correspondence of the Duke of Bedford*, iii. 84.

contrast between their own punctiliousness and the secrecy with which Frederick had shrouded his relations with Russia and Sweden. They had no intention of being moved from their course by advice or protests from Prussia.[1] And even their parade of disclosure was delusive and dilatory. While France, after the first overtures, took no step without consulting the wishes of Austria and Spain, Bute and Grenville—the latter took over the northern department on the 28th May—made no communication to Frederick, beyond the fact that negotiations had begun, until such progress had been made as to render futile any representations on his part. They were encouraged in their disregard of his wishes by the revolution in Russia, which removed Peter III and transferred the throne to his wife—and in a short time his widow—Catharine II, who was notoriously less inclined to idolize the Prussian king.[2] The blow to Frederick proved less serious than at one moment seemed possible, as Catharine was content to denounce Peter's treaty of alliance and to recall the Russian troops from the siege of Schweidnitz, but did not repudiate the treaty of peace with Prussia.[3] Still, Frederick's position was by no means so strong as it had been when Russia was openly on his side, and he could not afford to be as defiant of the British government as he would have wished to be. And the Russian revolution created a new difficulty for him. Catharine was eager to pose as a mediator and to gain the credit of putting an end to the German war. No mediator was acceptable to Frederick, but

[1] *Grenville Papers*, i. 464, Bute to Grenville, 12 July 1762 : 'Lord Bute . . . would have wished that Mitchell had been instructed to intimate to his Prussian Majesty that our peace must not be obstructed by any demur on his side: Lord Bute is sensible that this may be inferred from the colour of the dispatch, but perhaps this truth dressed in polite expression will not be without its utility.'

[2] *Pol. Corr.* xxi. 290, note 9. Mitchell reported to Frederick that Keith had warned him 'que l'Impératrice n'est pas si bien disposée envers Votre Majesté que l'est l'Empereur'. Keith to Mitchell, 20 February 1762, in *Add. MSS.*, 6825.

[3] Frederick, in a letter to Finckenstein (31 July), sums up the results of the Russian revolution: 'Tout le bien que nous avons attendu de l'alliance de Russie ne nous est pas arrivé; toutes les mauvaises suites que nous avons craintes de cette révolution subite n'arriveront pas non plus.' *Pol. Corr.* xxii. 92.

it taxed all his diplomatic skill to evade the suggestions of
Catharine, whom he could not afford to alienate, and whose
vanity was as sensitive as his own.[1]

It was certain from the first that the British ministers would
pay no excessive regard to the interests and wishes of the
Prussian king. If anything were required to demonstrate this it
would have been the selection as plenipotentiary to the French
court of the duke of Bedford, the earliest and the loudest
denouncer of the German war. On all the vexed questions
which had been discussed in the previous year the ministers
were ready to abandon the standpoint of Pitt, because that had
obstructed peace and prolonged war. Their desire was in all
these matters to find some middle course which would satisfy
France without too great a sacrifice of their own reputation
at home. And it did not prove very difficult to fix on the
via media of the Prussian problem. The first concrete proposal on the subject came from Choiseul, who had been carefully
tutored by Starhemberg behind the scenes. Choiseul drew a
definite line between the French conquests in Hanover, Hesse,
and Brunswick, which had been made in the Anglo-French war,
dating from the repudiation of the Kloster-Zeven convention,
and the French occupation of the Prussian dominions, which
had been effected in the name of the empress-queen, and
had nothing to do with the western war. The former territories could be returned to their rulers: the latter could only
be restored with the consent of Austria, and by agreement
between Austria and Prussia. Therefore Choiseul proposed
that they should remain in French occupation until the conclusion of a general peace. This was put forward on the 28th
June. On the 10th July the British answer was returned. If
France is bound by loyalty to Austria, Britain is equally bound
by loyalty to Prussia: therefore (without consulting their ally)
the British ministers suggest the magic formula which is to
demonstrate their absolute impartiality: as restoration is distasteful to France, let there be simultaneous evacuation of
Germany by both powers. Instead of repudiating the distinction
drawn between the Prussian provinces and the other German
conquests of France, the British government accentuated it by

[1] *Pol. Corr.* xxii. 193-4, Frederick to Goltz, 3 September 1762.

insisting that Hanover, Brunswick, and Hesse should be not only restored but restored in the same condition as before the war, i.e. with reparation. On the 14th July Grenville sent imperative injunctions to Mitchell to carry these precious documents, the French proposals and the British answer, to Frederick's headquarters before Schweidnitz. At the same time he was ordered to ascertain Frederick's views as to the terms on which he would make peace with Austria, Kaunitz having already communicated to Choiseul the Austrian demands, viz. the cession of Glatz and the compensation of Saxony.[1]

Mitchell made the toilsome and risky journey to very little purpose. Frederick received him immediately on his arrival (1st August), but would talk of nothing but the Russian revolution. When Mitchell at last endeavoured to carry out his instructions, Frederick turned the conversation to indifferent matters. On the next day Mitchell in a second audience produced the documents, together with those referring to the commencement of the negotiations, which had hitherto been kept back, but he could extract no answer from the king. On the third day the indefatigable envoy returned to the attack, but Frederick declared that he was too busy with his preparations for the siege to attend to political matters, and that he would send his reply through Finckenstein. So Mitchell, with his health 'sensibly altered by the fatigue I had in the mountains' returned to Breslau, whence he sent his rather rueful dispatch to Grenville on the 6th August.[2]

On the 7th August Finckenstein drew up his letter to Mitchell, which was forwarded to London on the 13th. After expressing, in the preamble, his master's preference of a secure and honourable peace to the continuance of the present horrible war, the Prussian minister fell foul of the French distinction between the Prussian dominions and the other German provinces, the cases

---

[1] *S. P. For.*, *Prussia*, 80, Grenville to Mitchell, 14 July. The documents enclosed by Grenville, but without the covering letter, are conveniently printed in Schäfer, ii. 2, App., pp. 751-3

[2] *Ibid.*, Mitchell to Grenville, 6 August. Mitchell's report is printed in full by Bisset (ii. 327-32), and also in *Pol. Corr.* xxi. 100-3. Frederick's account of the interview is given in a letter to his envoys in London (*ibid.*, pp. 114-15).

being in fact absolutely identical. Wesel and Gelderland were occupied by the French in 1757, partly to punish Prussia for its alliance with England (in the treaty of Westminster), and partly to facilitate the invasion of Hanover. Obviously the desire of the French ministers is to sow dissension between Britain and its ally, and at the same time to demonstrate their own superior fidelity to Austria. As to the terms with Austria, they cannot pass through any third hand, but must be dealt with by direct negotiation *cour à cour*.[1] A fortnight later, having learned in the meantime that France and Britain had practically adjusted the terms of a treaty, Frederick instructed Knyphausen to make a formal protest that, if the treaty should prove to affect his interests, and he had not been previously consulted, he would regard it as null and void.[2] This protest was made verbally to Grenville on the 8th September and a note taken of the protest, in which it was formally demanded that the king of Great Britain should stipulate for the restoration of Cleve, Gelderland, Wesel, &c.[3]

Grenville's answer to Finckenstein, forwarded through Mitchell on the 31st August, displays him as a more long-winded, pedantic, and ungenerous controversialist than Bute, and quite equally acrimonious. His great grievances were (1) the refusal to negotiate through Great Britain, which was ' a natural consequence of the recent exhibition of mistrust, but would otherwise appear extraordinary '; and (2) the irritating obstinacy of Frederick in replying to a request for his terms by vague and meaningless phrases such as ' a peace suitable to his interests and his glory ', or ' a safe and honourable peace ', declarations which he could have made to an enemy quite as easily as to an ally. Grenville then plunged into controversy. In spite of provocation, British candour and openness differed *in toto* from Frederick's distant and unfriendly conduct in Russia and Sweden. The evacuation of Wesel, Gelderland, &c., which Britain demanded from France, was an exact and scrupulous fulfilment of obligations to Prussia, yet no gratitude was expressed for this

---

[1] *S. P. For.*, *Prussia*, 81, Mitchell to Grenville, 13 August. Finckenstein's important letter is printed in Schäfer, ii. 2, pp. 753–4.

[2] *Pol. Corr.* xxi. 159–60.

[3] *Grenville Papers*, i. 466–8.

fidelity. The Prussian contention that the French conquests were caused by resentment at Frederick's alliance with England, and that their aim was to facilitate the invasion of Hanover, is rejected as untenable, because their real cause was ' the King of Prussia's irruption into Saxony, a measure totally disapproved of and earnestly dissuaded by his late Majesty '. On the contrary, Hanover was attacked on account of British fidelity to Prussia and to the treaty of Westminster. This treaty pledged both powers equally to oppose the intrusion of foreign troops into northern Germany, yet Prussia now demands, after Russia and Sweden have withdrawn, that Britain alone must oppose the French and force them to give up their conquests. Finally, Grenville declared that after Frederick's refusal to disclose the terms on which he is willing to make peace, Britain must wash its hands of the German problem, with the satisfactory assurance that it has been loyal to its ally and has facilitated his task by insisting on the withdrawal of the French troops.[1]

It is needless to dwell further on the scolding match, which was continued with increasing verbosity and vigour on both sides. On the 5th October Finckenstein sent to Mitchell a long and able *Mémoire raisonné*, in which, prompted by Frederick, he traverses the whole ground covered by Grenville and goes back to the old grievances about Bute's relations with Austria and Russia.[2] And on the 26th November Halifax, who had succeeded to Grenville's secretaryship, when the latter gave up the leadership of the House of Commons to Fox, replied in a still longer and more laboured dispatch.[3] The most interesting point raised in the debate was that of the origin of the war and the motives for the attack on Hanover. But recent experience has shown us how interminable a controversy on such a subject can be, and how useless it is as long as the war continues. The immediate settlement was in no way affected by the arguments or statements on either side, and in fact the preliminaries of peace had been signed at Fontainebleau (3rd November) before the last document was prepared. The two clauses which referred to Germany—No. 12, which stipulated

---

[1] *S. P. For.*, *Prussia*, 80, Grenville to Mitchell, 31 August 1762.

[2] Forwarded by Mitchell to Grenville on 8 October. *Ibid.*, 81.

[3] *Ibid.*, 81, Halifax to Mitchell, 26 November 1762.

for the restoration of Hanover, Hesse, and Brunswick, and No. 13, by which the French were to evacuate the Prussian provinces—were forwarded by Halifax to Mitchell on the 9th November. This gave rise to a further futile discussion, carried on with similar recriminations, as to whether the thirteenth article was a reasonable fulfilment of British obligations to Prussia, and as to whether Britain was justified in concluding it without Prussian assent. Frederick answered both questions in the negative, and adhered to the protest which, in accordance with his instructions, was renewed by Knyphausen and Michell after the signature of the preliminaries.[1] But all attempts failed to obtain a modification of the terms before the ratification of the treaty in Paris on the 10th February 1763.

That Frederick genuinely believed that France and Britain were in league to play him false, and that the Rhenish provinces would either directly or indirectly be handed over to Austria and used as pawns in the ultimate negotiations with himself, is proved by the elaborate precautions which he took to prevent or to redeem such a misfortune. Even if the provinces were honestly evacuated and left, as Halifax put it, to be scrambled for, Austria was in an advantageous position, as the southern Netherlands were adjacent, whereas Frederick had no troops in the neighbourhood. His first move was to suggest that the Dutch should occupy the provinces until the peace, in order to prevent their state from being completely hemmed in by Austria.[2] When that was rejected, he framed elaborate plans to have troops on the spot who should rush into Wesel the moment the French had departed, or, if they failed to anticipate the Austrians, should combine with the inhabitants to drive the intruders out. If this failed, he would risk a quarrel with Britain, occupy Münster on its evacuation by the British troops, and hold it as security for the restitution of his own territories. Ferdinand of Brunswick, whose mercenary troops Frederick hoped to take into his own service, and who shared the king's disapproval of the British ministry, was his confidant in all these projects.[3]

[1] Schäfer, ii. 2, App., p. 756.   [2] *Pol. Corr.* xxii. 258–61.
[3] For these projects see Frederick's letters to Ferdinand and his detailed instructions to his various agents in *Pol. Corr.* xxii, *passim*.

It is probable that Frederick's anxiety was exaggerated, and that his suspicions, both of Britain and France, had little justification. And two things occurred which rendered all his elaborate precautions unnecessary. His first reassurance came from the two suspected powers. Nivernais, the French plenipotentiary in London, against whose insinuating approaches Frederick had expressly warned his envoys,[1] and Halifax, whom the king had welcomed as unlikely to be so hostile as Grenville,[2] actually concerted a scheme, in January 1763, by which the Prussian lands were to be restored on condition of a double neutrality, guaranteed by Britain and France, both of these provinces and of the Austrian Netherlands.[3] Frederick eagerly and even gratefully accepted this proposal and authorized Knyphausen and Michell to sign the necessary convention.[4] But events occurred elsewhere which rendered this expedient unnecessary.[5] Austria, financially exhausted and intimidated by the progress of Prussian negotiations at Constantinople,[6] resolved that a German peace must accompany instead of following the French peace. Reluctant to undergo the humiliation of taking the first step, the court of Vienna employed Saxony to make the necessary overtures. Frederick, satisfied with the concession to his own self-esteem, and afraid that Catharine of Russia would succeed in forcing him to accept her unwished-for mediation, welcomed the overtures, fixed Hubertsburg as the place of negotiations, and sent Hertzberg there to represent him. But he himself remained close by at Leipzig, and kept the threads of the negotiation resolutely in his own hands. To the Austrian demands for the cession of Glatz and the compensation of Saxony he opposed an unflinching negative, and Austria gave way when Frederick promised his vote to the Archduke Joseph as king of the Romans. On these terms the treaty of Hubertsburg was concluded (15 February),

[1] *Ibid.*, xxii. 251, 254, 256, 385.   [2] *Ibid.*, pp. 309, 426.
[3] *S. P. For., Prussia*, 82, Halifax to Mitchell, 15 January 1763.
[4] *Pol. Corr.* xxii. 483 (26 January 1763).
[5] *Ibid.*, p. 532, Frederick to Knyphausen and Michell (22 February). In this letter Knyphausen was instructed to quit London.
[6] *Ibid.*, p. 515. Frederick to Prince Henry (9 February). 'Un corps de Turcs de 110,000 hommes sur les frontières de la Hongrie, la paix séparée des princes de l'Empire, et une convention conclue avec les Français pour les provinces du Rhin a fort accéléré la négociation.'

and the whole of Frederick's territories were recovered as before the war. Andrew Mitchell, in his letter of congratulation, declared, ' I have long recognized your Majesty as the greatest of warriors, but to-day, when you have restored tranquillity to Germany in so short a time and so brief a treaty, I admire you as the most skilful negotiator that has ever lived.'[1]

The congratulations of the British government were far less warm. The alliance, which had effected so much both for Europe and for the world, had been fatally strained for the last eighteen months, and was now at an end. Twenty-three years were to elapse before it was renewed, and it was never again so cordial as it had been during Pitt's tenure of office. The agents of the alliance were no longer needed. Knyphausen was recalled in February 1763. Michell, who was left alone for a year, was recalled in 1764 at the request of the British ministry, and Andrew Mitchell, broken down by incessant labours during the war and depressed by the continued misunderstandings which he was unable to remove, quitted Berlin in the same year. His services were grudgingly requited by the British government. In 1759 he had been promoted, but only on his own request, to the rank of plenipotentiary with its increased emoluments. Since then he had made frequent demands through various channels for the ' red ribband ', but it was not given him until 1765. After his departure from Berlin the two embassies were left in the hands of obscure secretaries who were useless for any but formal business.

[1] Schäfer, ii. 2, App., p. 762 ; *Add. MSS.*, 6831. Mitchell to Frederick, 7 March 1763. Mitchell, who knew the attenuated conditions of Frederick's army, believed to the last minute that Austria would never make peace unless Prussia consented to sacrifices. On 1 February he wrote to Halifax of the preposterous rumours of terms ' such as his Prussian Majesty might with honour have accepted after a complete victory obtained over the Austrian army '. And on 3 February he wrote again : ' If the King of Prussia has been able to conclude an honourable and advantageous peace for himself with the courts of Vienna and Dresden, it is of all the miracles he has performed since the beginning of the war by much the greatest.' *S. P. For.*, *Prussia*, 82.

V

THE PERIOD OF ALIENATION
1763–86

THE period covered by this lecture is lacking in unity, and as regards my main subject is largely a blank. It is, indeed, largely a blank in the history of British foreign policy. Few things in our history are more startling than the sudden obliteration of British influence in Europe after the Seven Years' War. It was the most successful war we had ever waged; the peace of Paris, in spite of all contemporary criticism, was the most advantageous peace we had ever concluded; and yet for the next twenty-three years British influence in continental affairs is practically negligible. No doubt this was partly due to intense absorption in domestic affairs; the efforts of George III to free himself from the Whig domination of the last two reigns and from all coercion in the choice of his ministers; the frequent changes of ministry to which he resorted before he found what he wanted under Lord North (Frederick, who kept his own ministers till they died or till he was tired of them, said scornfully that 'he changes his ministers as he changes his shirts'[1]); the growing popular antagonism to the exclusive oligarchy, of which antagonism John Wilkes was the mouthpiece; and as time went on the increasing dangers and difficulties of American discontent. Wilkes and America! The reports of foreign envoys and the scanty pages of foreign newspapers are full of nothing

---

[1] *Pol. Corr.* xxv. 353. In the eight years following the peace of Paris there were nine holders of the northern secretaryship : (1) Halifax, who took both seals on the death of Egremont; (2) Sandwich, from September 1763 to July 1765 ; (3) Grafton, under Rockingham, in July 1765 ; (4) Conway succeeded Grafton in May 1766, and remained in office under Chatham ; (5) Weymouth, from January till November 1768 ; (6) Rochford, till December 1770; (7) Sandwich again ; (8) Halifax again, from February 1771 till his death in the following June ; (9) Suffolk.

else when they deal with Great Britain. And in the later years came the disastrous American war, in which we had to face the hostility, avowed or ill concealed, of all the powers of Europe.

It is clear from the history of this war that the loss of influence was not solely due to domestic or colonial complications. It was also due to our isolation. Frederick laid it down (it is impossible to avoid quoting him when speaking of the eighteenth century) that ' l'Angleterre ne jouera qu'un chétif rôle en Europe sans être fortifiée d'alliances '.[1] That was our position after 1763. We had to face two obvious and declared enemies, France and Spain, which were still united by the Family Compact of 1761. So far as British ministers turned their attention from home or colonial affairs to the Continent, it was to this danger that their gaze was directed. Such quarrels as did arise, on the Manilla ransom, on the French occupation of Corsica and the suppression of Paoli, on the Falkland Islands, were all quarrels with the Bourbon courts. Choiseul subordinated all other interests to the desire for revenge, and his policy was resumed in the next reign by Vergennes. Frederick in his correspondence constantly anticipated renewal of war between Britain and France, and this was one of his reasons for fighting shy of a British alliance.

Against this danger the natural and instinctive precaution was to fall back upon the old system and the Austrian alliance. But the British ministers had ruefully to admit that the necessary severance of Austria from France was for the time impossible. The alliance between the two powers had not been brilliantly successful from the point of view of either. France had not rendered the efficient military assistance that had been looked for at Vienna. It had neither produced nor borrowed a Villars or a Marshal Saxe, its officers had displayed remarkable inefficiency,[2] and its troops had been disgraced by a ruinous lack of discipline. On the other hand, the war had been costly to

---

[1] *Pol. Corr.* xxvi. 305.

[2] *Ibid.*, 356, Frederick to Prince Henry (who was suspected of pro-French sympathies), 5 April 1758 : ' Leurs officiers ont un jargon militaire qui en impose ; mais ce sont des perroquets qui ont appris siffler une marche, et qui n'en savent pas davantage.'

France, which had spent in the service of Austria money and men that might have been employed against Britain, and had thus lost both its American possessions and its chance of founding an empire in India. Still the alliance persisted; it was even strengthened by the marriage of Marie Antoinette to Louis XV's grandson. France could not afford to drive Austria back to the British alliance; Austria regarded the French alliance with pride and complacency because it secured its ill-guarded and exposed extremities in Italy and the Netherlands. So long as Maria Theresa and Kaunitz controlled the policy of Austria, they were likely to cling to an agreement which they regarded as their masterpiece. For a moment there was some hope, when Joseph II succeeded his father as Emperor and as joint ruler in the Austrian dominions, that he would free himself from 'the tutelage of his mother and from the ferule of Kaunitz.'[1] He was supposed to be not over friendly either towards France or towards his sister, and he certainly made efforts during his mother's lifetime to direct the foreign affairs of Austria. But his independence did not lead him in the direction desired by Britain, and after his mother's death Kaunitz remained in office for another twelve years.

Not only was Austria lost, but another familiar prop had gone. The 'maritime powers' had ceased to be a unit in Europe. In the late war the Dutch had steadily refused to give any assistance to Britain, and they had shown themselves bitterly hostile to the restrictions placed by their old ally upon neutral trade. The republican party was now completely in the ascendant, and in accordance with seventeenth-century traditions its leaders looked to France for support against the house of Orange and its English connexions. One of the most fatal weaknesses in the European position of Britain during these years was the steady growth of French ascendancy in the United Provinces.

There remained, as a last resource, Russia and Prussia. An unexpected result of the Seven Years' War was the sudden elevation of Russia to ascendancy in Europe. While all the other belligerents on the Continent were paralysed by exhaustion,

[1] *Pol. Corr.* xxviii. 209: 'L'Empereur se trouve sous la tutelle de sa mère et sous la férule du comte Kaunitz.'

Russia had suffered comparatively little. Its resources were immense and as yet unmeasured, it had no vulnerable point within easy reach of any assailant, and its rapid emergence from barbarism gave it the terror associated with mystery. It had a ruler who in ability and strength of character had no superior and only one equal among contemporary sovereigns. And Catharine II was forced by her origin and the circumstances of her accession to gratify Russian prejudices and Russian ambitions. In the days of Peter the Great, as we have seen, Britain was inclined to resent and even to resist the growth of Russian power. But we had not been able to prevent it, and since those days we had rather endeavoured to profit by it. We had never been actually at war with Russia, we had a lucrative trade with it, especially since its acquisition of a Baltic coast, and there had been a time when with the help of Bestoujew, British influence had been dominant at St. Petersburg. The fact that Catharine, after the revolution, recalled Bestoujew from exile and disgrace seemed to open a prospect of recovering that influence. This was the more probable because at so many points the interests of Russia were opposed to those of France. Russia and France had never been cordial allies, even while they were fighting on the same side. The Russian occupation of East Prussia, its determination, disclosed in the later years of Elizabeth, to retain possession of that province, its oppressive domination in Poland during the war, had all caused exasperation in France. For these reasons it was natural for British statesmen to seek to escape from isolation by an alliance with the colossus of the north. But there were three difficulties in the way. Russia wanted subsidies, and Britain had made up its mind that it was wasteful and often useless extravagance to pay subsidies in time of peace. Russia wanted a guarantee of assistance against the Turks, and Britain was not prepared to jeopardize its Levant trade by risking a rupture with Turkey. In addition, Russia already had an ally in the person of the king of Prussia, who had no desire to share the alliance with Britain. The guidance of Russian policy under Catharine fell into the hands, not of Bestoujew, but of Panin ; and Panin became the close, and probably the bribed, confidant of Frederick the Great.

This brings us to the real cause of British isolation, the quarrel with Prussia, which was the direct result of Bute's short-sighted —if no harsher term is used—policy in the peace negotiations. In order to appreciate this it is necessary to recall the substance of the previous lectures. Great Britain had had no previous quarrel with Prussia except about the captured ships and the Silesian loan. All the old animosity and friction had really arisen with Hanover, and Hanover had fallen into the background with the accession of George III, who 'gloried in the name of Britain'. On the other hand, Prussia was under a very considerable burden of debt to Britain. All its acquisitions since the beginning of the century, except East Friesland, were due in considerable measure to British support. Gelderland in the peace of Utrecht, Stettin in the treaty of 1720, Silesia in the treaties of Breslau and Dresden, all these cessions had been largely due to British influence. In the late war Frederick, in spite of all his heroic efforts, must have succumbed if Britain, with the help of Ferdinand of Brunswick, had not taken the French off his hands. There was, therefore, every reasonable prospect that the Prussian alliance, if it were desired, would be attainable. And in these twenty-three years that alliance was constantly sought, at some times more vigorously than at others, but always desired, and could never be obtained. The might-have-been is an idle speculation, but the future history, possibly of Europe and certainly of Britain and Prussia, would have been profoundly altered if the policy of Pitt towards Prussia had been pursued to the end of the war.

At the outset the actual quarrel continued. The persons against whom Frederick had the greatest antipathy were, in order of demerit, Bute, the princess dowager, and the duke of Bedford. Bute's alleged offences have been already dealt with. Augusta of Saxe-Gotha was suspected by Frederick of a bitter grudge against Prussia and of having taught it to her son.[1] Bedford was not only the negotiator of the peace against which Frederick had protested, he was also the man who had openly and vigorously denounced the German war even while he was the colleague of Pitt, and he had materially contributed to Pitt's downfall. So long as any of these remained in power Frederick would have no truck with a British ministry, and would do what

[1] See S. P. For., Prussia, 102, Elliot to Suffolk, 22 February 1778.

he could to overthrow it. When Bute resigned and Grenville became first minister, he was in no way appeased, as he rightly regarded Grenville as a mere cloak for the continued domination of Bute. There was a momentary excitement in September 1763 when overtures were made to Pitt, 'a change', said Frederick, 'which has always been one of the first objects of my desires.'[1] But they came to nothing, and when Grenville's ministry was reinforced by the adhesion of Bedford and the 'Bloomsbury gang' matters became worse. And so Michell continued his close intercourse with Pitt and other opposition leaders. This was as intolerable as it had been when Knyphausen was his colleague. Mitchell was instructed to make complaints at Berlin. Finckenstein and Hertzberg attempted to defend Michell, and warned Mitchell that a formal complaint would complete Frederick's exasperation. At last, losing all patience, Sandwich told Mitchell that if the Prussian ministers would not carry the British complaints to their master he must do so himself, that he should remind Frederick of the recall in 1751 of Hanbury Williams, 'though his rank, abilities, and connexions were altogether superior to those of Michell', and that, if he could get no satisfaction, he must present his letters of recall, which were enclosed, as his remaining in Berlin was obviously useless.[2] Mitchell obeyed these instructions, though without any reference to Hanbury Williams, of whose case he confessed to rather extraordinary ignorance.[3] Frederick at once agreed to recall Michell, but added with some warmth, 'that it was not his ministers but him that we were angry with.' Frederick further showed his anger by sending to London as secretary of legation a Frenchman called Baudouin, who had no previous experience of diplomacy. By way of retaliation the ministers gave leave to Mitchell to go to Spa for the waters, leaving his secretary, Burnet, a fellow Scot, to carry on routine duties, and then sent his recall from there. In spite of this deliberate rudeness, Frederick presented to Mitchell a snuff-box with his portrait set

---

[1] Frederick to Michell, 11 September 1763, in *Pol. Corr.* xxiii. 118-19.

[2] *S. P. For., Prussia*, 83, Sandwich to Mitchell, 6 January, 9 March, and 13 April 1764.

[3] *Ibid.*, 83, Mitchell to Sandwich, 5 and 8 May 1764. *Pol. Corr.* xxiii. 368-9.

in diamonds, worth 3,000 thalers, 'more out of consideration for his own worth than for that of his employers '.

The quarrel, acute as it was, would not have been long-lived if Prussia had been as isolated as Britain was. Such a position was bad enough for an insular power, it would have been intolerable for a continental state. But, with the uncanny foresight which he sometimes displayed, Frederick had anticipated the danger and had provided against it. He had been disconcerted by the Russian revolution of July 1762, and by Catharine's prompt abandonment of her husband's close alliance with Prussia, and he was immensely relieved when she refused to return to Austria and to re-open the war. In spite of his desire to conciliate Russia at all costs, he would not gratify Catharine's vanity by admitting her mediation, and he hustled the negotiations at Hubertsburg in order to keep her out of them. Nevertheless he clearly realized that his only hope of future peace and security lay in a Russian alliance as soon as peace was made, and he had made up his mind as to the expedient for gaining it.[1] A vacancy in the Polish throne was imminent, and he proposed to co-operate with Russia in bringing about the election of any native Pole whom Catharine might select. This would secure the termination of the union of Saxony with Poland, always distasteful to Prussia; it would be a blow to Brühl, almost as great a bugbear to Frederick as Bute; and it would sever Russia, both from France, which desired to exclude a Russian nominee, and from Austria, which aimed at the maintenance of the Saxon dynasty. Everything turned out as he had planned, and with even greater ease than he could have expected. The death of Augustus III (5th October 1763) was followed two months later by that of his son Frederick Christian (17th December). The latter event completely disconcerted the plans of Austria and France, as they had agreed to support the candidature of Frederick Christian. An alliance for eight years was concluded between Russia and Prussia on the 11th of April 1764. Frederick promised assistance against any power which should actively oppose Russian intervention in Poland. No such opposition was forthcoming at the time, and Stanislas Poniatowski, one of Catharine's former lovers, was elected on the 7th September.

---

[1] Frederick to Goltz, 3 September 1762 (*Ibid.*, xxii. 194).

The Russo-Prussian alliance was cemented by its success, and Frederick established a claim to Russian gratitude by using his recently gained influence at Constantinople to keep the Turks quiet. Thus, although Catharine and Panin were not ill-disposed to an alliance with Britain,[1] Prussian interest at St. Petersburg was strong enough to frustrate the negotiations.

There seemed to be a prospect of better relations between London and Berlin when the Grenville-Bedford ministry was dismissed in July 1765, and George III reluctantly accepted a Whig administration under Rockingham. The hereditary prince of Brunswick, during a visit to London, was employed to play the part of mediator, as his father had played it in the autumn of 1755. But all that resulted from the British overtures was an agreement to resume normal diplomatic arrangements by the sending of envoys of suitable rank, though there was an ominous punctiliousness in Frederick's insistance upon exact reciprocity in the minutest details of the exchange. The British ministry had no difficulty in the choice of an envoy, and sent back Mitchell, now Sir Andrew Mitchell, K.C.B., in the hope that his personal friendship with Frederick would produce greater harmony between the two courts. Frederick on his side sent Count Maltzahn, previously employed in Dresden, but would not let his envoy embark until Mitchell, delayed by illness, had actually landed on the continent. Nothing resulted from this exchange of envoys. Mitchell had no definite offers to make, and Frederick, though he received him kindly enough, would only talk generally about the affairs of Europe and the exhaustion of the Bourbon powers.[2] He admitted in his letters that he preferred the Whigs to the Tories, but he doubted their continuance in power, and he was disappointed that Pitt held aloof. To his nephew, who had urged the need of defending Protestant interests, he replied that it was out of date to sound 'that trumpet of discord',[3] and that as to an alliance he 'waited to see what consistency the British government would gain, and whether the influence of Bute was completely expelled. If then

---

[1] See *Pol. Corr.* xxvi. 40.

[2] *S. P. For., Prussia*, 85, Mitchell to Conway, 21 June and 12 July 1766; see *Pol. Corr.* xxv. 136-7 and 153-4.

[3] *Pol. Corr.* xxv. 8.

a firm administration could be solidly established, one might consider what could be done.'[1]   It was a misfortune that just at this time one of the few remaining links between Britain and Prussia was snapped by the resignation of Ferdinand of Brunswick from the Prussian service. Frederick told Maltzahn to say that it was because he was growing too stout to mount his horse, but it was notorious that the two brothers-in-law had quarrelled.[2]

A new situation was created in the summer of 1766 when Pitt actually formed a ministry, the famous 'tesselated' non-party ministry which Burke denounced so vigorously in the 'Present Discontents'. Pitt at once determined to press forward his plan of a 'northern system', based upon a triple alliance of Russia and Prussia with Britain, which he had sketched out in a private colloquy with Mitchell in 1763, and which was therefore quite familiar to Frederick.[3] This system was to balance the alliance of Austria with the Bourbon powers, 'the most formidable combination ever yet formed, and the most dangerous to the liberties of Europe.'[4] The negotiation at St. Petersburg was to be taken out of the hands of Sir George Macartney, the resident envoy, and entrusted to Hans Stanley, who had been employed at Paris in the futile negotiations of 1761. Stanley was to go to Berlin on his way, and to concert measures with Mitchell, who in the meantime was to sound Frederick on the feasibility of the scheme. Mitchell, who had now at last a substantial proposal to make, obtained an interview at Potsdam, but could only report a discouraging reception. Frederick began by repeating his previous contention that the Bourbon courts were at the moment powerless, and added that the proposed northern league would create alarm and disturb the present harmony. 'Chi sta bene non si muove.' Mitchell, not to be beaten by Frederick's Italian, replied, 'Chi sta solo non sta bene', but he failed to see that he was describing the position of Britain rather than that of Prussia. After this inter-change of platitudes in a foreign tongue, Frederick 'then hinted at the treatment he had met with from us when the last peace was

---

[1] *Pol. Corr.* xxv. 42.   [2] *Ibid.*, p. 139.
[3] *Ibid.* xxiii. 192.
[4] Conway to Mitchell, 30 September 1760, in *S. P. For.*, *Prussia*, 85.

made, and talked of the instability of our measures and sudden changes in our administration, which made it almost impossible to transact business with us with any sort of security. I answered him as well as I could, allowing at the same time that he had some reason to complain.' To Frederick's questions as to details Mitchell could only reply that they would be disclosed by Stanley.[1] On the 30th September Conway answered this report, saying that what they wanted was not details but to know whether Frederick accepted the principle of the alliance. As no answer came to this, Conway wrote an angry letter to Mitchell, pointing out that the affair was of primary importance, that it was treated as if it were ordinary office correspondence, and that he would doubt Mitchell's honesty and capacity if they had not been previously proved.[2] To this diatribe Mitchell sedately responded that Frederick's delay did not surprise him, that Conway had given him no new proposals, and that the king could not endure mere repetitions. However he applied for a second audience, and reported on the 4th December that the British overture had been virtually declined. Conway accepted the decision as final, and the whole scheme was dropped.[3] Stanley never went to St. Petersburg, and no attention was paid to Mitchell's acute suggestion that a beginning should be made there, and that if Russia were gained, Prussia would not hesitate to follow.

Frederick's motives for rejecting overtures from a man to whom he was under great obligations, whom he profoundly admired, and to whose return to office he had long looked forward,[4] could not be expounded in an interview with Mitchell.

[1] S. P. For., Prussia, 85, Mitchell to Conway, 17 September 1766; printed in Pol. Corr. xxv. 217-19, and in Bisset, ii. 312 (an extract).

[2] S. P. For., Prussia, 85, Conway to Mitchell, 30 September and 14 November 1766.

[3] S. P. For., Prussia, 85, Mitchell to Conway, 8 November and 4 December 1766 (the latter is in Pol. Corr. xxv. 316-18); Conway to Mitchell, 2 January 1767 in S. P. For., Prussia, 86.

[4] On 2 June 1765 Frederick wrote to his minister at the Hague that a ministerial change in England 'n'aura pas de l'influence sur les grandes affaires de l'Europe, à moins qu'il n'arrive que le sieur Pitt rentrât dans le ministère' (Pol. Corr. xxiv. 213). Frederick to the hereditary Prince of Brunswick, 26 October 1765: 'Je regarde M. Pitt comme un des plus grands ministres de ce siècle' (Ibid., p. 338).

The new ministry was not in the least what he had expected. Pitt himself by accepting an earldom forfeited that popularity which was the chief source of his strength. His colleagues were a mixture of his own personal followers with the new party of ' king's friends '. The formation of the ministry was a virtual surrender to the principles of Bute, and Frederick could have no confidence either in its policy or its stability. That he was justified in his estimate is proved by the later history of this strange administration. It gradually abandoned all that Pitt had stood for, revived the question of American taxation, raised Wilkes to greater prominence and popularity than ever by its preposterous dealings with the Middlesex election, and was slowly transformed by royal dexterity into the purely Tory administration of North. In no respect did it depart more completely from the principles of its first head than by turning its back completely on the affairs of Europe. Chatham, whose breakdown in health had allowed all control to slip out of his hands, returned to public life to be the vigorous assailant of the abortion he had originally fathered.

For the next four years Sir Andrew Mitchell lived a very quiet and uneventful life at Berlin. He had no pressing business to negotiate, no need for special audiences of the king, or for exciting interviews with Finckenstein and Hertzberg. He attended the court ceremonies, he played his eminently respectable part in the not very lively distractions of Berlin society, and every three days or so he sent off his—generally meagre—budget of news and comment. He saw the young William V of Orange married in 1767 to Frederick's niece, Wilhelmina, ' a very beautiful and well-educated young lady ', but he could not foresee that this event was destined to bring Britain and Prussia once more into alliance. He chronicled the divorce proceedings against the young Frederick William's first wife, the one bride from Brunswick who was a failure, the second marriage of the prince with Frederica Louisa of Hesse-Darmstadt, and the birth of their first child, afterwards Frederick William III, who lived to see Prussia humbled at Jena and Auerstädt and reduced to impotence by the treaty of Tilsit. But the main topic of his dispatches was the diplomatic and military drama—far more diplomatic than military—which preceded the first partition of

Poland. It was always an interesting drama, especially when Frederick sought to free himself from the too irksome yoke of the Russian alliance by his famous interviews with Joseph at Neisse and Neustadt; and it became an exciting drama when the revolt of the harassed Poles and the entry of the Turks into the war seemed to give Austria and France a chance of redeeming their past failures and of putting a limit to the detested advance of Russia. But it was a drama which did not seem to give much concern to Mitchell's employers, who were occupied elsewhere. They occasionally asked a question of their envoy, but paid little attention to his replies. And Mitchell himself did not live to see the *dénouement*. On the 26th January 1771 he signed very feebly his last dispatch, announcing that a Prussian cordon was being established on the Polish frontier. Two days later he died, and was buried by the faithful Burnet, his secretary and companion for fifteen years, in one of the vaults of the principal French Church of the Reformed Religion.[1] Frederick expressed his appreciation of his old friend in a letter to Hertzberg: 'His talents and character had wholly gained my esteem, and he retained it to the end of his days. It will be difficult for the court of London to find a successor of such distinguished and recognized merit '.[2]

Mitchell's two successors in the Berlin embassy were in complete contrast to him, two of those young and rather dashing men of fashion who seem in those days to have had a sort of vested right to step at once with the minimum of training into first-rate, or at least second-rate, diplomatic posts. The first of them, who held the embassy for four years, 1772–6, and who was in his twenty-sixth year when he was appointed to Berlin, was James Harris, afterwards the first Lord Malmesbury, the best-known diplomatist of his generation, and one of the principal actors on the European stage during the next fifteen or twenty years. But his stay at Berlin was uneventful and practically useless, except that it gave him a knowledge of the Prussian

[1] On 10 December 1770 Mitchell signed an undertaking to pay to Alexander Burnet younger of Kemnay the sum of £3,000 for his faithful services for fifteen years. It is interesting to note that one of the witnesses was 'Louis Michell, ci-devant Ministre en Angleterre'.

[2] *Pol. Corr.* xxx. 473. Compare pp. 30, 415, 429.

court which was not without value to him in later years. He
was at Berlin when Frederick succeeded in averting a European
war by adjusting the partition of Poland, and by purchasing with
the cession of Galicia the reluctant but ultimately the greedy
complicity of Austria.   Harris was the recipient of those remarkable dispatches[1] from Lord Suffolk which record the singular
aloofness with which the British government regarded an
episode, which has deeply affected European history for a
century and a half and whose results are not yet exhausted.
And while he was at Berlin two other important events occurred.
Gustavus III ascended the throne of Sweden, and with the secret
encouragement of both Prussia and France, defied Russia by
effecting the first of his *coups d'état*, by which he depressed the
oligarchy and revived the authority of the crown.   And in 1774
the Russo-Turkish war was closed by the epoch-making treaty
of Kutchuk Kainardji, and Austria sought to balance the gains
of Russia by seizing the province of Bukovina.   Whatever might
be thought of Sweden or Poland, there can be no doubt that
British interests were directly involved in the settlement of the
eastern question.   But there was not even a suggestion at
the time that this country should be either consulted or
considered.

The second of the youthful envoys was Hugh Elliot,[2] who
arrived at Berlin in 1777, and who was then only twenty-four
years old. He belonged to a distinguished family. His aunt,
Jane Elliot, was the authoress of *Flowers of the Forest*, and his
elder brother, Sir Gilbert, afterwards the first Lord Minto, was
brother-in-law of James Harris, and one of the most distinguished
of the able young politicians who grouped themselves round

---

[1] See especially the dispatches of 5 June 1772, in which he speaks of the
partition as 'this curious transaction', and of 2 October, in which he says
of his answer to the formal intimation from the three partitioning courts,
'the utmost caution has been used not to convey any favourable sentiments
of a transaction which, from its inconsistency with national equity and public
honour, must engage his Majesty's disapprobation ; though it has not been
so immediately interesting as to deserve his interposition'. They are printed
in *Diaries and Correspondence of First Earl of Malmesbury*, i. 81–2, 91–2.

[2] A memoir of Hugh Elliot was written by Lady Minto (Edinburgh, 1866).
It is a readable book, and not without historical value, but it is not so good
as her Life of his brother, the first Lord Minto.

Charles James Fox. A sister was married to William Eden, afterwards Lord Auckland, a rising member of Parliament who supported the administration. Elliot was in many ways quite as able a man as Harris, but he lacked Harris's composure and self-control, and was probably better fitted to be a soldier than a diplomatist. Young and very good-looking he pleased the ladies and married the richest heiress in Berlin. But he was not a *persona grata* to Frederick, and he did not make the most of the chances of a reconciliation between Britain and Prussia. He believed that Frederick was a bully, and that he should be answered by ' demonstrations of vigour ' and not by concessions.[1] He arrived at an unfortunate time. The American war compelled us to appeal to Frederick for permission to allow our hired troops from Hesse and Hanover to pass through his Rhenish provinces on their way to embarkation. Frederick's reception of these requests was a barometer of his good or ill-will towards Britain. At the time of Elliot's arrival his hostility was as great as ever. He publicly declared his disbelief in Britain's ability to put down the rebels, and his conviction that the American republic was ' now to be considered as a rising, independent, and powerful state '.[2] Two American delegates were received in Berlin, and were allowed to purchase stores for the rebel army. There was even some talk of sending Prussian officers to serve against Britain, and of joining France in acknowledging the republic. In these circumstances Elliot found Berlin a by no means attractive place of residence, and his impetuosity involved him in an awkward scrape. One of his servants, hearing his master express a desire to see the papers of the American delegates, promptly broke into their house and returned with the desired documents. Elliot had to restore them at once with profuse apologies to the Prussian Government. It was no wonder that he suggested a temporary absence from Berlin, while Robert Liston, formerly his tutor and now his secretary, was to take charge of the embassy.

But two events occurred in 1778 which altered the whole situation, and compelled Elliot to remain at his post. One was

[1] *S. P. For., Prussia*, 102, Elliot to Suffolk, 22 February 1778.
[2] *Ibid.*, 101, Elliot to Suffolk, 16 August and 27 December 1777.

the outbreak of war between Britain and France, which at once raised the old question of the security of Hanover and rendered the alliance, or at any rate the friendly neutrality of Prussia, of imperative importance. The other was the outbreak of a double quarrel between Austria and Prussia.[1] The immediate and obvious cause of quarrel was the Bavarian succession, which for many years had loomed large in Europe as a possible source of trouble. The last of the Bavarian Wittelsbachs died on the 30th December 1777. His heir was the Elector Palatine, Charles Theodore. Austria had long been prepared for the contingency, and announced to the world a convention by which Charles Theodore recognized various Austrian claims which amounted in the aggregate to nearly half the Bavarian inheritance. Everybody instinctively looked to Frederick to oppose such extraordinary pretensions, and he promptly accepted the challenge. Having obtained a formal protest from the next heir to the Palatinate and Bavaria, he appealed for support to the princes of Germany and Europe. Among them was George III in both his capacities. The other quarrel was about the succession in Anspach and Baireuth. The two questions were not really associated together, but they became mixed up by the action of Austria. The latter question had also been under consideration ever since it had been raised in the negotiations at Hubertsburg. In outline it is simple. The two Franconian principalities were the oldest possessions of the Hohenzollerns, and since the acquisition of Brandenburg, they had always been held by junior branches of the family. By a deliberate family agreement, whenever the principalities fell in to the main line they were always granted out again to younger sons or brothers. This Frederick was determined to break. Baireuth was now united with Anspach, and the two provinces were held by the last male of the latter branch. On his death Frederick proposed to retain them in his own hands, i.e. to unite them with the kingdom of Prussia, and had obtained from his brothers an express renunciation of their claims. This Austria asserted to be illegal. When Frederick replied that one family agreement could be altered by another family agreement, Austria declared that the original

[1] A good account of these disputes is to be found in H. W. V. Temperley, *Joseph II and the Bavarian Succession.*

agreement was a 'pragmatic sanction', that it had received the approval of the emperor and the diet, and that without their consent it could be neither altered nor repealed. The two quarrels were intermingled when Austria offered to withdraw its Bavarian claims if Frederick would admit that Anspach and Baireuth must always be a *secundo-genitur*, as Tuscany was to the Austrian house. Frederick refused, on the obvious ground that there was no real connexion between the two problems, and that they were of a wholly different nature. He would not surrender his right to purchase the undoing of Austria's wrong. The result was the outbreak of the short war between Austria and Prussia which is known as the War of the Bavarian Succession, or sometimes as the *Kartoffeln-Krieg*, because the combatants were more absorbed in eating up each other's resources than in fighting.

The simultaneous outbreak of a maritime war between Britain and France, and of a land war between Austria and Prussia, together with the fact that the alliance of Versailles between Austria and France was still in force, seemed to bring Europe back to the conditions of 1756 when the Seven Years' War began. It appeared probable that the conditions which had produced an Anglo-Prussian alliance twenty-two years earlier would have the same result again. This was what Suffolk and Elliot had to play for. But there was one fatal difference between 1756 and 1778. When Prussia attacked Saxony, France not only admitted that the *casus foederis* had arisen, but that it was so monstrous an aggression that her full forces, not a mere contingent of 24,000 men, should be employed to punish it. When Austria appealed to the same treaty in 1778, France replied that the assertion of claims to new territories, which were not guaranteed in the treaty of Versailles, could not be regarded as a defensive war, and that therefore the *casus foederis* did not arise. Thus the two wars could not be linked together as they had been before. France remained neutral in the German quarrels, and wisely abstained this time from the attempt to harass Britain by attacking Hanover. To Frederick it was much more important to weaken the alliance of France with Austria than to be reconciled with George III. And so, while he expressed his gratitude for the moral support which Britain gave him in the Bavarian dispute,[1] he did nothing more. The mediation of France and Russia put an end to the war by the treaty of Teschen (13th May 1779). The Austrian claims were bought off by the cession of a fragment of territory, and all opposition was withdrawn to Frederick's claim to deal as he pleased with Anspach and Baireuth when they fell in. The Bavarian Succession did not reconcile Prussia with Britain, but it took some of the bitterness out of the quarrel, and it showed that conditions might arise in which co-operation would be possible. While the dispute lasted Elliot had no difficulty about the transit of hired troops.

The decade which followed the treaty of Teschen is as regards diplomacy the most complicated in the whole century. The threads of conflicting interests and motives cross each other at so many points, and become so tangled together, that it is as difficult for the historian as it was for the contemporary politician to pick out the main lines of continental relations. The whole system created by the diplomatic revolution seemed to be on the verge of destruction, and no one could foresee what was to take its place. The only stable conditions were the hostility of France and Britain, which were at war with each other, the impossibility of a cordial understanding between Austria and Prussia, and the continuance of the Family Compact. Everything else was in the melting-pot. British difficulties were constantly increasing. Spain joined France in the war in 1779, and Holland was added to the list of our enemies in 1780. Harris at St. Petersburg was authorized to make the most lavish offers to gain Russia.[2] But the northern courts were in the old state of exasperation against the right of search, the confiscation of enemy goods in neutral ships, the arbitrary declarations of often unreal blockade, aud the extensive definition of contraband.

[1] *S. P. For.*, *Prussia*, 103 : Finckenstein wrote to Elliot on 19 June 1779, 'regretting that he cannot personally express Frederick's appreciation of the obliging good-will of his Britannic Majesty, of the part which he has played in bringing about a happy settlement, and of the patriotic sentiments which have animated him during the whole of the German troubles'. The word 'patriotic' is maliciously used, as it leaves it dubious whether the patriotism was German or British.

[2] Extracts from Harris's interesting correspondence during his Russian mission are given in his *Diaries*, &c., vols. i and ii.

Catharine II took the lead in voicing their grievances, and her declaration of the rights of neutral powers was accepted by Sweden and Denmark in 1780, and became the basis of the Armed Neutrality. By this act Russia served the interests of France, and drew closer to that power than it had been since the close of the Seven Years' War.

But while western events tended to unite Russia with France, eastern interests tended to divide them. In recent years a struggle had been going on at St. Petersburg between Panin and the rising favourite Potemkin. The question of Poland had fallen into the background since the completion of the partition, and Russia had no reason to revive it, so long as the diminished kingdom left to Stanislas was reasonably docile. This Polish question, however, had been the basis of the Russo-Prussian alliance, and as it receded the need for Prussian help steadily diminished. On the other hand, the Turkish problem was becoming more acute. Constant disputes arose as to the carrying out of the treaty of Kainardji, and a renewal of war seemed to be sooner or later inevitable. In such a war an Austrian alliance would be more useful than a Prussian alliance, or conversely, Austrian hostility would be more dangerous than Prussian hostility. Frederick had always shown an invincible reluctance to diminish Turkish power or territories, whereas Austria, except in the late war, had always been the ally of Russia against the Turks. Hence Potemkin, the advocate of aggressive action against Turkey, was inclined to an Austrian alliance, while Panin clung to Prussia. Frederick began to feel that he was losing the sheet-anchor of his security. The death of his old enemy, Maria Theresa, was in the end a blow to him, because she steadily adhered to the French alliance and distrusted Russia. Joseph II, now both Emperor and sole ruler in Austria, was more inclined to take risks. He put down his defeat in the Bavarian succession to the Russo-Prussian alliance, and believed that if he could gain Russian support his difficulties in Germany would disappear. The result of these common interests was the famous interview of Joseph and Catharine in 1780, and the exchange of letters in the next year which constituted an alliance. The gist of the bargain was a free hand in the east for Catharine and in the west for Joseph. Frederick made great efforts to regain his hold upon Russia, and sought Catharine's favour by joining the Armed Neutrality, though his maritime interest was microscopic. But as Joseph, also the head of an inland state, followed his example, no advantage was gained by the move.

The transfer of Russia from a Prussian to an Austrian alliance was a change of the greatest magnitude. And it at once raised a question of equal importance. Would France follow the lead of Austria, and repay Russia for the Armed Neutrality by sacrificing Turkey? It soon became clear that France did not intend to make such a sacrifice of its traditions for the sake of Austria. Vergennes had been for many years ambassador at Constantinople, and regarded the Turks as invaluable allies of France. Other questions arose which accentuated this decision. Joseph, the most restless of rulers, began in 1781 to pick a quarrel with the Dutch, which went on for four years. He repudiated the Barrier treaty, and he wanted to open the Scheldt and to add the border fortress of Maestricht to the southern Netherlands. If France allowed him to do all this, it would lose the hold it had acquired over the republican or so-called patriotic party. Patriots and followers of Orange would, as in the past, combine against a common enemy, and the party dissensions, so invaluable to France, would disappear. So here again France had to part company with Austria.

If France and Austria separated, then the diplomatic revolution would be undone, and the treaty of Versailles virtually annulled. No wonder the diplomatic dovecots were fluttered. The difficulty was to know what was going to happen. If the two courts fell apart then the result was clear. Prussia would at once return to France, and Britain might recover Austria, and possibly Russia with it. But if they remained united in spite of their differences, then Britain could not gain Austria, Prussia could not gain France, and therefore Britain and Prussia must be almost forced to come together. This was what actually did happen, but Frederick refused to the end to give it his absolute belief. There can be no doubt that in his last years his mental as well as his physical faculties were failing. Even his ministers ventured to have policies of their own, a thing which they had never presumed to do when their master was in his

full vigour. There can be no doubt that Hertzberg was in
favour of a British alliance, and that Finckenstein, like his master,
was resolute to do nothing that would forfeit the chance of
detaching France from Austria. The Prussian court was divided
upon similar lines. Prince Henry, who was regarded as likely
to guide his young nephew, was an avowed partisan of France.
As for the young Frederick William himself, he had probably no
strong convictions, but was believed to trust in Hertzberg and
to share his views. This division, combined with the king's
vacillation, kept the representatives of Britain on tenter-hooks
throughout the later years of Frederick's reign.

Meanwhile it must be borne in mind that Britain itself, quite
apart from foreign politics, had been passing through troubled
times. A few short words will recall them. The European
coalition, the temporary loss of maritime superiority and the
consequent surrender at Yorktown, convinced the most resolute
optimists that a triumphant peace was out of the question, and
that Britain must surrender either to the colonists or to the
house of Bourbon, or to both. The ministry of Lord North,
which had continued in office long after its chief had wished to
resign, came to an unhonoured end in 1782. The Whigs
returned to office, but the death of Rockingham split them into
two sections, and the preference of the king for Shelburne drove
Fox and his friends into secession, and ultimately into a factious
coalition with Lord North and the Tories. The treaty of
Versailles was concluded during these disputes, and it is largely
due to the troubled conditions of Europe that its terms were not
worse. No sooner was peace concluded than the coalition forced
Shelburne to resign and themselves into what they deemed a
durable tenure of office. But they reckoned without George III.
By a last desperate bid for autocracy the king procured the
rejection of Fox's India Bill in the House of Lords, on that inadequate pretext dismissed the hated ministry, and called the
younger Pitt to office in face of a hostile majority in the House
of Commons. The errors of the coalition leaders delivered them
into their rival's hands, and the general election of 1784 con-
doned the king's action and made Pitt the most powerful minister since the days of Walpole. During these quick transitions
the conduct of foreign affairs passed through several hands, and

this contributed to the failure to obtain any secure continental support. One change is of such importance for my subject that it must be specially mentioned. When Fox and Shelburne took the two Secretaryships under Rockingham their functions were radically changed. The distribution between the northern and southern departments, long obviously inconvenient, was abolished. Shelburne undertook home and colonial affairs, and the whole department of foreign affairs was undertaken by Fox. Henceforward there has only been one Foreign Secretary in the British Government. Lord Carmarthen received the seals of this office under Pitt.

Frederick's obstinacy in clinging to the futile hope of a French alliance was the more remarkable because two events towards the close of his reign seemed to make co-operation with Britain almost inevitable. The first was the aggressive policy adopted in Germany by Joseph II after the conclusion of his alliance with Catharine. While Russia was coercing the Turks and substituting the annexation of the Crimea for the protectorate established at Kainardji, the emperor was gaining one advantage after another at the expense of German princes. Frederick was powerless to do more than protest. It was now his turn to realize the truth of Mitchell's maxim, *chi sta solo non sta bene.* He had lost Russia, he had not gained France, and if he could have made up his mind to bid for British support, that State had not yet emerged from its disastrous war. But in 1785, after Britain had secured peace, came the final provocation. With the avowed approval of Russia, Joseph revived the old project of exchanging the Netherlands for Bavaria, and once more obtained the consent of the complacent Charles Theodore. France was not likely to object to the reversal of a settlement which had been devised to erect a barrier to French aggression. But Britain and Holland were entitled to protest by the terms of the Barrier treaty of 1715, and the German princes were not likely to tolerate such a vast increase of the territorial predominance of Austria as would be gained by the annexation of the Bavarian electorate. Frederick set himself to organize the famous *Fürstenbund*, which was joined even by the Roman Catholic princes whose traditions bound them to the side of Austria. In the formation and organization of the League, his most active and

efficient aid came from Hanover. It was only fitting that
Hanover, which had so often and so fatally divided Prussia from
Britain, should now serve to link the two powers together.
And the League was successful. Joseph II found himself compelled by the general opposition to abandon the exchange project. Frederick sardonically exclaimed, ' Nous avons réussi à
intimider César Joseph '.[1] But while it was the second check to
the ambitious Emperor, it was the first check to Catharine II, and
she did not like it.

The second great impulse towards Anglo-Prussian co-operation came from events in the United Provinces. Joseph's exchange project and his quarrel with the Dutch were pressed
simultaneously, and were in fact closely associated. If he could
open the Scheldt and acquire Maestricht he made the Austrian
Netherlands a more tempting morsel to offer to Charles Theodore.
France, which had supported him in one scheme, gently dissuaded
him from the others, and in the end French mediation saved the
Dutch. The Barrier, which France detested as part of the evil
Utrecht settlement, was already gone, but Joseph agreed by the
treaty of Fontainebleau (8 November 1785) to leave the Scheldt
closed and to withdraw his claims upon Maestricht. Since the
exchange had been dropped, the desire for these gains had
sensibly diminished. In return for his complaisance he was to
receive ten million Dutch florins, and France generously undertook to pay half of that sum. By this politic intervention
Vergennes secured the slavish devotion of the republican
patriots, and a second treaty two days later than that with
Austria established the long-sought alliance of the United Provinces with France. Harris, who had been sent to the Hague
after the conclusion of peace with the Dutch, did all in his power
to obstruct the French treaty, and induced three out of the seven
provinces to protest against it. But he had to acknowledge
himself beaten in this matter, and all his energies were called for
to avert another and final defeat. Already, before the Fontainebleau treaty had been signed, the patriots had begun, with
encouragement from France, to complete their triumph by
wresting from the House of Orange the powers which had been
restored to it in 1747 and confirmed in 1766. The lead was

[1] *F. O.*, 64. 7, Ewart to Fraser, 14 June 1785.

taken by the province of Holland, always the stronghold of the republican party, and Harris hoped to save the stadtholdership by appealing to the jealousy with which Zealand and other lesser provinces regarded their predominant partner. In this struggle he had good reason to expect the support of Prussia. The stadtholder's wife was Wilhelmina, the niece of Frederick and the sister of the heir to the Prussian throne, the 'beautiful and well-educated' lady whose wedding Andrew Mitchell had attended. She supplied the intellect and the courage which William V conspicuously lacked, and she confidently appealed to the uncle who had chosen her inadequate husband for her. It seemed hardly possible that Frederick should allow a family so closely connected with Prussia to be deprived of all political power. Here at last was the obvious opportunity for that co-operation which the Hanoverian partnership in the *Fürstenbund* seemed to deserve.

During these exciting years, contrasting so strongly with the long interval of tacit alienation, the embassy at Berlin passed through several hands. One of the first acts of Charles Fox when he took over the Foreign Secretaryship was to recall the impetuous Hugh Elliot, either because he was distasteful to Frederick, or, as the victim believed, because he had identified himself too closely with the late administration.[1] Grantham (Foreign Secretary under Shelburne) sent Sir John Stepney as his successor, and he remained at Berlin from October 1782 till June 1784, when he got leave to return for the general election, and was still absent when ill-health induced him to resign, in August 1785. Stepney's chief importance is that he induced to enter his service a young Edinburgh graduate, Joseph Ewart, who was acting as tutor to the son of a Scottish laird on the grand tour. During Stepney's absence Ewart was left in charge at Berlin, and acquitted himself with such remarkable industry and ability that, when it was decided to send Lord Dalrymple to fill Stepney's place, Ewart, in spite of his youth and previous

---

[1] *Journal and Correspondence of William, Lord Auckland*, i. 396, Elliot to Eden, 15 July 1782: 'I am singled out as the first victim in the foreign line because I was the most obnoxious, from my avowed attachment to better men and better principles.' It may be added that he received a snuff-box from Frederick and a testimonial from Hertzberg.

inexperience (he was born, of course a son of the manse, in 1759), was raised to the rank of Secretary of Legation. And though he was technically superseded by the arrival of Dalrymple in November 1785, Ewart continued to be the most influential representative of Britain at Berlin, and it was to him that Harris wrote (even after Dalrymple's arrival) to arrange for concerted action with regard to Dutch affairs. Ewart was a convinced and most consistent advocate of a Prussian alliance as a good thing in itself, whereas Dalrymple had quite different opinions.

The most definite bid for an Anglo-Prussian alliance was made in the spring of 1785, when both the exchange project and Joseph's quarrel with the Dutch were the main objects of attention. It had already been agreed that the British and Prussian envoys at St. Petersburg should act together to induce Catharine to oppose the Bavarian exchange, and on the 14th May Carmarthen wrote to Ewart that this co-operation should be extended into a greater and more comprehensive system, and especially that the two powers should act in unison to 'emancipate the Republic from the shackles of slavish dependence upon France'. It was added that if Frederick was willing, a confidential envoy should be sent to him.[1] Frederick returned a discouraging answer, and deprecated any special mission as likely to give undue publicity to the negotiation.[2] In spite of this, or perhaps because of it, and in the desire to create the impression that an understanding existed, Lord Cornwallis was sent on a special mission in September. The account of his interview with Frederick is an interesting document, though it cannot be accepted as an honest avowal of the king's motives. He declared in substance that the balance of power was gone, that France, Spain, Austria, and Russia were allied, and Holland was under French control; that Britain and Prussia were isolated and, even if combined, were no match for such a coalition; that he had fought one Seven Years' War in similar conditions and did not want another. But, with another reminiscence of that war, 'detach Russia and I will join the triple alliance to-morrow'.[3] Unfor-

---

[1] *F. O.*, 64. 7, Carmarthen to Ewart, 14 May 1785.

[2] *Ibid.*, Ewart to Carmarthen, 28 May 1785.

[3] Cornwallis, in forwarding the report to Carmarthen on 20 September, states that the duke of Brunswick is always active in trying to bring Prussia

tunately, and Frederick had reason to know it, Russia, with her eyes fixed on Constantinople, could not be detached from Austria, whose opposition might block the way to the Bosphorus.

And so matters remained till the end of Frederick's reign. It is usual to lay the blame upon Frederick and upon the insane permanence of his grudge against Bute. And no doubt it is unusual to cherish a grudge of that kind for twenty-three years. It was not, however, the old quarrel which held Frederick so aloof from Britain, or made him so deaf to the appeals of his niece. The real motive was that he clung to the hope of gaining over France, and would not commit himself to any step which would complete the alienation of France. The British alliance, in his eyes, was not a good in itself, it was a last resource, and, so he believed, a resource available at any time when it was absolutely needed. But there is another point of view. The responsibility for the failure to come together does not rest wholly upon Frederick; it must be shared by the British government.[1] If the British alliance was a *pis aller* to Frederick, so the Prussian alliance was a *pis aller* to Britain. As long as Prussia had a chance of detaching France from Austria, so long Britain had a chance of detaching Austria from France. And if there was a choice between an Austrian and a Prussian alliance, no orthodox diplomatist could hesitate for a moment. Certainly neither Harris nor Carmarthen would have hesitated. Carmarthen wrote as late as the 24th July 1786, only four weeks before Frederick's death, ' My own manner of thinking, with respect to

and Britain together, and praises the 'merit, assiduity and intelligence of Mr. Ewart' (*F. O.*, 64. 7). The report is printed in *Malmesbury*, ii. 151-2. In his first interview with Dalrymple, Frederick also expressed his dread of another Seven Years' War. *F. O.*, 64. 9, Dalrymple to Carmarthen, 3 December 1785.

[1] In an interesting letter to Harris, of 19 September 1785, Carmarthen tells him that Count Lusi, the Prussian envoy in London, had incurred Frederick's displeasure by advocating an agreement with Cornwallis. The Foreign Secretary adds that the king need not have been alarmed, as Cornwallis was instructed to get information, 'but not to commit this court in the smallest degree by the remotest idea of anything like an alliance' (*Malmesbury*, ii. 152-3). It is difficult to reconcile this assertion with the instructions to Ewart of 14 May.

Austria and Prussia remains, and probably ever will remain, unshaken: the first ought to be the *perpetual*, as it is the *natural* ally of England; the second can, I apprehend, be but an *occasional* one'.[1] And Harris wrote an almost apologetic letter to Ewart on the 8th August to explain that ministers cannot so decidedly favour Prussia 'as to shut the door entirely against Austria', and expresses his own view that a Prussian connexion is only to be desired when 'Austria is irrevocably cemented to France'.[2]

Thus, in spite of substantial impulses towards union, beginning with the Bavarian Succession, and ending with the party strife in Holland, the period of alienation lasted till the death of Frederick the Great, on the 17th August 1786.

[1] *Malmesbury*, ii. 211.   [2] *Ibid.*, pp. 218–19.

THE RECONCILIATION IN 1787 AND THE TRIPLE ALLIANCE OF 1788-91

AT the death of Frederick the Great the attention of both Britain and Prussia was still largely concentrated upon the affairs of the United Provinces. The question at issue was whether both powers conjointly or either of them separately should intervene actively to oppose the growth of French ascendancy, and to prevent the republican or 'patriotic' party, who were the tools of France, from carrying out their efforts to abolish the hereditary stadtholdership, or at least to reduce the holders of that bundle of offices to impotence and to make them actually, what they were held to be in law, the servants rather than the masters of the Republic. The difficulties in the way of the patriots were, that the existing constitution could only be overthrown by a revolution or by a *coup d'état*; that for such a purpose they could not rely upon the support of the regular army, which looked to the prince of Orange as its head; that three of the provinces, Zealand, Gelderland, and Friesland, were against them; that they could not command a majority in the States-General, the central authority of the federation; and that, if the whole population was counted, and not merely the privileged classes, they were in a minority. On the other hand, they were well organized under resolute leaders;[1] they could count on the Provincial Estates of four of the provinces, including Holland, which in wealth and population was equal to the other six; they might at any moment, by bribery or intimidation, gain over the Estates of one or more of the loyal provinces, and thus alter the unstable balance in the States-General; and, if they could not undermine the loyalty of the regular troops, they could organize

[1] The leaders were the three pensionaries of Amsterdam, Dort, and Haarlem, Van Berkel, Gyslaer, and Zeeberg. See *Malmesbury*, ii. 76, 85, 87-9.

a formidable force of volunteers or ' free corps ', as they called them.   The only absolutely loyal province was Gelderland, and there, at Nimeguen, William V and his wife took up their residence, as the Hague was too completely in the hands of their opponents, who had already deprived the stadtholder of the command of the garrison in the capital.   Sir James Harris set himself to strengthen and encourage all the loyalist elements in the Republic, and hoped by this means to prevent anything like unanimity either in the attack upon the stadtholder or in submission to France.   There was, however, one fatal defect in his position.   In April 1786 Vergennes declared that France would actively resent any foreign interference in the internal affairs of a state to which it was bound by the defensive treaty of the 10th November 1785,[1] and the French envoy at the Hague assured the patriots that they could count upon efficient support from France. The Orange party dared not take any decisive measures against the hostile faction unless they were also assured of external aid. Harris could not, and the Prussian envoy, Thulemeier, neither would nor could, give such an assurance.   So long as this state of things lasted, the ultimate triumph of the republicans and of France seemed to be inevitable.

Hitherto all attempts to bring about united action on the part of Britain and Prussia had failed, and neither was prepared single-handed to risk a quarrel with France, which would probably, in existing circumstances, lead to a rupture with Austria and Russia.   In my last lecture I examined some of the causes of the absence of agreement between London and Berlin. The two courts had long been estranged from each other, though the antipathy was stronger in Prussia than in Britain.   Both had other inclinations.   Prussia desired a reconciliation with France. British statesmen longed for a reconciliation with Austria.   Only when they were absolutely convinced that the realization of these aims was impossible would they contemplate the possibility of agreement with each other.   Among British politicians only Chatham and Charles Fox, and among British diplomatists only Horace Walpole (the elder), Andrew Mitchell, and Joseph Ewart, regarded a Prussian alliance as desirable in itself.   In the particular Dutch problem, though the interests of the two states

---

[1] Harris to Carmarthen, 7 April 1785, in *Malmesbury*, ii. 195.

partially coincided, they were by no means identical. Prussia was primarily concerned in defending the house of Orange because William V had married a Prussian wife. Britain was mainly interested in thwarting France. Prussia wanted to maintain the office and rank of the stadtholder, but cared comparatively little for his prerogative. Britain was concerned to uphold the powers of the office because they alone stood in the way of French domination. As William V put it to Harris, with unwonted clearness of apprehension, the motives of the one power were personal, of the other public.[1] And both courts with good reason distrusted each other. Each wanted to remain aloof itself and to induce the other to incur the expense and the risks of intervention. The strongest argument of the powerful French party in Berlin was that Britain would involve Prussia in a ruinous conflict with France and then refuse all assistance,[2] and their argument was justified.[3] Pitt, who kept the ultimate decision in his own hands, was determined to give his country a prolonged period of peace in which to recover from the American war. He would run no risk of war with any power, and least of all with France, with which state he was engaged in 1786 in negotiating his famous commercial treaty. Finally, Finckenstein could point to the strain and the terrors of the Seven Years' War. Even if British support was secured again, as in 1756, it was unthinkable that Prussia should wantonly throw itself into another such war.

In spite of all these obstacles, there were slight symptoms of improved relations between Britain and Prussia in the ultimate days of Frederick the Great. It was regarded as significant that

[1] Harris to Carmarthen, 1 September 1786, in *Malmesbury*, ii. 224.

[2] *F. O.*, 64. 10, Dalrymple to Carmarthen, 11 October 1786: 'French partisans urge that a Dutch war will drive France into indissoluble union with Austria, and that England can and will give no assistance.'

[3] *Ibid.*, Carmarthen to Dalrymple, 22 September 1786: 'Prussia should be encouraged to prevent Holland being sacrificed to France, without England being at least for the present committed.' Compare Harris to Carmarthen, 3 October 1786 (*Malmesbury*, ii. 240). Carmarthen had written on 26 September to say that Britain cannot risk an immediate war. Harris replies, 'To commit France and Prussia in a military quarrel is my first wish; my second, to encourage them in a political one,—England in both cases to remain quiet'.

the king took with him on his last retirement to Sans-Souci, not Finckenstein, his usual associate, but Hertzberg, the known advocate of a better understanding with the Court of St. James. It is said that the king died in Hertzberg's arms.   But the chief confidence of the pro-British section in ministerial circles was placed in the supposed inclinations of the heir to the throne, who was regarded as hostile to France and as an ardent partisan of his sister's cause.   At the outset of the new reign these hopes seemed likely to be realized.   Frederick William gave Hertzberg the Order of the Black Eagle and raised him to the rank of Count.   The minister, who was confident that he could henceforth dispense with the concurrence of Finckenstein, accompanied the king on his tour to the outlying provinces.   Goertz, an experienced diplomatist and a confidant of Hertzberg,[1] was sent to the Hague to explore the best methods of defending the stadtholder.   Goertz at once put himself in confidential relations with Harris, and virtually quarrelled with the arrogant French envoy.   But a speedy disillusion followed the king's return to Berlin.   Frederick William was a weak man, and like all weak men he was afraid of having a master.   Hertzberg was too much of a pedant to be a good courtier, and the king refused to allow him to become a first minister.   Departing from his uncle's traditions, who had kept all departments under his own direct supervision, Frederick William revived his grandfather's 'general directory', in which the heads of the various departments met together to discuss public affairs in the presence of the king. And in these discussions the French party, with the powerful support of Prince Henry, the king's uncle, and of Marshal Möllendorf, regarded as Prussia's greatest native soldier, speedily gained the upper hand.   Goertz at the Hague found his hands tied and his intercourse with the British envoy severely blamed.[2]

[1] Dalrymple, in a letter of recommendation to Harris, says of Goertz, 'he is, besides, embarked with Mr. Hertzberg, and must sink or swim with him' (*Malmesbury*, ii. 224).

[2] Harris to Carmarthen, 24 October 1786, quotes from a letter to Goertz from the ministers at Berlin : 'On dit, M. le Comte, que vous négligez l'ambassadeur de France . . . et ne vivez qu'avec le ministre Anglais et le parti Anglais.   Le Roi est persuadé que ce n'est qu'un bruit suscité par vos ennemis' (*Ibid.*, ii. 244).

Frederick William, inconstant both as a brother and as a king, chafed at his sister's over-confident appeals and thought his brother-in-law far too pertinacious in clinging to his prerogatives. He declared that it was his duty as a Prussian king to watch the emperor, that if he intervened in Holland Austria would at once attack him in Silesia, and that Dutch affairs were of quite secondary importance.

Harris at the Hague and Ewart at Berlin were in despair : Harris because Prussian inaction meant British inaction, Ewart because the Anglo-Prussian alliance, on which he built all his hopes, seemed to be as far off as ever.   The French party in the United Provinces was jubilant and aggressive.   A new French envoy declared to Goertz that ' a hereditary stadtholder was of too new a creation to have acquired a constitutional sanction '.[1] At a meeting of the Provincial Estates of Holland, in September, a direct and bitter personal attack on William V was made by Gyrslaer, the pensionary of Dort, and one of the triumvirate which guided the republican party.   On his proposal a resolution was carried to suspend the prince's tenure of the offices of stadtholder and captain-general within the Provinces.

During the months that followed all prospect of Prussian intervention steadily declined, and the influence of Finckenstein and the French party became almost absolute.   A triangular correspondence was carried on between Berlin, Versailles, and Nimeguen as to the possibilities of devising some compromise on which the patriots and the Orange party could agree.   But the stadtholder and his wife, guided by Harris, refused all proposals which did not include the revocation of the acts passed in September by the Provincial Estates of Holland, and to this the patriots could not agree.   Frederick William, always indolent, became more and more tired of Dutch affairs,[2] and said that if the stadtholder chose to ruin himself he could not help it.[3] Goertz was recalled, an act which Wilhelmina interpreted as the

[1] *Malmesbury*, ii. 238.

[2] *F. O.*, 64. 10, Dalrymple to Carmarthen, 23 December 1786 : ' It appears that the affection the king formerly had for the house of Orange is considerably diminished, and that he is grown extremely tired of Dutch affairs.'

[3] *Ibid.*, 64. 11, Dalrymple to Carmarthen, 13 January 1787.

desertion of her cause by Prussia.[1]   When the omniscient Hertzberg tried his hand at drafting a new Dutch constitution,
Wilhelmina replied in a bitter letter that further intervention
would only redound to the dishonour of Prussia and the ruin
of the house of Orange.[2]   Her brother coldly replied that he
wished the house of Orange would show more moderation and
common sense.[3]   So completely did Prussia seem to have turned
her back upon Holland that Dalrymple, in April 1787, obtained
leave of absence for private business, and once more Ewart was
left as the sole representative of Britain at Berlin.

Meanwhile, in the United Provinces things were steadily drift-
ing towards civil war.   Harris set himself to organize an association whose members would pledge themselves to support the
constitutional authority of the stadtholder.   The opposition at
once formed a rival Patriotic Association to maintain the purity
of the republic from every taint of monarchy.   Riots occurred
in Amsterdam and other towns, and it was clear that the available forces were so equally balanced that the intervention of
foreign troops would decide the issue.   So far the only power
which had given assurance of such intervention was France, and
the French envoy continued to encourage the patriots by repeating his former promises.   But an important event had taken
place in France during the winter.   Vergennes, the real author
of the alliance with the United Provinces, died in January 1787.
His successor, Count Montmorin, ostensibly carried on his predecessor's policy, but acute observers could trace henceforth a
weakening in the French decision to support the patriots at all
costs, and a tendency to leave the Dutch to settle their own disputes.[4]   Harris became convinced by the financial troubles which
necessitated the calling of the Assembly of Notables that after all

---

[1] *F. O.*, 64. 11, Dalrymple to Carmarthen, 6 February 1787.

[2] *Ibid.*, Dalrymple to Carmarthen, 7 April 1787.

[3] *Ibid.*, Dalrymple to Carmarthen, 14 April 1787.

[4] This was first disclosed to the unfortunate patriots in June, just before
the arrest of the princess.   Verac, the French envoy, when pressed as to
whether France would send troops to support the party, had to reply that
' he had no authority to say she would. . . . He was for proving that the
party was strong enough of itself and wanted no exterior assistance '
(*Malmesbury*, ii. 320).   This was in complete contrast to his previous
assurances.

France would not fight, and that Britain might safely intervene
to thwart French designs in the United Provinces. Carmarthen
declared himself a convert to these views in January,[1] and in
May, when the civil war seemed in sight, Harris determined to
take upon himself the responsibility of urging the British Cabinet
to undertake an active policy.[2] He was so far successful that,
instead of being blamed for his presumption, he was invited over
to attend a Cabinet meeting in London. From the minutes of
what passed it appears that a majority of the members were in
favour of Harris's contentions, but Pitt maintained that though
war was possible rather than probable, yet the mere possibility
imposed caution, and intervention was limited to permission for
Harris to expend up to £20,000 in his campaign against the
patriots.[3] With this rather inadequate comfort he returned to
console and encourage William V and Wilhelmina. They needed
all the encouragement they could get, as Frederick William at
this time refused a request for a supply of munitions from Wesel
which were urgently needed for the loyal troops.[4] Carmarthen
intimated to Harris, on the 12th June, that all idea of acting with
Prussia must in present circumstances be abandoned.[5]

The events which followed this simultaneous refusal by the
two possible allies of the only assistance which really counted
are dramatic and well known. The Provincial Estates of Holland
dismissed a number of officers who regarded their oath of allegiance
to the federal authority as stronger than their obedience to the
province of Holland. The States-General by a majority rein-
stated them. This created a definite split; it 'set the States-
General and the States of Holland at open defiance of each
other'. But the balance was very even. An illegal assembly in
the city of Utrecht sent deputies to the States-General, and their

---

[1] *Malmesbury*, ii. 268, Carmarthen to Harris, 8 January 1787.

[2] This important dispatch is dated 1 May 1787, and is printed in full in
Malmesbury, ii. 294-8. In a private letter to Carmarthen, of the same date,
he adds, ' if we will be *bold* enough to assume the style and tone which belongs
to us, *I will pledge my head on the event*.'

[3] The minutes of the two Cabinet meetings, held on 23 and 26 May, are
in *Malmesbury*, ii. 303-7.

[4] *F. O.*, 64. 11, Dalrymple to Carmarthen, 19 May 1787. See also
Malmesbury, ii. 368.

[5] *Malmesbury*, ii. 312.

admission gave a majority for rescinding the resolution. Then the intruders were excluded, and the resolution was restored. At this crisis the princess of Orange resolved, with the hesitating approval of Harris, to risk a journey to the Hague in order to encourage her supporters. On the frontier of Holland, at a village called Haestricht, near Gouda, she was arrested by a body of the free corps, carried a prisoner to Schoonhoven, and then released by orders from the Hague, but only to return to Nimeguen. Harris, strained by the long struggle and by the sense of responsibility, thought all was lost. ' *Check to the Queen*, and in a move or two checkmate is, I fear, the state of our game.' Carmarthen, calmer and more distant, saw other possibilities, and replied, ' Don't be so disheartened by a check to the Queen ; let her be covered by the Knight and all will be well. . . . If the King her brother is not the dirtiest and shabbiest of kings, he must resent it, *coûte que coûte*.' [1]

Carmarthen was right. Frederick William II was not a competent ruler, but he was not the dirtiest and shabbiest of kings, and the insult to his sister touched his personal and family pride. He at once ordered Thulemeier to demand a humble apology and complete satisfaction from the Provincial Estates, the punishment of the actual criminals, and the withdrawal of all opposition to Wilhelmina's journey. To enforce this demand he ordered the troops in Wesel and his other border fortresses to be ready to march, and appointed the duke of Brunswick to command them. He declared that he was going to exact satisfaction, even if he had to go to Holland to get it, and added, ' Je ne crains pas la France '.[2] Then came a sudden cold fit, which Ewart traced to two causes. (1) Thulemeier reported that ' the court of London was actually determined not to interfere at all in Dutch affairs, in consequence of representations made by Mr. Pitt against it '.[3] (2) France flattered Frederick William's vanity by inviting him to take part in a joint mediation to restore peace in the United Provinces. Both moves were promptly countered. Ewart pointed out that Thulemeier's report suspiciously resembled previous rumours to

[1] These interesting letters are in *Malmesbury*, ii. 329.
[2] *F. O.*, 64. 11, Ewart to Carmarthen, 14 July 1787.
[3] *Ibid.*, Ewart to Carmarthen, 7th July 1787.

the same effect, and obtained authority from London to repudiate it. Hertzberg induced the king to attach conditions to the joint mediation which France could not accept without alienating the Dutch patriots. Still the French party continued the struggle: they urged the danger from the emperor, and the risk that Britain would leave them in the lurch at the last moment. But Hertzberg, who co-operated cordially with Ewart in these critical weeks, had the stronger cards in his hands, and he obtained valuable support from Bischofswerder, a Saxon who had entered the military service of Prussia and had gained a great influence over Frederick William while he was crown prince.[1] The conversion of Pitt to an active policy after he was assured of Prussian intervention gave Ewart an immense advantage over his opponents at Berlin. Another great aid to him was rendered by the maladroit conduct of France. The obvious game for France to play was to draw a hard and fast line between the insult to the princess of Orange, in which Prussia was concerned, and the constitutional disputes, which mainly interested Britain. If France had compelled the Estates of Holland to offer a full and frank apology, Prussia would have been disarmed and Britain isolated. Instead of doing this, France tried to make light of the episode at Haestricht, and allowed the Estates to give the haughty answer that 'a sovereign body cannot apologize to the wife of its first servant'. The French envoy was instructed to demand imperiously that the march of the Prussian troops should be countermanded, and to threaten a complete rupture of relations with Prussia. At the last moment a second courier arrived with orders that the envoy should moderate his tone, entreat the stoppage of the troops, and withhold the ultimatum. Nothing could be more ill-judged. Threats and dictation exasperated the Prussian king, and entreaties only convinced him that France would not risk a war. Hertzberg assured Frederick William that the late king 'never had so fortunate a moment as the present for establishing the power and political consequence of this country'.[2] All hesita-

---

[1] Bischofswerder is described by Ewart in the above dispatch as 'at present the only person who possesses the entire confidence of the king relative to foreign affairs'. It was characteristic of Frederick William II to be guided by other advice than that of his regular ministers.

[2] Ewart's dispatches during August, which give a graphic account of the

tion was removed when Britain gave a formal assurance of assistance by land and sea if France should go to war with Prussia,
and when news came on the 7th September that the Turks had
declared war against Russia by imprisoning the Russian ambassador in the Seven Towers.   The latter event was regarded as
a practical guarantee against any danger from Austria,[1] and the
Anglo-Prussian agreement was embodied in a convention by
the exchange of mutual declarations on the 2nd October.   This,
the first compact between the two states since the quarrel of
1762, was signed by Ewart for Great Britain and by Finckenstein and Hertzberg for Prussia.[2]

Nearly three weeks before this convention was signed Brunswick had crossed the Dutch frontier, on the 13th September.
On the same day Montmorin intimated to William Eden at
Versailles that French aid had been requested by the Estates of
Holland, and that this would be given in the most efficacious way
in case of a Prussian invasion.   On the 16th a formal notice to
the same effect was made in London by the French envoy.
Between these dates Pitt had written to Eden, on the 14th, that
the French must give up their preponderance in the Dutch
republic or they must fight for it.   He pointed out clearly that
the French treaty was with the States-General, and that it was
impossible to plead that treaty as an excuse for aiding a party
in a single province whose conduct the States-General had
disavowed.[3]

vacillation of the Prussian king and of the steady advance of the pro-British
party, are in *F. O.*, 64. 11.   I have abstracted the main gist of them in
the text.

[1] *F. O.*, 64. 12, Ewart to Carmarthen, 8 September 1787: Finckenstein
'communicated to me, with strong marks of satisfaction, the intelligence
he had just received from Vienna of the Porte having declared war against
Russia, which he said was particularly fortunate at the present conjuncture
as it would make it impossible for the Emperor to intermeddle in Dutch
affairs'.

[2] The British declaration was sent by Carmarthen to Ewart on 21 September,
with instructions to keep it secret.   On the 28th Carmarthen wrote that the
declaration, though now otiose, might be signed if Prussia wished it.   On
2 October Ewart reported that he had signed it, though the authority
to do so cannot have reached him.   *F. O.*, 64. 12.

[3] *Journal and Correspondence of William, Lord Auckland* (London, 1861),
i. 194-7.

Events soon proved that the French threats were mere empty bluster. The military camp at Givet, of which there had been so much talk during the last year, had never been occupied, and no adequate preparations had been made to resist such a combination as that of Prussia and Britain. After all its past assurances France left its allies to their fate. Brunswick's march was a military procession. The Orange partisans welcomed the troops as deliverers. The free corps, so truculent in their dealings with civilians, fled from an encounter with regular forces. William V and Wilhelmina returned in triumph to the Hague. Harris, who had been execrated and threatened by the bellicose patriots, found himself suddenly the most popular and influential personage in the United Provinces. The Provincial Estates of Holland, filled with new deputies, hastened to rescind all the past measures against the stadtholder and to erase from their register the appeal for French assistance. Harris wrote to Carmarthen that 'the Revolution in this country is as complete as it was in 1747. I wish it may be as lasting.'[1] The surrender of Amsterdam, the last stronghold of the patriots, on the 10th October, completed the triumph of the house of Orange.

All this was a bitter humiliation for France. And Pitt, who had not forgotten the late war, was not willing to allow the French government to escape with a mere rankling sense of defeat. It must be made to swallow the leek in public. To Eden, with the assistance of William Grenville (later Lord Grenville), was entrusted the ungracious but not very difficult task of trampling upon the fallen. It was distasteful to Eden, who was on friendly terms with the French ministers and who had negotiated the commercial treaty with them in the previous year; but Pitt was a stern taskmaster, and his instruction was carried out. On the 27th October Montmorin had to sign a formal declaration that France would not take any steps to carry out its declaration of the 16th September and that it would not retain any hostility for past events in Holland.[2] Prussia was a passive

[1] *Malmesbury*, ii. 376.

[2] *Auckland Correspondence*, vol. i, contains the British Declaration and the French Counter-Declaration, with a translation (pp. 255-7), and also the preliminary letters between Pitt and Eden. Harris, a thorough Gallophobe, blamed Eden for his partiality towards France. Eden's policy was probably the sounder of the two.

party to this act of humiliation, but may well have doubted its prudence. Few things did more to discredit the French monarchy, to increase the antagonism to the Austrian connexion, and to encourage the growth of revolutionary forces in France, than this open acknowledgement of impotence by the government of a proud state. And the doubt as to Pitt's wisdom in the matter is increased when we remember that at the very same time he proposed to employ French influence in the east to protect Turkey from its threatened partition by Austria and Russia.

It is clear that the immediate gainer by the intervention in Holland was Great Britain. Prussia had no substantial quarrel with France; Britain had. A powerful party in Berlin regretted and resented the alienation of France; in London opinion was practically unanimous in vengeful hostility to France. Europe was startled by the sudden re-emergence of a state which for a quarter of a century had stood aloof from continental affairs, and only four years before had seemed to affix the seal to its decline by the extorted grant of independence to its revolted colonists. And the recovery of its position in Europe had been achieved at a minimum of cost. All that the British government had done had been to increase its military and naval forces for a few weeks, and this was dropped as soon as France had signed the agreement of the 27th October. The work had been done by Prussia, and Prussia was not likely to forget it or to allow her fortunate colleague to forget it. For the first time since 1740 Prussia had waged a disinterested war, and the idolaters of Frederick the Great were not pleased to have no more solid recompense than an increase of barren reputation. If Hertzberg wished to commend a British alliance to Prussian opinion, he must associate it with some more obvious and tangible gain. This motive gives us the key to his policy in the tangled series of events which followed.

One very natural and necessary result of the counter-revolution in Holland was the alliance of the Dutch Republic with the two states which had combined to save it from the domination of France. The treaty of Fontainebleau had been concluded when the republican party was in the ascendant; it was practically torn to pieces by their overthrow. As that treaty had been primarily a blow to Britain, its nullification was an additional gain to that power. The negotiations which followed were conducted at the Hague by Harris, and at Berlin by a Dutch envoy, Baron van Reede, but it was agreed that the terms of the two treaties should be as far as possible identical and their signature simultaneous. Unexpected difficulties arose because both Holland and Prussia wished to include in the treaties a recognition of the doctrines laid down in the Armed Neutrality, and the Dutch also wanted the restoration of Nega-patam, which had been retained by Britain when peace was made at the end of the late war. Harris, however, succeeded in evading both demands, though he was personally willing to complete the conciliation by restoring Negapatam, and the two treaties were signed on the 15th April 1788. The United Provinces concluded a defensive alliance with the two liberating powers, and the latter guaranteed the maintenance of the restored constitution of 1747, including the hereditary stadt-holdership. The ' maritime powers' were once more a unit in Europe, and in the partnership Britain had more than regained its past predominance.

All that remained to complete the work begun in 1787 was to determine the future relations of Britain and Prussia. The com-pact of the 2nd October[1] was a purely *ad hoc* agreement; it was obsolete when it was signed, and was still more obsolete now that its professed object had been securely achieved and had been buttressed by the April treaties. It contained nothing to bind the two powers to future co-operation, and, unless they wished to revert to their former isolation, some further and more extensive agreement was obviously needed. To bring about such an agreement had been Hertzberg's aim all along. He was a con-vinced supporter of that 'northern system' which Chatham had propounded in 1766, and which Frederick the Great had then rejected. It is usual to describe Hertzberg as a pupil of Frederick, and so in a sense he was. But he was too self-confident to be a slavish follower of his master's methods, of which, by his own account, he had often disapproved. To under-stand Hertzberg's policy, and to grasp the problems with which

---

[1] Carmarthen informs Ewart on 2 October (*F. O.*, 64. 12) that this compact has been regularly sealed, in spite of the formal difficulty of sealing a secret document.

an Anglo-Prussian alliance would have to deal, it is necessary to
glance at the European situation in 1788. The primary fact is
that a great war had broken out in the east. Joseph II, after
some vacillation, had decided that he dared not sever his hitherto
rather unprofitable alliance with Russia. So he threw himself
into the Turkish war, not as a mere auxiliary but as an equal
partner, hoping to profit by the expected conquest of Turkey's
European dominions, which it was now too late to avert, and
from which it would be dangerous to allow Russia to reap the
whole gain. It is impossible to say how the eastern war would
have terminated if there had been no external complications.
But the news that the two great allies were committed to the
war was the signal for a general outbreak of forces which in
time of peace they had been able to restrain. There were three
great centres of disturbance. (1) Sweden under Gustavus III
seized the opportunity to attempt the complete recovery of
Finland and to undo the treaty of Abo. (2) In the Austrian
Netherlands Joseph II's reforms had exasperated the champions
both of provincial liberties and of clerical immunities and privileges, and they were now free to extort compliance with their
demands by rebellion. (3) Most dangerous of all to Russia, and
to the concert between Russia and Austria, was the beginning of
disturbance in the long submissive Poland. If the Poles threw
off the Russian yoke, and celebrated the recovery of independence by reforming their constitution, it would be difficult to
retain the provinces annexed in 1772, and especially difficult for
Austria to keep Galicia, which lay on the farther side of the
Carpathians and was easier to attack than to defend. In addition Austria had to face the chronic insubordination of the
Magyars in Hungary, who were almost certain to rise if they
heard of movements in Poland and the Netherlands.

To Hertzberg and to Frederick William these disturbances
seemed to offer a chance, which it would be criminal to let slip,
of raising Prussia to a dictatorship in Europe almost as absolute
as that which they had gained in Holland. If they played their
cards well, they might impose terms in the east as they had
already imposed terms in the west. For the last eight years
Prussia had been on the defensive against Joseph II, it was now
her turn to humble her inveterate opponent. But in order to

secure the maximum of gain with the minimum of risk they must have adequate backing, and they must especially secure Prussia against a western invasion by France and against attacks on its Baltic coast by the Russian and Danish fleets. Such backing and such security could be supplied by the maritime powers, and Prussia not unnaturally thought that it had established a claim to their assistance. Hence the eager demand for a Triple Alliance came, not from Britain, but from Prussia. As early as the 27th September 1787, after the triumphant occupation of the Hague but before the fall of Amsterdam, Frederick William intimated to Ewart his desire for such an alliance.[1] The motive at that time was to secure protection against the expected hostility of France. But on the 20th October, when all fear of French opposition had disappeared, Ewart reported that Finckenstein and Hertzberg, after consultation with the king, had agreed to press the conclusion of a Triple Alliance, not merely as a defence against France, but also as a foundation ' of the northern alliance which his Prussian Majesty has so much at heart '. Finckenstein's change of front is attributed by Ewart to the same timidity which had made him previously shrink from any rupture with France, and he is said to have ' become a most zealous advocate, not only for entering into a partial agreement with Great Britain relative to Holland, but also to form a particular intimate alliance '.

These overtures from Berlin were received in Whitehall with as much coyness as Prussia had previously shown towards British approaches. Carmarthen did not reply till the 2nd December, when he intimated that ministers were willing to continue co-operation with Prussia, not only as to Holland, but also ' in respect of the many other important points which are now in agitation and those which will very probably arise at no distant period '. But they think it premature, in the present uncertainty, to frame a binding treaty on these latter points, which might alarm and alienate other courts. Therefore they propose to limit the agreement in the first instance to the guarantee of the Dutch settlement.[2] Finckenstein and Hertzberg were profoundly disappointed by this cool answer, and

[1] *F. O.*, 64. 12, Ewart to Carmarthen, 27 September 1787.
[2] *Ibid.*, 64. 11.

continued to urge the conclusion of a general treaty, in which the Dutch guarantee would be one of the articles. On this and other lesser points Ewart carried on a controversy with the Prussian ministers for the next six months. Behind the immediate topics of discussion lay that still existing divergence of view which had so long kept the two courts apart. The ultimate enemy to Prussia was Austria. Russia was a power which was to be detached from its ally and brought into the new northern system at the earliest possible moment. To Britain, on the other hand, the most desirable settlement was the gaining over of Austria and the restoration of the old system. The eagle with two heads was always more attractive than the eagle with one head. Pitt had not yet formulated his foreign policy, but he was steadily tending towards that antagonism to Russia and that fixed determination to maintain Turkey as a barrier to Russia, which became such a cherished tradition of the British Foreign Office. With such divergence of view it was difficult to see how any alliance, however skilfully drafted, could keep Britain and Prussia permanently together.

While Ewart was maintaining with equal skill and discretion the discussion as to the character and content of the proposed treaty, a new subject of debate arose, which was not likely to increase the desire of Britain to tie itself too closely to Prussia. The Dutch invasion had given to Hertzberg an unquestioned predominance in the official councils of the Prussian king. Finckenstein, who was growing old and infirm (his signature is now absolutely undecipherable), retired more and more into the background and left both the burden and the responsibility of foreign affairs to his younger colleague. Hertzberg, who was in many ways more fitted to be a professor than a politician, had already, not merely decided to interfere in the eastern question, but had drawn up a doctrinaire scheme for the settlement of peace to which, with occasional slight modification, he clung with a passionate paternal affection. On the 9th of January 1788 Ewart transmitted the famous plan, which had been submitted to him and to Frederick William without any communication to Finckenstein. The main points are as follows. (1) There was to be 'armed mediation' on the part of the Triple Alliance (which was not yet in existence). (2) Russia was to have

Oczakow and Bessarabia, and restore Finland to Sweden.   (3)
Austria was to give up Galicia and take instead Moldavia and
Wallachia, which were much more convenient and defensible, and
which Austria would have preferred to take at the time of the
partition of Poland.   (4) Poland, out of gratitude for the
recovery of Galicia, was to cede to Prussia the palatinates of
Posen and Kalisch (which Prussia ought to have got in 1772 to
equal the gains of the other powers), including Danzig and
Thorn.   (5) The Turks were to be reconciled by pointing out
that but for the armed mediation they would have lost much
more, and by giving them a guarantee of their remaining possessions.   The essential points in the scheme, as appeared later,
were the expulsion of Austria, so far as might be possible, from
Galicia, and the Prussian acquisition of Danzig and Thorn.
Ewart characterized the scheme as 'equally extravagant and impracticable', but says that the king was attracted by it.   He
concluded an unusually interesting dispatch by expressing the
opinion that, in view of ministerial divisions and Frederick
William's indolence and neglect of business, Britain can direct
the policy of Prussia, 'as it has done during the last six
months'.[1]

The British ministers paid little attention at the time to
Hertzberg's draft suggestions, which they regarded as both
premature and presumptuous, and which involved sacrifices on
the part of Turkey which they were not prepared to sanction
except under compulsion.   They declared it unnecessary to
anticipate the close of war before the first campaign had been
fought, and they guarded themselves by insisting that co-operation in the east must be interpreted as diplomatic co-operation
and not any measure of actual hostility to the two imperial
courts.[2]   At the same time they went so far as to admit that,
if the rival powers should make acquisitions of territory, Prussia
would be entitled to some proper equivalent.[3]   This was a
distinct approach to approval of Hertzberg's scheme, and it
was quoted against them more than once in subsequent negotiations.   Meanwhile they adhered to their contention that a special

[1] F. O., 64. 12, Ewart to Carmarthen, 9 January 1788.
[2] Ibid., 64. 13, Carmarthen to Ewart, 2 April 1788.
[3] Ibid., Carmarthen to Ewart, 14 May 1788.

treaty about the Dutch guarantee should precede the general treaty, and on this point they carried the day. The negotiations at Berlin had come to a deadlock, when in June Frederick William II paid a long-promised visit to his sister and brother-in-law. At the palace of the Loo, Harris, taking advantage of the absence of the Prussian ministers, succeeded in obtaining the king's consent to the provisional treaty of the 13th June, which was signed on behalf of Prussia by Alvensleben, the Prussian envoy at the Hague.[1] The two contracting states agreed to guarantee the Dutch settlement and constitution, and to aid each other if attacked on that account. Harris wrote a very apologetic letter to Ewart to excuse the apparent taking out of his hands of a matter which properly belonged to the Berlin embassy, pleaded in defence the tempting opportunity and his instructions from London, and expressed the hope that his action would facilitate the conclusion of the general treaty, which was to be left entirely to Ewart.[2]

The Treaty of Loo contained a secret clause that a general treaty of alliance was to be concluded within six months, and the terms of this had now to be settled in Berlin. Finckenstein and Hertzberg were profoundly annoyed that the king had abandoned their approved policy behind their backs, but they could not undo the accomplished fact, and Hertzberg had to admit that a substantial advantage had been gained by the discomfiture of the partisans of France. On the 15th July Carmarthen wrote to Ewart that Lord Dalrymple, who had been absent since May 1787, had now formally resigned, and that the active Secretary of Legation was to have the rank and pay of Envoy Extraordinary. This was remarkably rapid promotion for a young man of twenty-eight, who had had no diplomatic training, no experience of other courts, no social rank or influence, and who owed his rise entirely to his unaided talents. Ewart gratefully set to work to merit his promotion, and by the 13th August had adjusted all the contested points to the satisfaction of his employers.[3] The signature of this

---

[1] Harris's account of the way in which he obtained Frederick William's consent during a ball and after midnight is in *Malmesbury*, ii. 424-8.

[2] Harris to Ewart, 13 June 1788, in *Malmesbury*, ii. 421-2.

[3] The most acutely contested point was as to the character of the assistance

treaty on that date completed the Triple Alliance, and constituted the first complete contract of union between Prussia and
Britain since the abortive Treaty of Westminster of November
1742.   The convention of Westminster of the 16th January 1756
was merely an *ad hoc* agreement, and the subsidy treaty of
April 1758 was only made from year to year.

The most important clause of the treaty of Berlin was a secret
article by which the two powers undertook 'to act in perfect
and intimate concord in relation to the war between the two
imperial courts and the Ottoman Porte'.   This agreement was
promptly tested by events in the north.   The war opened in
1788 with disastrous reverses to the Austrian troops, who were
commanded by Joseph II in person and were inadequately
supported by Russia.   The unexpected feebleness of the Russian
effort, which was limited in this year to the six months' siege
of Oczakow, was largely due to the action of Sweden.   Gustavus III, eager to prove himself another Charles XII, concluded
a secret treaty with Turkey, made a surprise attack on Russian
Finland, threatened St. Petersburg, and compelled Catharine to
recall a considerable part of her forces from the southern
campaign.   But before these troops had arrived Russia was
saved by other means.   A mutiny of Swedish officers, organized
by the nobles who had never forgiven Gustavus for his *coup
d'état* of 1773, compelled the king to beat a hurried retreat from
Finland.   On his return to Sweden, without an army, he found
that the Danes, bound to Russia by a treaty made in 1773,[1] were
invading Sweden from Norway and were preparing to attack
Gothenburg.   It was a critical moment.   The Triple Alliance
could not afford to allow Sweden to be forced into a humiliating
peace, which would destroy such balance of power in the Baltic
as still existed.   But the allies had no forces that could act in
time, and could only employ threats.   Even concerted threats
could not be drawn up in time, and thus the responsibility of

---

which Prussia should render in case of an attack on the overseas dominions
of George III, and as to which power should have the decision on this point.
The ultimate compromise was drafted by Ewart.

[1] This was the treaty by which the Grand Duke Paul confirmed the cession
of Sleswick and Holstein to Denmark, which his mother had provisionally
sanctioned in 1767 (see p. 71).

averting disaster was thrown upon Prussia as the nearest power to the scene of disturbance. With Ewart's approval a declaration was drawn up at Berlin to the effect that Prussia would invade Holstein, that Hanoverian troops would assist, and that a British fleet would be dispatched to the Baltic. The Prussian envoy, Borcke, was to carry this to the Danish camp. At the same time Ewart sent an urgent letter explaining the situation to an old friend, Hugh Elliot, who was now stationed at Copenhagen. Always ready for adventure, Elliot, without any instructions from home, at once crossed the Sound and, after an agitated search, found the Swedish king prepared, like James II, to abandon his kingdom. Elliot, never at a loss for a telling phrase, said, ' Sire, lend me your crown, and I will return it to you unsullied'. The king threw himself into Gothenburg to encourage the feeble garrison, while Elliot hastened to the Danish camp. There, acting without any authority and as a mere traveller, he extorted by sheer bluff a short armistice. Before it expired Borcke arrived with the Prussian ultimatum. The armistice was prolonged, and Elliot, with the help of his Prussian colleague, extorted the convention of Uddevalla, by which the Danes were to evacuate Sweden. Gustavus was able to return to his capital, to punish his opponents by a second *coup d'état*, which gave him supreme control over peace and war, and to continue his invaluable diversion of Russian forces. The two venturesome envoys were officially rapped on the knuckles, Ewart for allowing Prussia to claim disposal of a British fleet and—more monstrous still—of Hanoverian troops, and Elliot for having left his post without leave and for acting rather as a knight-errant than as a diplomatist. But both were unofficially praised for saving the situation, and Elliot, to his intense gratification, was hailed in Sweden as ' the saviour of the north'.[1]

Thanks largely to Ewart and Elliot, the Triple Alliance had successfully grappled with its first difficulty, and Denmark was reduced to a rather sullen neutrality. But a far more searching test was applied to its stability when the allies came to deal with

[1] The story of Hugh Elliot's dramatic intervention in Sweden is told in chapter xi of his *Memoir* by Lady Minto (Edinburgh, 1868), which has been already referred to. His interesting letters to Ewart are in *F. O.*, 64. 14, and deserve publication.

their two great opponents Russia and Austria.   As usual,
Hertzberg had a cut-and-dried plan for dealing with the problem,
which he communicated to Ewart in September 1788.[1]   Britain
and Prussia—Dutch assent was taken for granted—were to offer
the joint mediation of the three powers to terminate the eastern
war.   If the offer were accepted, then the mediating powers would
be able to guide the settlement both in the east and in the north
of Europe.   If it were refused, then further steps must be taken
in order to secure practically dictatorial powers for the allies.
Treaties must be made with Sweden, with Poland, and with
Turkey, who will all be drawn into 'the system'.   It is unlikely
that so imposing a confederacy will be resisted, but in the last
resort it may be necessary to employ force.   The British Foreign
Office is far more opportunist, refuses to accept any such
elaborate scheme, and prefers to suit its conduct to circumstances
as they arise.   Its aims are not formulated in any single dispatch,
but have to be collected from its rather destructive criticisms
from time to time of the concrete proposals that came from
Berlin.   These criticisms are necessarily of a negative character.
Britain will not join in any offensive war.   Britain is opposed
to any extension of the matters in dispute.   Britain does not see
why Turkey should be curtailed or injured in any way to serve
the interests of a non-belligerent power.   Britain will not admit
that the Polish question is directly connected with the Turkish
war, and rather cruelly refuses to take much interest in Poland.
This is the more annoying, because Prussia regards Poland as
the pivot of the whole settlement, and is much elated that Poland
has repudiated the Russian alliance, insisted upon the withdrawal of all Russian forces, and refused a passage through
Poland to Russian troops on their way to the Turkish war.
And Russia, afraid of driving the Poles into a Prussian alliance,
has been compelled to acquiesce in the restored independence
of what had been since 1775 a docile client state.   Another
difference between the allies is that Prussia, in order to have as
many pawns to play with as possible, wants to have all disputes,
both in north and east—and later in the west—settled in one
general pacification, whereas Britain, anxious to minimize quarrels

---

[1] *F. O.*, 64. 14, Ewart to Carmarthen, 12 September 1788.

as much as possible, is quite willing to settle one dispute at a time. Finally Britain, while quite ready to assent to any Prussian gain that may come naturally and by consent, is not prepared to support any artificial system of exchanges which are designed to give to Prussia Danzig and Thorn—a scheme, as Carmarthen, now Duke of Leeds, cruelly puts it, of which the object 'appears to be aggrandisement rather than security, and which from its very nature is liable to provoke fresh hostilities, instead of contributing to the restoration of general tranquillity '.[1]

This rather critical and negative attitude of the British government placed Ewart in an extremely difficult position. The Anglo-Prussian alliance was largely his creation, and his reputation and career were bound up with its success. He must, of course, carry out his instructions, but, on the other hand, he would be useless if he lost his influence at Berlin. And that influence rested, in the main, on his alliance with Hertzberg. If he aspired—as he did—to guide the Prussian government, he must do it through Hertzberg. If Hertzberg fell from power and a successor were appointed, all Ewart's work might have to be done over again. Hence, while he had to curb and even to thwart the Prussian minister (now practically single-handed) in the details of his policy, he could not afford to quarrel with its root principle, the demand of some adequate reward to Prussia for its exertions on behalf of the liberties and the balance of Europe. Hence his dispatches during 1789 often read like apologies for or defences of Hertzberg's proposals, especially with regard to Turkey, and might well have incurred the usual reprimand given to subordinates who try to dictate to their masters. And it is probable that Ewart really desired a more tender treatment of his associate. But Leeds was tolerant enough to appreciate Ewart's dilemma, and to give him the more credit for his success. On the 11th August Leeds intimated that he was to receive 'the additional character of Minister Plenipotentiary at the Court of Berlin '.[2] On the 25th he writes in strong commendation, 'The very able manner in which you have conducted yourself in your communications with the Prussian ministers on these several

[1] *F. O.*, 64. 15, Leeds to Ewart, 24 June 1789.
[2] *Ibid.*, 64. 16, Leeds to Ewart, 11 August 1789.

points has met with the king's most gracious approbation, and it is but justice to assure you that his Majesty's ministers have observed with particular satisfaction the ability with which you have so effectually supported his Majesty's interests in successfully combating those ideas which a mistaken, though laudable zeal, on the part of Count Hertzberg, seems to have given rise to.   I can assure you that General Schlieffien does ample justice to your conduct, and observed to me to-day that you had proved yourself the best friend Count Hertzberg ever had, by preventing his plans from being carried out '.[1]

Ewart's difficulties were not diminished by the fact that during the winter of 1788-9 the attention of ministers was distracted from foreign affairs by the king's illness and the exciting debates on the Regency bill, and in the following year was absorbed in the dispute with Spain about Nootka Sound.   Every apparent neglect or delay in dealing with its affairs was bitterly resented by Prussia.   And in 1789 a new subject of differences between the allied courts was introduced by the final rebellion in the Southern Netherlands ending in the proclamation of a Belgian Republic.   Van der Noot and the other leaders of the rebellion naturally appealed to the courts of the Triple Alliance as the avowed opponents of Austria.   Prussia eagerly welcomed a new weapon against Austria, and urged the formal recognition of the Republic in order to prevent its being forced to appeal to France.[2]   The Dutch, who had been quiescent while eastern affairs were under discussion, began to be more active when their own interests were so closely touched, and the Grand Pensionary obtained a subsidiary agreement between the three powers (9 January 1790) that they would act together in the Belgian question and would oppose the intervention of any other state.[3]   The Dutch had not forgiven Austria for its hostility to their interests during the last decade, and were therefore inclined to follow the lead of Prussia and to recognize the Republic in the southern provinces.   But on this question Pitt and Leeds were adamant.   Such an act would give no

[1] *Ibid.*, Leeds to Ewart, 25 August 1789.

[2] *Ibid.*, Ewart to Leeds, 15 November 1789.   Also *F. O.*, 64. 17, Ewart to Leeds, 4 January 1790.

[3] *F. O.*, 64. 16 and 17, Ewart to Leeds, 8 December 1789 and 11 January 1790.

security against a subsequent union with France, and might indeed further it. It would render any reconciliation with Austria impossible.[1] It savoured far too much of the conduct of France in America. We had treated their recognition of the United States as a *casus belli*. Austria would be justified in doing the same.[2] The Barrier treaty of 1715 entitled the maritime powers to defend the constitution of the provinces then handed over to Austria, but it did not entitle them to exclude Austria altogether from their rule. On receipt of this unqualified refusal, Hertzberg agreed to the postponement of recognition, and expressed the willingness of Prussia to allow the Netherlands to be handed back to Austria on condition that Austria should cede Galicia to Poland. This monstrous assumption that an appeal for assistance created a right to dispose of the unfortunate Belgians without consulting them was too much for the British ministers. They replied curtly that the fate of the Netherlands had no connexion whatever with Galicia, and not obscurely hinted that Prussia had better confine its attention to eastern affairs and leave the settlement in the west to the maritime powers who were far more closely concerned. Finally, the British cards were laid on the table. Their policy was to restore the *status quo ante bellum*. Let Prussia abandon all its fantastic schemes and concentrate on this desirable aim. If they should be involved in a war waged for this purpose, Britain will come to their assistance.

It is clear that the Triple Alliance was wearing very thin. The Prussian king and ministers were reported by Ewart to be highly indignant at this last reply. Frederick William declared in a passion that ' unless the cession of Galicia could be obtained he would prefer that the Netherlands should fall into the hands of France '.[3] Catharine II, who had rejected the proffered mediation with a bitterness that surprised Prussia, watched with malignant joy the increasing split between Prussia and Britain, upon which, from the first, she had confidently reckoned. And in the early weeks of 1790 it seemed that a complete rupture was not far off. For a considerable time a strong anti-British

[1] *F. O.*, 64. 17, Leeds to Ewart, 9 February 1790.
[2] *Ibid.*, Leeds to Ewart, 26 February 1790 (comprehensive dispatch).
[3] *Ibid.*, Ewart to Leeds, 22 February 1790.

party had been growing up, especially among the officers of the army.[1] They denounced Britain as still hankering after the Austrian alliance, and as determined, out of jealousy of Prussia, to oppose all its efforts to profit by the unique advantages offered by the present situation of Europe. Why not cut adrift from these ungrateful and hampering allies ? They made Prussia do all the work in Holland in 1787, while they took all the pay. They are now playing the same game, but Prussia must not be their catspaw a second time. Prussia is strong enough to stand alone, especially now that France is rendered impotent by domestic troubles. Let us recognize Belgium, and make alliances with Turkey, Poland, and Sweden. Let us stir up revolts in Hungary and in Galicia. The Turks are our best allies. Let them give up hammering at the recovery of Oczakow and Belgrade. Induce them to guard the Danube and invade the Crimea, but their main forces should march through Bosnia and Croatia into Styria and Carinthia, where there are no fortresses and plenty of food. Then, leaving Russia to fight against Turks and Swedes, the Prussian army, 200,000 strong, can throw itself upon the hapless Austrian forces in Bohemia. Attacked on both sides, Austria must speedily succumb, and then it will be time to dictate terms to Russia. These were, in outline, the plans of the military party, and there was much to commend them to the impulsive Frederick William II.

These plans, however, had no attractions for Hertzberg, who had an instinctive antipathy to the risks of war. He had no desire to destroy the Triple Alliance, which he had helped to build up. He admitted the advantages of the Prussian position, but he thought they would be quite as useful in diplomacy as in war. His ideal was the conduct of Frederick the Great in 1772, when he had skilfully avoided going to war, and yet had obtained an extremely valuable gain to Prussia. He was confident that he could carry out his aims with regard to Galicia and Danzig and Thorn in spite of Britain, and that Britain would be pacified and even pleased if they were attained without active hostilities. He relied, perhaps excessively, upon certain

---

[1] *Ibid.*, Ewart to Leeds, 19 April 1790: ' Ill-humour and complaints against Great Britain continue very violent among the officers about his Prussian Majesty's person.'

expressions in past dispatches from London which Ewart had communicated to him. One of these has already been quoted. On another occasion Leeds had admitted that a strengthening of Prussia by the detachment of Galicia from Austria would be ' beneficial to our general system ', but it would be too dearly purchased if 'the attempt led to involve the allies or any of them in a war '.[1] It must be remembered that there was no party at Berlin for the *status quo* pure and simple. It was admitted, after the British declaration, to be a possible alternative, better than uncompensated gains for the hostile powers, but very inferior to that subtle scheme of exchanges which was to pacify Europe permanently by giving to everybody, if not precisely what they wanted, yet what they ought to have. There were many Hertzbergs at Versailles in 1919.

For the first three months of 1790 Europe was on the verge of a general war on the eastern question, and such a war would have altered the whole history of Europe by rendering intervention in France impossible. Everything depended upon Frederick William's decision between the aggressive policy of the military party, which would have broken up the Triple Alliance, and Hertzberg's plan of continued negotiation in such concert as could be maintained with the allies of Prussia. In February Ewart reported that nothing, in his opinion, would prevent the Prussian king from taking the field, and that any attempt to check him would only increase his mistrust.[2] Two armies were prepared, one in Silesia under Frederick himself and Möllendorf, the second under Brunswick on the borders of Saxony and Bohemia. A corps of observation was stationed at Tilsit on the Niemen to watch Russia. Dietz, the Prussian envoy at Constantinople, had concluded a treaty with Turkey on the 30th January, by which Prussia was pledged to join in the war. Lucchesini at Warsaw had everything ready for a treaty with Poland, and its signature was only delayed because the Poles obstinately refused to give up Danzig and Thorn, even in return for lowered tolls on the Vistula. But the treaty could be had at any moment if this condition was abandoned, and it was actually signed on the 29th March 1790.

[1] *F. O.*, 64. 16, Leeds to Ewart, 14 September 1789.

[2] *Ibid.*, 64. 17, Ewart to Leeds, 11 February 1790.

Two events occurred which turned the scale in favour of Hertzberg's policy and averted a general war. One was the death of Joseph II on the 20th February and the accession of his brother Leopold II, hitherto Grand Duke of Tuscany, who was said to have 'neither the same predilection for Russia, the same jealousy of Prussia, or dislike to the mediation of England, which so long prevailed in the mind of the late Emperor'.[1] The second was the arrival in Berlin on the 2nd of April of two autograph letters from Leopold, dated 25 March, in which he (1) asked for Frederick William's vote, and (2) expressed his willingness to terminate the Turkish war on reasonable terms, e.g. those of the treaty of Passarowitz, denied any views of aggrandisement in Germany, and stated his willingness to join the *Fürstenbund*. Frederick William continued his military preparations, but after the receipt of this letter it was difficult for him to find a reasonable pretext for attacking Austria.

The extreme tension was relaxed from the beginning of April. Prussia suspended the ratification of the treaty with the Turks, and declared that Dietz had exceeded his powers. Although the Prussian forces remained on a war footing, and Austria was compelled in self-defence to recall Laudon with a considerable army from the south to protect Bohemia, interest was mainly concentrated on the negotiations which the two leading members of the Triple Alliance carried on with each other and with St. Petersburg and Vienna. There were three vital questions at issue. Would Austria and Russia negotiate together for a general peace? If Russia persisted in its rejection of mediation, would Austria consent to make a separate peace? In either case, was the basis of the peace to be the *status quo* as advocated by Britain, or a scheme for the exchange of territories and re-adjustment of boundaries such as Prussia had suggested? There was a subordinate question as to whether the fate of the Netherlands, which Leopold was determined to recover, should be mixed up with the eastern settlement or treated quite apart from it. A further subsidiary question was whether any settlement as to the Netherlands should be guaranteed by the Empire or only by the Triple Alliance. The first two questions were answered comparatively quickly. Russia

[1] *Ibid.*, Ewart to Leeds, 19 March 1790.

determined to hold aloof and to settle its own terms with Sweden and Turkey. Austria, without any formal severance from Russia, continued the negotiations and tacitly accepted the principle of a separate peace. This rendered it more and more difficult for Prussia to employ force without forfeiting the support of its allies. There now remained the question of the basis of the peace, and the two subsidiary questions regarding the Netherlands. On these the Triple Alliance was divided. Britain adhered to the *status quo*, contended that the Netherlands had nothing to do with the eastern question, and rejected the idea of a guarantee by the Empire, on the ground that the members of the Triple Alliance, and especially the maritime powers, were the only states directly interested in coming to terms with Austria.

During April and May Hertzberg expounded his proposals to Austria, which had no objection to them in principle, and made frantic efforts to bring about that union among the allies which was necessary to make the requisite impression upon the states affected by his scheme—Austria, Poland, and Turkey. He compiled memorial after memorial and drafted note upon note to convince Britain of the superiority of his proposals over the strict *status quo*, urged the complete absence of any risk of war, dwelt upon the obligations of Britain to Prussia for its services in Holland, and added to those obligations by pledging Prussian support to Britain in the dispute with Spain about Nootka Sound.[1] In a private letter to Ewart he drew a piteous picture of Prussia, deserted by its allies on one hand, and on the other pressed by Turks, Poles, Swedes, and Belgians to fulfil the hopes which it had been forced by its efforts in the common interests to excite.[2] For some time he met with a very chilling response. At last on the 21st May Leeds used words which implied a slight willingness to make concessions to Prussia. This was apparently due to gratitude for Prussian backing against Spain. After repeating the stereotyped objections to any plans for gaining acquisitions for Prussia or Poland, and to the mixing up of the settlement in the east with that of the Netherlands, he professed the willingness of Britain to support

[1] Note of Finckenstein and Hertzberg, 20 May 1790, in *F. O.*, 64. 17.
[2] *F. O.*, 64. 17, Hertzberg to Ewart, 10 May 1790.

Prussia if it will drop these schemes and join in demanding the *status quo* or 'a slight agreed modification of it'. No definition was given of a 'slight modification' beyond the negative assertion that it could not cover an exchange of Galicia for the boundaries of the Passarowitz treaty, as that would weaken Turkey and diminish its usefulness as a future ally.[1]

Hertzberg hastened to draft a variant of his scheme by which he proposed a cession by Austria of a small part of Galicia, in return for which Poland was to give Danzig and Thorn to Prussia, and Austria was to receive a small equivalent territory from Turkey. This he assumed would answer to the British description of a slight departure from the *status quo*, and communicated the proposal to Austria as practically the agreed scheme of the Triple Alliance.[2] With this assumption still in his mind Hertzberg proceeded to meet the Austrian envoys in a conference at Reichenbach, which was fixed as the meeting-place because it was adjacent to the Prussian camp in Silesia, so that Frederick William could keep in touch with the negotiations as his uncle had done with those at Hubertsburg. Ewart and Reede, the Dutch envoy, also went to Reichenbach, and there discovered to their astonishment that they were to be excluded from the conference, which was to be limited to Prussia and Austria. This was a fatal blunder on Prussia's part, as it showed distrust of its allies, forfeited their support, and ultimately drove them into an opposition to the Prussian proposals more definite than they might otherwise have offered. It is difficult to determine whether the responsibility rests upon the king or upon Hertzberg, but it is probable that Frederick William, surrounded in camp by the military leaders, believed that he could force terms upon Austria by a threat of immediate war without having to appeal to the maritime powers. Hertzberg agreed to the plan because he knew that the allies still inclined to the alternative of

---

[1] *Ibid.*, 64. 17, Leeds to Ewart, 21 May 1790. In a previous dispatch of 30 March Leeds authorized Ewart to intimate that the *status quo* did not exclude 'reasonable modifications'.

[2] *Ibid.*, 64. 18, Ewart to Leeds, 4 June 1790, enclosing a note from Finckenstein and Hertzberg of 3 June, and their instructions to the Prussian envoy at Vienna. See also for Hertzberg's assumption that everything is practically settled, Ewart to Leeds, 16 June.

the *status quo*, and therefore his own schemes had more chance of success if their representatives were not present. Ewart at once drew up a strong protest against exclusion, stating the terms of the Triple Alliance, with the history of the negotiations, and concluding that Great Britain is the principal partner in the negotiations, that the accepted basis is the restoration of the *status quo*, and that there can be no cause for war with Austria, which has expressed its willingness to accept that basis. If the maritime powers are excluded, and Prussia rejects the *status quo*, then the Triple Alliance, with its assurances of co-operation and assistance, is done away with.[1]

In spite of this protest the first two sessions of the Conference on the 27th and 29th June 1790 were attended only by the Austrian and Prussian representatives. The basis of discussion was Hertzberg's last version of his scheme, and a draft agreement was drawn up for submission to Vienna. Prussia is to obtain from Turkey the cession of Croatia and a fragment of Wallachia. Austria, in return for this acquisition, is to resign to Prussia a substantial district in Galicia. This is to be handed over by Prussia to Poland in return for an equivalent including Danzig and Thorn. Meanwhile there is to be an armistice, and Austria is to give no further assistance to Russia. The Netherlands are to have an amnesty and their 'ancient constitution' under the guarantee of the maritime powers and the Empire. The terms to be proposed to Russia are the acquisition of Oczakow and the restoration of Russian Finland to Sweden as at the treaty of Nystad.

After this provisional agreement had been drafted for transmission to Austria, Ewart had an interview with Hertzberg, was allowed to read the minutes of the two sessions of the Conference, and at once pointed out that the Austrian demands involved a greater departure from the *status quo* and a greater weakening of Turkey than Britain could possibly assent to. During the necessary interval before the Austrian reply could be received, he set himself with equal energy and success to convince Frederick William that no cessions of territory could

---

[1] *F. O.*, 64. 18. Ewart's protest, dated 25 June, was forwarded by him to Leeds on the 27th. The following account of the Conference is mainly based upon Ewart's very full dispatches from Reichenbach.

secure peace unless they were voluntary cessions on the part of both Turkey and Poland. The interval was employed in ascertaining the wishes of these two powers. Ewart's hands were strengthened by the discovery that Prussia had actually decided to ratify the suspended treaty which Dietz had concluded on the 30th January, and he dwelt upon the obvious inconsistency between such a treaty and the proposal to deprive the Porte of 'such extensive and important possessions'. Considerable difficulty would have been caused if, as Ewart anticipated, Austria had accepted the generous terms proposed on the 29th June. Fortunately for the British envoy the reply of Kaunitz, drafted on the 7th July, was a characteristic analysis of the details of the scheme, contending that Austria would receive too little and would surrender too much. This contentious dispatch completed the conversion of Prussia to the *status quo*, which had already been partially effected by the discovery that Turkey and Poland would never consent to the proposed cessions, and that if they were forced to consent they would never become cordial allies of Prussia.[1] The military party assented to the change of policy in the expectation that Austria, after what had passed, would reject the *status quo* as a slap in the face, and that this would produce the rupture which they desired.

At the third session of the Conference on the 15th July the representatives of the maritime powers were present, and Ewart became the dominant personage. The Austrian envoys, on presenting Kaunitz's note, were astounded to find that it was now wholly out of date. When they tried to represent what had passed at the previous meetings as a virtual agreement between the two courts, Ewart coolly told them that the early sessions had been wholly irregular and informal. After a stormy discussion the session closed without any agreement, and the Prussian officers were exultant at the prospect of war. But during the

---

[1] *Ibid.*, Ewart to Leeds, 16 July 1790. Ewart reports that the king had directed Hertzberg 'to abandon entirely the plan of arrangement, since it could only serve to commit him with Great Britain as well as with the Porte and Poland, that the impossibility of reconciling the two latter powers to it was already a sufficient motive for setting it aside, and that it was probable the court of Vienna would furnish a further title by modifying the proposals already made'.

interval Ewart and his Dutch colleague succeeded in adjusting a compromise. To save Austria from the shame of complete surrender, it was suggested that the agreement as to the *status quo* should be accompanied by a reservation that it should not exclude a friendly readjustment of boundaries between Austria and Turkey. This was reluctantly accepted by Prussia with the *caveat* that if Austria gained any territory Prussia should have an equivalent. At the fourth session on the 24th July this was finally approved, and in a fifth session on the 26th terms were adjusted as to the Netherlands. On the 27th the various documents in which these agreements were embodied were formally signed and sealed, and these collectively constitute the Convention of Reichenbach.[1]

At first sight the Convention of Reichenbach appears to be a notable triumph for the Triple Alliance and a proportionate humiliation of Austria, and it was certainly regarded as such at the time.[2] Later, however, the ingenuity of Leopold II in evading the most distasteful restrictions imposed upon him succeeded in so completely restoring the prestige of Austria that the sense of humiliation disappeared, and men only remembered the dangers from which Austria was extricated by averting a war with Prussia. On the other hand, Prussia gained so little in the end that Reichenbach has a very unhonoured place in its annals, and most of its historians, following the lead of Hertzberg, have agreed to regard it as the beginning of the decline of Prussia from its imposing position under Frederick the Great. But from our immediate point of view the most important result of the Conference was a fatal weakening of the Anglo-Prussian alliance, and of the personal association between Hertzberg and

---

[1] *F. O.*, 64. 18. These documents, ten in number, were forwarded by Ewart on 28 July.

[2] *Ibid.*, Ewart reports on 5 August that Frederick William had expressed his gratitude to the allies for the support which had enabled him to bring the negotiation to 'so happy a conclusion'. More conclusive evidence is supplied by a report from Jackson to Leeds of 17 February 1791 that, when it was proposed at Sistowa to include the Convention of Reichenbach in the treaty with Turkey, the Austrian envoy objected to it as 'a humiliation'. The Prussian envoy, on the other hand, was unwilling 'to give up a point of honour which is said to have been obtained at so great an expense and by the disinterested sacrifice of so many real advantages' (*F. O.*, 64. 19).

Ewart, upon which it very largely rested. The whole antece-
dent history had created a distinct antagonism between Hertzberg's policy of exchanges and the British demand for the *status
quo*. A compromise, which seemed at one time possible, was
prevented by the fatal blunder of Prussia in trying to exclude
Ewart from the Conference, and also by the difficulty of despoil-
ing powers whom it was desired to conciliate. In the end the
British policy prevailed, but Prussia, though it assented, could
not but feel that it thereby ceased to be the predominant partner,
as it had aspired to be.

The rift which Reichenbach disclosed and partially enlarged
helps to account for the failure of the Triple Alliance in the
attempt to grapple with its next task, the forcing of similar terms
upon Russia. At the outset it seemed a simple matter. Russia
had exhausted its pecuniary resources, it had experienced great
difficulty hitherto in carrying on simultaneously both a Swedish
and a Turkish war, and now that it was deprived of Austrian
assistance it seemed inevitable that it must consent to resign all
its conquests to Turkey. But Catharine II, like Peter the Great
in 1720, refused to submit to dictation, and insisted on the retention of Oczakow with a large strip of territory reaching to the
Dniester and commanding the mouth and navigable channel of
that river. No sooner did she learn that Austria had broken
away from the Russian alliance than she took steps to deprive
Britain and Prussia of their most formidable weapon. Britain
had rejected the Prussian suggestion that Sweden should recover
the Nystad boundaries, and had insisted that in this as in the
other contests there should be no territorial gains or losses.
Catharine now offered to Gustavus III the *status quo ante
bellum*, which was all that the allies proposed to obtain for him.
It was obviously more flattering to his pride to obtain these
terms by the spontaneous offer of his opponent than to owe them
to the patronage of the allied powers. He gratefully accepted
Catharine's offer, and the treaty of Werela (14 August) not only
deprived Russia of a troublesome enemy, but also held out the
possibility of gaining a very useful helper.

In spite of the loss of Sweden, which seriously deranged their
plans, Britain and Prussia were resolved to compel Russia to go
back to the *status quo*. Against Russia Pitt was much more

bellicose than he had been against Austria, and his success in dealing with the Dutch, French, Belgian, Spanish, and Austro-Turkish problems inspired him with the conviction that a demonstration of British naval power together with the mobilization of the Prussian army would overawe Russia without any actual outbreak of war. There seemed, therefore, to be no obstacle to the cordial co-operation of the allies, and Ewart, whose health had suffered from the ceaseless activities of the last three years, obtained leave of absence in October, and left the Berlin embassy in the hands of a secretary, Jackson. On his way home Ewart had an interview with the Emperor Leopold at Frankfort, and obtained his repudiation of Kaunitz's ingenious contention that, while Reichenbach forbade any Austrian assistance to Russia in the Turkish war, it did not prohibit such assistance if any powers picked a quarrel with Russia for refusing the *status quo*.[1]

Besides the Russian problem there were three questions arising from the proceedings at Reichenbach in which the Triple Alliance was directly concerned. The most pressing in point of time was the settlement in the Netherlands. Ewart had succeeded in repelling the suggestion of an imperial guarantee, and it was agreed that the arrangements for granting an amnesty and restoring the ancient constitution should be made by a conference between Austria and the three allied states at the Hague. But while this conference was going on Leopold, freed from the eastern war, sent troops to put down the Republic and to restore his authority. Prussia had desired to prohibit the transport of these troops until terms had been adjusted at the Hague, but Britain had refused to concur. Thus Leopold was able to issue an ultimatum to his rebellious subjects and to compel them by overwhelming force to submit. Van der Noot and the other leaders sought safety in exile, but their followers were leniently treated, and the constitution was restored as it had been at the accession of Joseph II before his hasty and ill-considered reforms had provoked resistance. Meanwhile, however, the conference at the Hague had drawn up a convention, signed by the Austrian delegate, in which the 'ancient constitution' was defined as that which existed at the time of the Barrier treaty of 1715, when the

[1] *F. O.*, 64. 18, Ewart to Leeds, 2 October 1790; and 64. 19, Jackson to Leeds, 16 October, intimating Ewart's success.

provinces were originally transferred to Austria. Leopold ratified the convention with the exception of this clause. Prussia
was inclined to resent this as an insult to the allies, but the
maritime powers declined to disturb the accomplished settlement,
and Leopold had his own way.

The second question was that of Danzig and Thorn. The
British ministers had never opposed this gain to Prussia, but only
the mixing it up with irrelevant cessions on the part of Turkey.
They had suggested at Reichenbach that the coveted district
might still be gained by a direct bargain with Poland in return
for mercantile concessions, such as the lowering of the Vistula
tolls to two per cent. Negotiations were conducted on this
basis during the later months of 1790 and the early months of
the next year, but they never had much chance of success.
Prussia would not make such concessions as were suggested, and
suspected Britain of a desire to benefit its own trade at Prussia's
expense. But the fatal obstacle was the invincible reluctance of
Poland, where the Diet actually passed a law forbidding the
alienation of any part of the nation's land. As it was extremely
necessary to have Poland as an ally in any possible collision
with Russia, the whole matter was ultimately dropped by order
of the Prussian king himself.[1]

The third problem was the final conclusion of a treaty between
Austria and the Porte, of which the Reichenbach agreement only
laid down the preliminaries. The conference for this purpose
met at Sistowa, and like that at the Hague was attended by
representatives of Austria and of the Triple Alliance. The interest
of Prussia was to insist, so far as possible, on the literal enforce-
ment of the *status quo ante bellum*. Britain, as so often happened when Austria was concerned, was more leniently inclined.
As early as August 1790, just after Reichenbach, Leeds had told
Ewart that if it should appear necessary that Orsova should be
ceded to Austria he 'need not discourage the cession provided
the Porte can be induced to consent to it'.[2] One result of this

[1] *F. O.*, 64. 21, Ewart to Leeds, 6 May 1791. Ewart forwards a note of
the Prussian cabinet of same date, intimating that the negotiation is dropped
because 'elle rencontre trop d'opposition en Pologne et ne laisse pas de
causer discussions désagréables et une mauvaise disposition dans ce pays-là '.

[2] *Ibia.*, 64. 18, Leeds to Ewart, 14 August 1790.

divergence was the most exasperating delays in the proceedings at Sistowa. The Turks, past masters in the art of procrastination, excelled themselves in the hope that Prussia might be induced to carry out the treaty of January 1790. Austria emulated the Turks, in the expectation that a widening of the split between Prussia and the maritime powers might secure the support of the latter for the court of Vienna. In the end Austria drew a distinction between the *status quo de iure* and the *status quo de facto*, and claimed Old Orsova and district on the ground that they really belonged to the Banat of Temeswar and were therefore assigned to Austria by the treaty of Belgrade (1739). This demand, which had obviously been foreseen, led to a brief breaking off of the Conference, and to a renewed threat of war on the part of Prussia.[1] But there were strong reasons against a rupture, and in the end Austria gained the desired cession in the Treaty of Sistowa (5 August 1791). The equivalent, which at Reichenbach had been assured to Prussia, was never even claimed.

In none of these three negotiations had the Triple Alliance shown itself a very powerful or cohesive force. In none of them had failure involved any serious loss or humiliation. But the concurrent effect of even minor failures tends to weaken the foundations of any alliance or coalition. The major failure which finally wrecked the Triple Alliance was in dealing with the peace between Russia and Turkey. To the original demands of the allies Catharine returned an unflinching negative. She would not have mediation or dictation of any sort. She would make her own treaty with the Turks, and she would keep Oczakow with the whole district to the Dniester. Every success of the Russian arms served to increase her obstinacy. Obviously the allies must either acknowledge their defeat or they must bring pressure to bear upon Russia to accept their terms.

[1] *F. O.*, 64. 21, Ewart to Grenville, 20 June 1791, reports that Frederick William, on receiving the news that the Austrians had quitted Sistowa, exclaimed, 'Ma parole est sauvée et je remplirai mes engagements' [to the Turks]. He actually instructed Lucchesini to give this assurance to the Turkish envoy. In a private ciphered letter of the same date (*Fortescue MSS.*, ii. 104) Ewart advocates giving support to Prussia against Austria.

Prussia was the first to propose joint action after Reichenbach, and Prussia was the more bellicose of the two allies. The delays during the winter of 1790–1 were mainly due to British caution. Pitt and Leeds insisted upon getting the biggest possible consensus of opinion or action against Russia, and negotiated on the subject with Sweden, Denmark, Spain, and Poland. There was also a certain amount of dubitation at Berlin. Hertzberg, who attributed the failure of his schemes to British opposition, had begun to meditate on the possibility of a bargain with Russia, which in return for Oczakow might consent to the Prussian acquisition of Danzig and Thorn.[1] But in the end Frederick William stuck to the programme of coercion, and appealed to Britain to give him naval support in the Baltic. The British Cabinet, diligently coached in eastern affairs by Ewart, who was now in London and in better health, decided to back Prussia, prepared a fleet for action, and appealed to Parliament for the vote of the necessary supplies. Intimation was sent to Berlin together with the draft of an ultimatum, which Jackson was to adjust with the Prussian ministers, and which required Russia to give an answer within ten days. In spite of the vehement opposition of Charles Fox and the other opposition leaders, the ministerial demands were granted by adequate majorities in both houses. But outside Parliament public opinion was strongly opposed to a war with Russia, and especially to a war about a place and a district which nobody had ever heard of before. Members of the Cabinet began to hesitate, and to question the wisdom of their hasty decision. Little more than a fortnight after the virtual agreement to go to war, it was decided to send another dispatch to Jackson recalling the ultimatum and intimating a desire to find some compromise which might avert a conflict. The duke of Leeds refused to sign the dispatch, and the seals were hastily transferred to Lord Grenville, a resolute advocate of a peaceful policy. Ewart, with notable loyalty, agreed to return in haste to Berlin to explain and commend a climb down on the part of Britain which he most deeply deplored.

---

[1] For Hertzberg's opposition to hostile action against Russia see Jackson's dispatches of 23 January, 6 March, and 5 April 1791. In the last he says that Hertzberg represents Britain as 'aiming at the ruin of his country by engaging it in a useless and expensive war'. *F. O.*, 64. 20.

Ewart's final mission to Berlin was doomed from the outset to failure. The Triple Alliance had received a mortal blow when Britain decided to recall the ultimatum. The Prussian king and ministers were simply astounded by so sudden a change of front, for which at first no explanation nor excuse was offered. As the Dutch announced at this time their antipathy to a Russian war, Prussia was practically deserted by both its allies, and involved in dire humiliation by their timidity. Ewart returned to an estranged and an altered Prussia. Hertzberg, formerly his close associate, had never forgiven him for his successful opposition at Reichenbach. And Hertzberg, even if he could have been reconciled, was no longer in power. His complete failure to carry out his vaunted scheme, his obstinate adherence to it after its futility was obvious, and his recent opposition to all hostile action against Russia, had alienated the king. Finckenstein, old and nearly blind, counted for nothing, though he was still allowed out of respect to attach a wavering and illegible signature to state papers. In order to control Hertzberg, two new members, Schulenburg and Alvensleben, were added to the ministry of foreign affairs.[1] Ewart found it extremely difficult to carry on negotiations with a committee of four men, for whose unanimity there was no security whatever. And behind the ministers was the favourite Bischofswerder, once the loyal supporter of the British alliance, but now the advocate of a wholly new system. With elaborate and almost grotesque secrecy Bischofswerder had been banished from the court in order to lay the foundations of a future entente with Austria. In view of German grievances against revolutionary France it had become almost imperative that the two leading German states should agree upon some joint line of action. When the secret was at last disclosed, Ewart was informed that the Prussian aim was to complete the severance of Austria from Russia and to attach the Emperor to the system of the Triple Alliance. In reality the

---

[1] In a private letter to Grenville of 7 July 1791 Ewart states that Schulenburg was the dominant minister. Hertzberg retired from the cabinet at the beginning of July, but retained his other offices, and was allowed access to all state papers in order to write a history of the late reign. This enabled him to compose his well-known *Recueil*, which is of considerable value for the diplomatic history of the eighteenth century. See also *F. O.*, 64. 22, Ewart to Grenville, 9 July 1791.

intention was to form entirely new connexions which would free Prussia from all dependence on the maritime powers, and to enable Prussia, as Ewart saw later, to return to Russia by way of Austria.[1]

But even if Prussia had been as well as it was ill disposed, the Triple Alliance was doomed. Ewart was instructed to formulate a new demand by which Russia was either to keep Oczakow and the whole district on condition that the fortress was dismantled and the country left an uninhabited desert, or the frontier of the ceded district must be curtailed so as to leave the east bank of the Dniester securely in the hands of Turkey.[2] Prussia pretended to acquiesce in this new plan, and Ewart for a moment believed that he could regain his old ascendancy at Berlin. But there was no force behind this demand. When Frederick William asked what Britain would do if Russia was still recalcitrant, Ewart could only give evasive replies.[3] The fact is that Pitt and Grenville had made up their minds that they would not go to war on this Turkish question. They rejected all suggestions that they should send a fleet to the Black Sea or even to the Baltic. It would have been much more honest and much fairer to Ewart if they had from the first admitted that they could not oppose a complete surrender to Russia. As it was the unfortunate envoy was compelled to continue to force upon Prussia the concurrence in proposals which Catharine treated with the contempt which they deserved. At last he had to incur the supreme humiliation of urging the court of Berlin to put pressure upon the Porte to obtain acquiescence in the terms dictated from St. Petersburg. This was too much for Prussia, still bound by an unfulfilled treaty with the Turks, and the request was unhesitatingly refused.[4]

---

[1] *F. O.*, 64. 22, Ewart to Grenville, 21 August 1791. Ewart was acute enough to foresee that this *rapprochement* of the two German courts to Russia would lead to the partition of Poland, 'Austria and Prussia being unable to stop the progress of Russia '.

[2] Ewart's instructions, dated 20 April 1791, are in *F. O.*, 64. 21.

[3] *Ibid.*, Ewart to Grenville, 30 April. Ewart reports in this dispatch his interview with the Prussian king, in which he had to explain the British change of front. He expresses gratitude to Frederick William for his candour 'on this trying occasion '.

[4] *F. O.*, 64. 21, Ewart to Grenville, 5 June 1791. See also his private letter of 6 June in *Fortescue MSS.*, ii. 91. Ewart evidently regarded the

By this time disillusion had come both to the British ministers and to their envoy. In July Bischofswerder paid another, and this time an undisguised, visit to the Emperor, and returned with a preliminary treaty, signed on the 25th July, by which the two sovereigns were to adjust a common policy towards France at a personal conference at Pillnitz, and they further agreed to give joint support to Poland, which had finally defied Russia by adopting a reformed constitution on the 3rd May. This treaty was disclosed by Schulenburg (Hertzberg had finally quitted the foreign ministry in July) to Ewart as a profound secret.[1] Ewart at once drafted a note pointing out that it was in direct contradiction to the previous assurances that Austria was to be brought into a common system, and that the principles of the Triple Alliance were completely abandoned. Schulenburg carried the note to Potsdam, and returned the answer that the king knew of no engagement with Britain 'which could prevent him from negotiating separately or making what separate alliance he might think proper'. Ewart added in cipher that the Prussian king 'seems no longer to consider any concert or concurrence of his Majesty as necessary, or that the system of the alliance is to be kept up on the footing it has been hitherto'. Some days later he wrote that Schulenburg and Alvensleben hold ' that the alliance with England has been hitherto very disadvantageous to this country '.[2]

Ewart was now an outcast at Berlin where he had once posed as a dictator. He was no longer consulted by ministers nor courted by their adherents. Not only did he receive no invitation to Pillnitz, but he was given to understand that his attendance would be distasteful. He wrote home ruefully that

demand as preposterous ' after all that has passed between the Prussian king and the Porte '. It is characteristic of Grenville's diplomacy that he is quite unable to understand the point of view of another court.

[1] The demand for secrecy was speedily withdrawn, but Reede in a secret dispatch expressed the belief that very imperfect disclosures were made to Ewart. The experienced Dutch envoy realized how fatal the Austrian treaty was to the Triple Alliance. ' Voilà donc le grand système du Nord et d'alliance qui s'écroule comme un château de cartes.' An extract from the dispatch was forwarded by Auckland to Grenville on 19 August. *Fortescue MSS.*, ii. 170.

[2] *F. O.*, 64. 22, Ewart's successive dispatches to Grenville of 9 August (enclosing copy of his note) and 21 August.

'England is actually more disliked in this country than any other court, Austria not excepted'. To make his position more intolerable, he had lost the confidence of the British Foreign Office, where he had recently been an oracle. During the whole of his last embassy he was compelled, against his own will,[1] to forward his dispatches under flying seal through the Hague, where the British envoy was Lord Auckland (the William Eden of the French commercial treaty), a vigorous opponent of any rupture with Russia, and a personal enemy of Ewart, to whose advice he attributed the decision to send the ill-fated ultimatum of March. Auckland forwarded the dispatches to Grenville with a running commentary, in which he accused Ewart of departing from his instructions and of encouraging the warlike temper of Prussia instead of restraining it.[2] There can be no doubt that Grenville, who had not been in direct touch with Ewart during his earlier and more successful mission, was gradually converted to Auckland's views. The result was that when Ewart asked for another leave of absence on the ground of ill-health, Grenville assumed that he was too ill to return to diplomatic activity, accepted his request as a virtual resignation, and obtained for him a pension of £1,000 a year. Ewart remained at Berlin to witness the marriages of two daughters of Frederick William, one to the duke of York, the second son of George III, the other to the young prince of Orange, who became in 1815 the first king of the Netherlands. These marriages were the product of the Triple Alliance; they should have been an assurance of its continuance; but in fact they provided a funeral ceremony for the league, which had virtually ceased to exist. After their celebration Ewart finally quitted Berlin, whence his last dispatch was dated on the 21st October 1791. His final mortification was to learn that Lord Auckland's brother, Morton Eden, had been selected to succeed him. He retired to Bath, a disappointed and broken man, and there he died three months later, on the 27th January 1792, at the early age of thirty-two.

Ewart's departure from Berlin may be regarded as closing the

---

[1] Ewart tried to evade this. Auckland complained to Grenville, and the latter politely informed Ewart that departure from the usual practice was inconvenient. See *Fortescue MSS.*, ii. 72 and 76.

[2] Auckland's letters to Grenville are in vol. ii of the *Fortescue MSS.* For his animus against Ewart see his exultant letter to his brother,

history of the Triple Alliance, which he had done more than any other single man to create and maintain. During three eventful years it had played a great and in some ways a dominant part in Europe. It had enabled Britain and Prussia to emerge from that isolation, which had paralysed the former power in Europe for a quarter of a century, and had reduced the latter to impotence since 1780. It had in its infancy saved the Dutch Republic from subjection to France. It had rescued Sweden from destruction and enabled Gustavus III to suppress the turbulent and unpatriotic oligarchy. It had aided Britain to triumph over Spain about Nootka Sound. It had encouraged Poland to make a last bid for an independent national existence, and if the alliance had continued Poland might have survived. By putting an end to the eastern war it rendered possible the co-operation of Austria and Prussia against revolutionary France, with all its momentous consequences both to France and to Europe. Its most obvious achievement, however, was the preservation of the Turkish dominions in Europe from the most formidable attempt yet made to effect their partition. This may appear in the present day to be an achievement of little value, but in the eighteenth century it was very differently regarded, and the tradition then started in Britain lasted for nearly a hundred years. But the whole history of the alliance proves that there existed in those days no adequate binding force to hold Britain and Prussia permanently together. Probably the strongest link in international relations is the need of facing a common enemy. This link never existed between Britain and Prussia in the important half-century which we have traversed from the accession of Frederick the Great. The two states might combine for the moment to secure some common end or to face some common danger, but such an alliance could not serve as the basis of a permanent system. To Prussia during these years Austria was the obvious and the irreconcilable enemy. In the eyes of Britain Austria, even though ungrateful and estranged, was still a natural friend. The French Revolution destroyed many eighteenth-century traditions, and it necessitated a new grouping of European states in which there was no place for the Triple Alliance.

Morton Eden, in *Auckland Correspondence*, ii. 392–4. He says, among other things, that, if Russia had given way, 'the world would not have been large enough for the political importance of Mr. Ewart'.

APPENDIX

JOSEPH EWART

AN adequate memoir of Joseph Ewart is a *desideratum* in the history of British diplomacy. He was unquestionably the ablest and the most notable of the young Scotsmen who in his generation found a career in the diplomatic service. His rapid rise to eminence is the more remarkable in that, unlike his countryman and contemporary, Hugh Elliot, he had no social or political claim to patronage or promotion. He owed his introduction to diplomacy to a mere accident. He was the son of a minister of the Church of Scotland at Troqueer in Dumfries-shire. After completing his studies at the University of Edinburgh, he started life, as did so many young Scotsmen at that time, by accompanying a young laird, Macdonald of Clanronald, on the grand tour. According to Wraxall, he separated from his pupil at Vienna and obtained secretarial work at the embassy there from Sir Robert Murray Keith, who was an Edinburgh man, the son of 'Ambassador' Keith, who played an important part both at Vienna and St. Petersburg during the Seven Years' War. Wraxall is the only authority for this Vienna episode, and, though there is no inherent improbability in the story, the balance of evidence shows that Ewart began, as he ended, his diplomatic career at Berlin. At any rate he was serving there under Sir John Stepney in 1784, and had shown such capacity that he was allowed to act as *chargé d'affaires* when Stepney obtained leave of absence from Berlin.

To his contemporaries Ewart was for a short time a personage of no small interest and importance, and the correspondence of his fellow diplomatists, like Harris and Hugh Elliot, proves that they regarded him with both esteem and respect. The fullest account of his career is given by Wraxall (*Memoirs*, ed. Wheatley, vol. iv, pp. 219-25), who tells us that Catharine II of Russia tried to poison him before Reichenbach, and rather reluctantly rejects the story that she was ultimately successful in bringing about his

untimely end. The mere fact that such rumours were spread
abroad is no small tribute to Ewart's importance. But to the
modern student of history and, it would seem, to most modern
historians, Ewart is, at best, little more than a name. German
writers are apparently more familiar with him and more appreciative of his merits. This neglect is partly due to the fact that
in British history as normally told foreign relations are subordinated to the domestic records of party struggles and ministerial
changes, and the former only emerge into prominence when they
are associated with actual warfare. Also the particular foreign
transactions in which Ewart played a dominant part, the formation of the Triple Alliance and the Convention of Reichenbach,
were so completely obliterated by the French Revolution and its
results that they have attracted far less attention from posterity
than they did from contemporaries. It is rather startling to discover that these events were regarded by most people before
1792 as infinitely more important than the happenings at
Versailles and Paris.

From the general assertion as to modern historians, I must
except Dr. J. Holland Rose. In his volume on *William Pitt
and National Revival*, he has given a full and careful account
of foreign affairs at the time of the Triple Alliance, and he has
called special attention to the career of Ewart. In preparing
these chapters he had the advantage of access to the diplomatist's
private papers, about which there was some dispute after his
death (see *Fortescue MSS.*, ii, p. 253), but some of which have
been transmitted to his descendant, Lieut.-General Sir Spencer
Ewart, K.C.B.

Joseph Ewart must have been a masterful man. It was a
notable achievement for a young and unfriended Scotsman to
rise from mere private employment at an embassy to the rank of
envoy and plenipotentiary before he was thirty years of age.
But it was a still more remarkable feat that for three years he
dominated the court of Berlin and directed the policy of the
Prussian ministers. Such things have been done at times in
Constantinople, or even in St. Petersburg, but very seldom at a
western court. On this point Wraxall, whose emphasis is not
always to be trusted, is borne out by Lord Malmesbury. And
Ewart's ascendancy at Berlin was gained in spite of three very
serious handicaps. (1) He had no experience of any other
court (*Malmesbury*, ii, p. 226), and therefore lacked that variety
of experience, that insight into the complicated tangles of diplomacy, and that wide outlook, which are usually regarded as the
indispensable outfit of a successful ambassador. (2) He lacked
social training and social aptitudes. A Scottish manse and a

Scottish university did not in themselves fit a young man for the life of a court. With characteristic insight and intrepidity he sought to remedy the defect by marrying in 1785 Elizabeth Countess of Wartensleben. This doubtless improved his position at Berlin, but it gave him no status in English society, where the lady was plain Mrs. Ewart. The eighteenth century, an age of aristocracy, was not partial either to Scotsmen or to men who had risen from the ranks. (3) Ewart had an irascible temper and a somewhat dictatorial manner, and in his last year these defects were aggravated by a sense of failure and by the struggle against novel and unforeseen obstructions in his way. William Lindsay, the secretary who took over the embassy between Ewart's departure and Morton Eden's arrival, wrote to Grenville on the 29th October 1791 that Ewart was 'universally detested at this court on account of the haughtiness and arrogance with which he carried himself towards all ranks of men' (*Fortescue MSS.*, ii, p. 219). This may be taken with several grains of salt. It was Lindsay's cue to disparage Ewart, who had incurred the displeasure of the ministry at home, and to curry favour with Morton Eden, who was sent to pursue a different policy. And it was natural for the Prussian ministers to lay as much blame as possible for recent alienation upon the departed envoy, who could not refute their charges. But, after making these allowances, it is probable that there was some element of truth in the denunciations, and Ewart, like other men, did not find it easy to be a suppliant where he had once been a dictator, These faults of temper and manner help to explain the suddenness and completeness of his downfall.

It is this downfall which supplies the element of drama and of tragedy in Ewart's brief story. In 1790 he seemed to be the one possible rival to the fame and achievements of the first Lord Malmesbury. For the moment at the beginning of 1791 he was even more consulted and listened to than his brilliant competitor. And then, within a few short months, came failure, bitter disappointment, and dismissal from the service. A few weeks later still he was dead, and when he died he was already forgotten except by those with whom he had been directly associated and those who had to consider the provision for his wife and three children, left practically without any resources (*Fortescue MSS.*, ii, p. 253). He died at Bath,where his brother was a surgeon [Wraxall says that Joseph Ewart was trained for the same profession], and was buried in Bath Abbey. My quondam colleague, Professor Saintsbury, has been kind enough to send me a copy of the inscription on the tablet put up in his memory.

Sacred to the Memory of
JOSEPH EWART, Esq.
His Majesty's Envoy Extraordinary and Minister
Plenipotentiary at the Court of Prussia
from the year 1787 to 1792
A station to which he was called
At an important crisis of public affairs
And in which he approved himself
During many arduous negotiations
An enlightened Statesman
A zealous Minister
And (what is more than these)
A truly honest man.
He died on the 27th day of January 1792
Aged 32 years
A public loss
A premature victim
of the exertions of an ardent and superior mind.

For the benefit of the future biographer I may correct the chronological inaccuracies to which brevity has condemned the author of the above inscription. In June 1784 Stepney quitted Berlin on leave of absence and never returned. Ewart was left in charge from that date till the 29th November 1785, when Lord Dalrymple arrived. On the previous 21st October he was appointed Secretary of Legation. From the 25th July 1786 Ewart was again in charge while Dalrymple went to Hesse Cassel to confer the garter on the Landgrave, but the latter returned just in time for the death of Frederick the Great. In May 1787 Dalrymple went away on leave and did not subsequently return. Ewart was not again disturbed by the presence of a superior. On the 15th July 1788 he was made Envoy Extraordinary, and on the 11th August 1789 Minister Plenipotentiary. He was absent on leave from September 1790 till April 1791, but during that time he was in frequent consultation with ministers in London. His final stay in Berlin was from the 29th April till the 22nd October 1791.

It is clear that Ewart should not have been sent back to Berlin in 1791, and that he should not have consented to return. He had an impossible task to perform, and he was of all men the least fitted to perform it. From the moment that the British government resolved not to risk a war with Russia and to withdraw the joint ultimatum the Triple Alliance was doomed, and it was cruel to send its author to preside over its obsequies. Ewart was definitely committed to the forward policy, and he could not whole-heartedly acquiesce in its abandonment. In Leeds he had found a sympathetic and appreciative superior. Grenville, the chief author of the change of policy, was neither. And Grenville's natural distrust of Ewart was increased by the mischief-making letters of Auckland, which are not creditable either to the writer or to the recipient. When it was finally decided to get rid of Ewart, it was not easy to find a plausible pretext. Pitt tried to find one in the fact that Ewart had sought to gratify the Prussian king by hurrying on the marriage of the duke of York without allowing sufficient time for the formalities required by the Royal Marriage Act or for a parliamentary grant of an annual income to the bridegroom. (See on this subject the dispatches in *F. O.*, 64. 22, and the correspondence between Pitt and Ewart in *Fortescue MSS.*, iii, pp. 454-7.) But this was too venial an offence to justify the dismissal of a distinguished subordinate, and Grenville had to fall back upon Ewart's ill-health as the reason for his retirement. This proved to be a quite ample reason, but it was widely known that it was not the real reason, and that the resignation had a penal character.

As to whether Ewart was right in his contention that Russia would have given way if the original policy of the ministry had been adhered to, or whether the object to be obtained was worth the risks involved, it is impossible to dogmatize. There can be no doubt that Britain was humiliated by the course adopted, and Pitt unquestionably yielded with the greatest reluctance. Dr. Holland Rose (*William Pitt*, i, p. 617) quotes an interesting letter from Ewart to Jackson (14 April 1791) describing how Pitt 'with the tears in his eyes' explained the change of policy to Ewart. And Lord Malmesbury, in this matter both a competent and an impartial critic, was clearly on the side of Ewart. His comments are sufficiently illuminating to merit quotation. 'I thought it [the original decision] at the time a measure of sound policy, and everything I have seen since I have been on the continent makes me lament the weakness of our ministry in giving way on that occasion; we have lost a powerful friend, and made a powerful enemy by it.

'It is foreign to the subject of this letter to dwell on the consequences it will produce on the side of Russia. As to Prussia, we have for the time, if not irrevocably, lost it. Our influence, which before was all-powerful, is entirely gone, and his Prussian Majesty is piqued at our desertion of him, as he calls it, and has formed a connexion with the Court of Vienna in direct opposition to our interest.

'His Prussian Majesty, although as gracious and kind to me

as possible, studiously avoided talking to me on public concerns; and he observes the same reserve with His Majesty's minister [Ewart], who, instead of being as he was a few months ago in the whole secret, and in a manner the director of the Prussian Cabinet, is now neither consulted nor trusted. How long this unnatural connexion with Austria may last, after the first moment of pique with us is over, I do not pretend to say. It is very unpopular at Berlin, and Bischofswerder, being a foreigner, is loudly murmured against, and taxed with having sold his master to the Emperor. In the meantime, however, it has broken up our continental system, and let us down from that high situation in which we stood. It appears very clear to me, from some confidential communications which were made to me, that Lord Grenville was the cause of Mr. Pitt's giving way, and that he acted, not from the reason which was given, the nation's being against it, but from its being his fixed opinion that we should not interfere at all in the affairs of the continent' (*Malmesbury*, ii, p. 441).

An exactly opposite view was expressed by Lord Auckland in an exultant letter to his brother, Morton Eden, on the 1st November 1791 : 'Your nomination will not diminish Mr. Ewart's anger. He has been very absurd, nearly, I think, to insanity ; and if he had been allowed to drive on as he wished, would have forced the whole world into a state of war, upon the short-sighted and silly speculation of placing the power of England upon a colossus for the admiration of the present age and of posterity; of which colossus he, the architect, was to have received an unbounded tribute of fame and honour. In the whole idea there was a total ignorance of our finances, and of the disposition of this country, and a total disregard to all collateral consequences. The only wonder is, how he contrived to lead the minds of many individuals so much wiser than himself, and to commit them in his enterprise so far that it became impossible to get out of it without getting into a degree of ridicule, reproach, and inconsistency. He had one merit in that transaction—an unwearied activity. . . . I understand that he retires with a pension of £1,000 a year, and with a supreme and avowed contempt for the talent of many of the King's domestic and foreign ministers' (*Auckland Correspondence*, ii, pp. 392-3).

Auckland was correct as to the pension. Ewart was to have £1,000, and his widow £500 a year. After his death the king also granted £100 a year to each of the three children.

INDEX